CW01666880

A PAINTER'S PILGRIMAGE THROUGH FIFTY YEARS

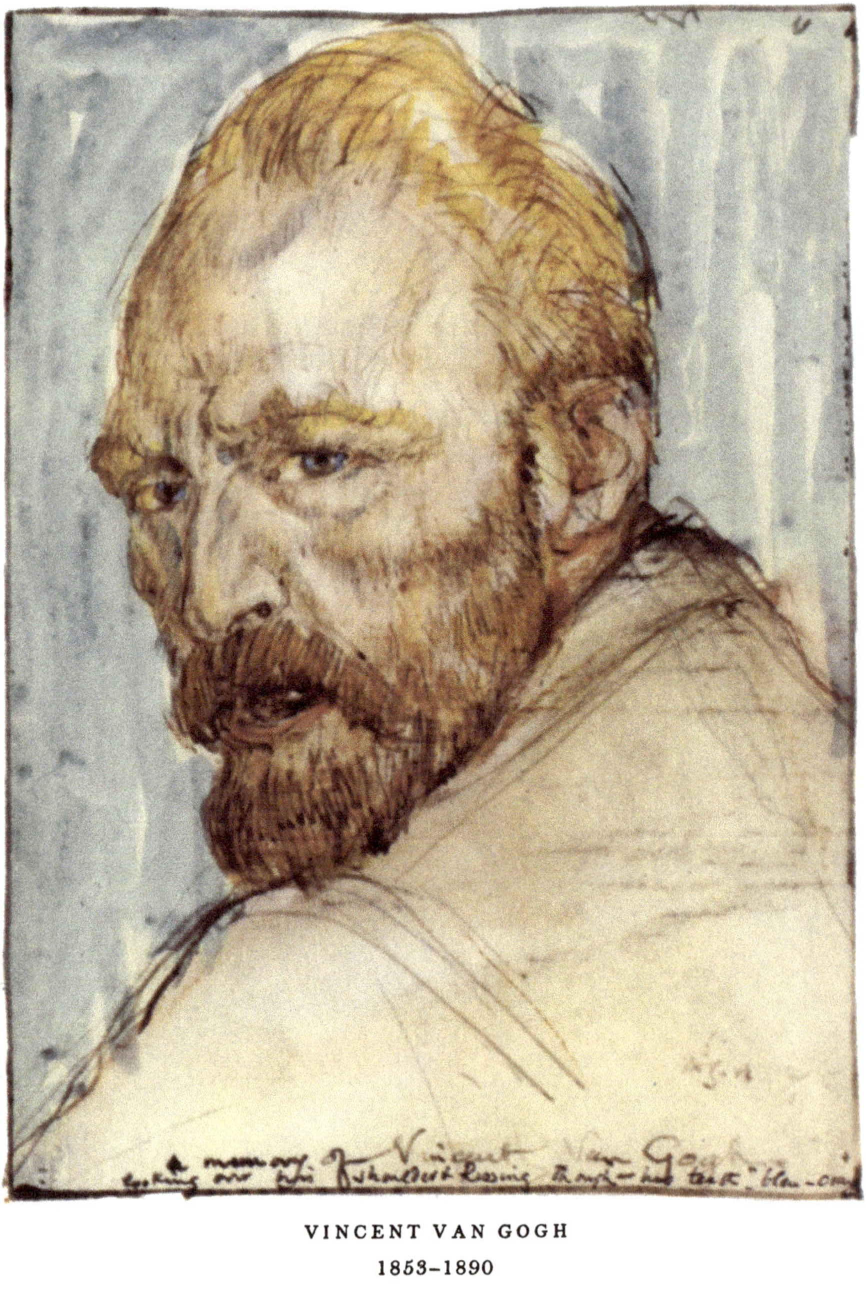

VINCENT VAN GOGH

1853–1890

by A. S. HARTRICK

A PAINTER'S PILGRIMAGE THROUGH FIFTY YEARS

by

A. S. HARTRICK
R.W.S.

CAMBRIDGE
AT THE UNIVERSITY PRESS
1939

CAMBRIDGE
UNIVERSITY PRESS

University Printing House, Cambridge CB2 8BS, United Kingdom

Cambridge University Press is part of the University of Cambridge.

It furthers the University's mission by disseminating knowledge in the pursuit of education, learning and research at the highest international levels of excellence.

www.cambridge.org
Information on this title: www.cambridge.org/9781107559783

First published 1939
First paperback edition 2015

A catalogue record for this publication is available from the British Library

ISBN 978-1-107-55978-3 Paperback

To

THE LADY PATRICIA RAMSAY

who gave me the title of my book,

in homage

CONTENTS

ILLUSTRATIONS

Except where otherwise stated all the illustrations are by the author

PREFACE

For fifty years, beginning with my student days in Paris, when I was fortunate to stray into the orbits of Paul Gauguin and Vincent Van Gogh, I have, from behind the scenes, participated in, or at least observed, the changes of standards and reputations in art. These changes were as violent and puzzling, though probably less harmful, than those we have all suffered from in the same period—War, Revolution, Politics. I loved my job, and have known it as a workman desiring no other. Therefore I have no apologies to make for recording those facts and appearances that have interested me, in the hope that, as they are sincere, they may prove instructive or amusing to others.

I kept no diary; and although I have looked at some papers and letters, I preferred not to burden what I wished to say with details already forgotten, and, except in their broad effects, better left so. In any case, my publisher said my original manuscript was too bulky and must be cut. I agreed that it should be treated "as if I were dead" for I have no pretensions as a writer and I gladly take advice from those who know. The writing proved a more formidable task than I expected. Like many others, I discovered that it is no easy matter to convey in words that which belongs to the eye. Fromentin, himself a painter, is the most successful writer on painting that I know. Somehow he is able to describe the processes, emotional and technical, that go towards the making of fine painting—so accurately that we feel it has been revealed to us why Rembrandt, Rubens, Hals and even Paul Potter are called great painters; his word-painting can always be made to work again with a brush.

The encouragement of some good friends and pupils has carried me through to the end and I hope they will not be disappointed. I feel specially grateful to my friend Mr Arthur

Morrison who not only read all the MSS. but did his best to make straight what was crooked and advised me on his own art of authorship; and also to Mr S. C. Roberts to whose skill and experience the final form of this book is due. Something more than thanks I owe to John Copley and his wife Ethel Gabain, two artists who tread the narrow way of sincerity in life and art. By their enthusiasm they sustained me in apparent defeat, and found the ideal publisher for my work. Lastly, I would like to thank Mr and Mrs Kerr Lawson as well as Mr F. E. Hansford, who all have helped in their various ways, and Vincent Lines, my friend and pupil who has drawn my portrait.

A. S. H.

March 1939

CHAPTER I

THE PAINTER

"Artists are dull dogs." Thus spake Benjamin Jowett, sometime master of Balliol, as reported to me by my housemaster at Fettes when I tentatively proposed "painting" as my "life" career. And the verdict was reinforced in growls to my mother, then a widow, by the headmaster, W. A. Potts, to the effect that they were "an uneducated lot". Doubtless this criticism and resistance was based on experience of the world, such as they had, and was well meant—but the immediate result for me was that my effort to make a serious attempt at beginning as an artist was postponed until after I should have passed the matriculation examination for medicine at Edinburgh University. This, however, I accomplished successfully, even with some honours, if I remember aright; though indeed I remember little of it, for in my mind that examination was no more than another obstacle to my purpose, now safely overcome.

But as this writing is by way of autobiography, and as there are always with us those who demand facts, apart from the majority who prefer fiction, I must go back from Fettes for a little while to Bangalore in India, near which place my father, Captain William Hartrick, was stationed with his regiment, the 7th Royal Fusiliers, on 7 August 1864, where and when I was born. As to my ancestry (if it matters), it was Scots, Welsh and Irish, so should be called mongrel, like that of most people in these islands, I suppose. The Hartricks, I have been told, came from Holland with William III, and were given land in New Ross as military settlers after the Battle of the Boyne. My father was a cousin of Charles Lever, the novelist: these are all my contacts with Erin that are worth recording. On my mother's side I may claim a connection with sufficient of romance in it to have attracted the attention and the pen of Sir Walter Scott. For the Rose Bradwardine in *Waverley*, as Scott himself testifies in his introduction to that novel, was moulded on Mary Stewart of Invernahyle in Appin, who, as a child of eight years old, for weeks after Culloden evaded the soldiers who were hunting her wounded and fugitive father, Alexander Stewart, and fed and tended him in a cave hidden in a thicket on his own property. That Mary Stewart became the great-grandmother of my own grandfather. Much more of the romantic history of Stewart of Invernahyle can be read in that same introduction to *Waverley*. Of Welsh blood, I remember a grand-uncle, Joseph Peers, the last of his race, who was Clerk of the Peace for Denbigh in North Wales. There is, or used to be, a public memorial to him in the town of Ruthin. The memory of him remains green with me, for his custom was to send my parents at Christmas a cake from Bolland of Chester and a Stilton cheese. As I write I wonder if there be anything in this Celtic ancestry to account for my juvenile artistic tendencies, or whether the whole belief of some artistic strain in any trickle of Celtic blood be mere superstition. I have no other reason to account for it in myself.

At two years of age I came home permanently to the land of my fathers and mothers in a troopship; and, of course, as needs be in those days, by way of the Cape. We touched at St Helena, where I am informed, and perhaps remember, that I was held up by the French sentry, there stationed, to kiss the bust of the great Napoleon.

This makes a sufficient introduction of myself to bring me back to Fettes. Notwithstanding the unfavourable view of the artist's vocation in high authority at that school, a drawing-master was kept there. He was an elderly Bohemian named Bohuslav Kroupa. His skull had been bashed in by a blow from a Prussian needlegun at the battle of Königgrätz in 1866, and since then he had wandered the earth a political exile. How he came to be appointed to Fettes I have no idea. He was a good friend to me, giving me prizes for drawing and nursing my enthusiasm for art, though he remained a "butt" for the majority of the school, who cheeked, tormented and told funny stories about him, as boys will do with foreigners. There was no proper equipment for teaching art in public schools at that time, and, truth to tell, Kroupa was an amateur in art who could not take one far. The most valuable art teaching I had at Fettes was acquired from a study of the early numbers of the *Graphic* newspaper, bound volumes of which were in my house library. There I used to copy from the works of Boyd Houghton, E. J. Gregory, W. Small and others. Both Thomas Hardy and Van Gogh have pointed to their value as education in art, so by instinct or accident I wrought better than I knew. I have learnt recently, from Col. M. W. Douglas, a contemporary at Fettes, that the news that I, a favourite pupil, had gone to study in Paris, was a nightmare to old Kroupa. "He is lost. He will return an impressionist!" he wailed; a matter fully as shocking in those days to the well brought up as a post-impressionist of yesterday or to-day.

Further, the decision was that I must remain at school for yet another year, presumably to acquire more culture. The net result, profit or loss, to me was that I got my cap for the 1st XV at Rugby football, and was in the school VIII for gymnastics; at cricket I was an indifferent performer, being short-sighted. Such is, or was, my education for that period, and honestly, I doubt if I can ever complain. What mind I possess is, thank God, contained *in corpore sano*, which was certainly encouraged. Nevertheless, that dismissal of all artists as "dull dogs" rankled with me at the time and still does.

The education of an artist is a much more personal matter than that of a schoolmaster or a don. What others know or can teach is of little use to him. Only what his own eye and hand and brain can together create will serve him in the end. "Though we can become learned through another man's knowledge, we can never be wise except in our own wisdom" is how Montaigne puts it.

The lives of artists, as written by themselves or other people, do not fare badly beside the biographies of the eminent who have been conventionally educated. It is doubtful if an autobiography exists more vivid and more widely acclaimed by the verdicts of every nation that counts than that of Benvenuto Cellini, artist, egoist, ruffian and even scoundrel though he may appear in the eyes of the righteous.

Leonardo da Vinci's notebooks are still yielding ideas and possibly gold to investigators, and William Blake, already, has as many books written in English about himself and his mysticism as St John the Divine.

Even the failures have a saving quality about them, for Benjamin Hayden's autobiography and Van Gogh's letters have a vitality that seems to have evaporated from the life of Benjamin Jowett and his like, eminent and important though they were in their own time.

Finally, on this subject I would like to quote the opinion of Ellen Terry, who must have met the pick of all the men of her day; it is written in her own autobiography that of the two most brilliant men she had ever known Whistler was one.

For what my own experience is worth, I can confirm her statement about Whistler. He had the quickest brain of anyone I have ever known and he used it like an artist to be perfectly charming or perfectly impossible. To this I would like to add that it amuses me to remember that although Whistler, in his impatience, mocked and abused England and the stodginess of the English as compared with the politeness and polish of the inhabitants of Paris or West Point, his perspicacity did not fail him at the end; for in spite of all temptations, when his time drew near he retired into the bosom of a real British family to die, and left all the money he had to his English sister-in-law in gratitude for her care of him with the certainty that his last wishes would be punctiliously obeyed. Few so faithful would be found to-day, for nearly all would think that they "knew better!"

"Qui s'excuse s'accuse", but having got this grievance off my chest I will proceed with my narrative.

In the last year of my time at Fettes, my mother made her second marriage to Dr Charles Blatherwick, a widower with a family mostly grown up, who lived near my home at Rhu on the Gareloch, in Dumbartonshire. He was Chief Inspector of Alkali Works for Scotland, and also an amateur painter in water-colours of quite professional ability—indeed, he had been one of the founders of the Royal Scottish Society of Painters in Water-Colour about the middle of the eighteen seventies, and was President of the Glasgow Art Club; thus he was at home in all art circles of the West of Scotland. Socially, he was the most gifted man I have ever known—musician, writer, painter, as well as doctor of medicine; and each of a standard that was remarkable. He had been in practice at Highgate until his health broke down, living in what was still known as Coleridge's house; and after an interval was appointed to this Inspectorship, which had just been created under the Local Government Board.

At last the opposition to my aspirations, so far as authority was concerned, passed away. After various inquiries as to ways and means I found myself in London at the Slade School of Art under Professor Legros. Those were the days of the apotheosis of the Barbizon School of painting for the English and American public. More pictures signed Corot than the artist had painted in his lifetime had been sold in America alone.

J. F. Millet's picture, "The Angelus", after a series of rapid rises in value, was bought for 553,000 francs (the franc was then worth 10*d.* in sterling) from the estate of a Parisian stock-broker Secretan, who had made a fortune speculating in copper, and lost it. The name of Millet was in the news of the world, a competition having been cleverly started by the picture-dealers and worked up by the press in the fashion still approved by publicity. The moneybags of Europe and America were set in competition. We were told that the honour of nations was at stake; and dramatically the picture was saved for France by

Mons. Proust, the Government agent, from the bids of two American dealers who arrived after the sale had started! But this was not the end of "sensations" in regard to it. The French Government refused to ratify the deeds of its agent, so the picture was surrendered to the Americans, who took it home and exhibited it in New York and all the principal American cities as the most expensive picture in the world! At long last it was bought for £32,000 and brought back to France by a Mons. Chouchard, proprietor of the Magazins du Louvre, the chief French collector of Barbizon pictures, and by him was bequeathed to the Louvre, where it now hangs. Through reproductions, in every form and shape, it has become one of the best-known pictures in the world. I was surprised at its small size when I saw it for the first time, and even more astonished to learn that when first painted it earned for the painter the reputation of a dangerous anarchist together with much accompanying abuse. While agreeing that the motive really is touching and the design impressive, most painters will agree also that it is not the artist's finest work—indeed, the Louvre already possessed in the "Gleaners" and the "Church at Greville" two unchallenged masterpieces. The most marvellous painting by Millet I have ever seen is that lovely nocturne called "A Shepherd in the Fold by Moonlight" painted in 1861. About four feet square in size, it was exhibited at the International Exhibition in Paris of 1889, when it belonged to a Belgian collector. The luminosity and quality of the moonlight in this picture is extraordinary; quite as startling as the first sight of a Van Gogh to me, but with a reserve that is absent from the latter. The moonlight really floods everything and the flanks of the sheep seem to heave, while their breath goes up like smoke in the frosty air; there can be no reservations—it is a masterpiece.

The most striking memory I have of the art world, in my early days at the Slade, is of Rodin and his "L'âge D'Airain". He was a personal friend of Legros, and for a week or two I seem to remember him a small energetic figure with a wispy beard hurrying about the passages of the Slade; very different from the stout, grave signor (with scented beard) of the International Society twenty years later.

The statue, already cast in bronze, had been placed in the corridor outside Legros's private room, which was not used as a studio but as an office. Rodin at that time had hardly become known in London, but the bronze excited considerable interest, not to mention criticism, among the students, especially on account of the story that it had been rejected from the Salon at first, because the jury believed that the torso had been cast from the life; a suspicion that was proved to be false. It disappeared from its place at the Slade for about a fortnight, then returned, and we students heard sinister rumours that it had been sent to the Royal Academy and was rejected from there also!

Legros was not a stimulating teacher for the ordinary, undistinguished student. In the first place he did not speak English, so there was a barrier between him and those who could not speak French. The teaching of the common herd was chiefly in the hands of Messrs Slinger and Durham, both elderly men. The former was cleverly caricatured as the "Vulture" in an early book called *The Wages of Sin* by the daughter of Charles Kingsley, who wrote under the name of "Lucas Malet": this description aptly conveys his appearance to the youth of that day. He used to follow Legros, when he made his somewhat rare rounds of the classes, to translate the words of the "master", and always began "the Professor says". What the Professor said was usually "pas mal", or something equally colourless; but in correcting the life drawing he had one peculiarity: on the smallest opportunity he cut down the size of the genitals, saying, "Michael Angelo always made them small".

Of Slinger many tales used to be told, of which an encounter with a student called Sturdee is worthy to be preserved from oblivion if possible. Coming up to the drawing, Slinger began his criticism: "A little more andante, Mr Sturdee, a little more andante", and he went on rubbing his hands together as was his wont. "Ah! I thought we were supposed to draw *à Legros*", was the *riposte* of the victim; and this indeed was the burden of most outside criticism of the period. The truth is that Legros, like other artists of strong individuality, had a very marked effect, perhaps too marked, on his favourite pupils, such as William Strang, Charles Holroyd and J. B. Clarke. Although, I confess, I did not see it properly at that time, it is my conviction now that his method of teaching drawing, based on that of the old Italian masters, to draw with the point and by the character of the contour rather than by the mass in tone, is the best, if not the only one for the proper training of a student. Drawing is the study of the representation of form, and the expression of form is the end of drawing.

For the purpose of teaching this art nothing can equal the point on white paper, and such was Legros's general instruction to his pupils. Charcoal and the brush, tools most suitable for the representation of tone and colour, should come later. A novelty, in those days of square drawing and the stump, in most art schools, Legros provided quantities of full-size photographs of drawings by the old masters, especially those by Leonardo, Michael Angelo and Raphael. These, all students were encouraged to study and to copy. "Nothing new in that" the expert will say, but it was new then and can easily be forgotten again. In the formation of taste as well as in training the eye this sort of unconscious discipline is invaluable.

Charles Holroyd (a future Director of the National Gallery, for which he was knighted) and Harrington Mann were the "high lights" in the life-room when I arrived at the Slade, with Charles Furse a little later. From the first the last-named displayed that mixture of energy and self-confidence which the prophets believed would have made him President of the Royal Academy had he lived a little longer. The quality of his wit is displayed in a story belonging to a few years later than these, his student days. The occasion was a meeting of the Art Workers' Guild in Clifford's Inn.

Frank Dicksee (who later *did* become P.R.A.), then at the height of his vogue as one of the attractions to Burlington House, had just read a paper on "Handling in Paint" to the members. When he had finished, Furse rose with deliberation to hurl this "bomb": "Master and brethren, it appears to me that there must be some mistake or confusion in the mind of the last speaker, because what he has been talking about is certainly not *handling* but *footling*."

Holroyd became a teacher of the life for a time, and it was from him rather than from Legros himself that I acquired the more valuable part of the instruction I received at the Slade.

Rossetti had but recently died, the Grosvenor Gallery in Bond Street had just been opened by Sir Coutts Lindsay, so the Pre-Raphaelites and the teachings of Ruskin were in the air and news. Holroyd's advice to us students remains with me as convincing, that when Ruskin praised it was safe to follow him, but that when he blamed we should look for ourselves. This is true of most prophets and valuable criticism for a beginner. I have never forgotten it, so now hand it on. Whether Ruskin is read by students to-day or not is not the question, but we could do with another Ruskin to-day.

At the Slade we were taught to draw on Michalet paper with the point, using the "natural" Italian chalk. When you had found a good piece this was delightful, but oftener it was little better than slate pencil. I recall another of Legros's little sensations: it was his pleasure, whenever he found a drawing carefully shaded up in the approved east-wind Slade fashion, to seize a piece of this slate pencil chalk and cut his corrections without pity into what the poor student considered, if not a masterpiece, something of the nature of a ewe lamb. I have seen a student in tears of rage, if not of sorrow, after such a visitation.

From time to time a special session was held, to which all the students both male and female were called together, in order to see the Professor paint a head from the "life".

He invariably used a canvas with a background prepared on it with a wash of raw umber and "turps". On this ground he rubbed in the main drawing directly with a brush, also in a raw umber, blocking in the main planes and tones rather carefully until the drawing was completely realized in monochrome. Next he worked with solid colours, leaving the shadows for the most part thin and transparent in the umber, while loading impasto in the lights. In an hour to an hour and a half the head was complete. This of course is an old and perfectly sound method of painting in oil colours, but it was also monotonous, heavy, and often dull. Some of us had heard of freer and more exciting methods which were being tried in Paris. Now Legros seriously objected to any of his pupils going to Paris—that was the *via damnosa*. Why? Apart from the implied reflexion on his own teaching I do not know. It was said he refused to have anything further to say or do with a pupil who took so false and insulting a way. Many years before this, Legros proposed to Courbet and others of his friends: "Let us form a school and I will be the head of it." Thus man proposes, but who disposes in these days the winds alone may tell.

After about two years at the Slade, hearing that Harrington Mann, Frank Emanuel, George Gascoyne and several others were about to migrate to Paris, the city of light as it then seemed, I determined to go there also, and joined up with a number of other English students from the Royal Academy School and elsewhere in the Académie Julian in Paris. Among them an impish figure stands out, Raven Hill (of *Punch*), aged nineteen and wearing a full black beard!

Julian's was the largest school of art in Paris and it had been started by a painter *manqué* and ex-strong man called Julian who, having hired a studio to work in, got together a number of students, engaged a model and finally persuaded certain well-known painters to come round and, for a fee, correct the efforts in drawing and painting of these students, who afterwards were known as "ses élèves", and as such acknowledged the fact in all catalogues and publications. When I joined up, there were about four hundred students in the Académie Julian, gathered from every country and nationality in the civilized world. Four Professors, Bougereau and Robert Fleury in one and Boulanger and Lefèvre in the other, divided the two main studios between them. All of them were well-known painters of the time and members of the jury of the Salon, the chief French picture exhibition of the year. It was important that the Professors should be members of the "jury" of the Salon, because the work of most of the pupils would pass before them as such sooner or later. I enlisted under Boulanger and Lefèvre.

Although we students did not know it, this was a time of change in the art world in Paris. The Impressionist Movement was coming into fashion and the Academicians of the Salons were being cast down from their pedestals.

I had a prize for painting landscape at the Slade, but my next bouquet arrived not long after I had entered the Académie Julian. Boulanger, the Professor, who with Lefèvre criticized the work of the division of the studio to which I was attached, gave me the prize of the monthly "Concours" for composition. He was delightfully complimentary about my effort and he finished by saying that I was "tout-à-fait l'artiste", but he added, as his little pill, that I must "learn to draw"! This of course was the soundest advice I could have received from anyone at the time.

There is an anticlimax to this of course. As soon as I started work on the next monthly "Concours", the subject of which was "The Prodigal Son", at least half-a-dozen men settled down with easels just behind me, watching every stroke I made. This time I did not get the prize!

A year or so later, after I had left Julian's to join the Atelier Cormon, a very French studio in the Clichy quarter, I think I must have carried out Boulanger's instructions to some degree, because an American called Van der Pool, the head of the Art School of Chicago, who was collecting life drawings to take back to his school, as specimens of contemporary drawing in the studios of Paris, bought two by me as representative of the work done in Cormon's atelier. Nor was this the end; nearly ten years after, I gave to Morley Fletcher, who asked for them, two other life drawings of this period, which he used when teaching life drawing at the L.C.C. Central School of Arts and Crafts, then just started in Regent Street. Later, these went with him to Reading, where he was head of the Art School at University College. From there they went with him to the College of Art in Edinburgh and finally to Santa Barbara in California, where he was called to start an art school under the Carnegie Trust. Altogether I might claim, through these two drawings, that I have had some responsibility in the teaching of young draughtsmen "how to shoot", if I may put it so, and I trust that from these examples of mine they, at least, learnt to shoot straight, so that I have handed on untarnished the advice of old Boulanger, my first master in Paris.

CHAPTER II

THE ATELIER JULIAN

In the hope of mitigating the too insistent presence of the ego, I am giving my memories of the Atelier Julian in the form of a sketch of the life of an ultra-British type whom I encountered there. A specimen of that pathetic class of hopelessly hopeful students struggling steadily against the insurmountable obstacle of an inborn incompatibility of nature with the task they had set themselves.

I suppose he must be classed as a specimen of that eccentric type of Briton—believed to have died out in these days when we are rather envied and therefore hated—who used to earn for his fellow-countrymen on the Continent the general title of "madmen".

His story, as told by himself, a mass of distorted facts and conclusions, was one of the most pathetically humorous histories it was ever my fortune to hear.

I can but give, in something of their real sequence, the bare outlines: to attempt more were hopeless, unless the whole air and eye of the original narrator were present to add the touches of quaintness and drollery native to an unusual personality and physique.

Gibbon, as he was called, was a Mancunian, broad of accent and of person, with a face that beamed at you over a short black pipe held close to his lips by a crooked fore-finger and shaded by a nose of bold proportions. For years he had been domiciled in Oldham, where he managed a cotton mill to the profit of his employers and the admiration of himself. When well past middle life and a married man, with a family practically dependent on his salary, of all possible madnesses, he was seized with the desire to pursue (in paint) that most fickle and *exigeante* of mistresses, the Goddess of Art.

As was only to be expected, his ideas of her ways and moods or even possible locality were of the queerest.

He had spent several summer holidays from time to time in a secluded haunt in Wales, where a number of generally speaking fifth-rate artists had retired to practice economy and loafing, as far as possible from the disturbing influence of a discriminating public.

There he learnt to make sticky-looking little landscapes, the best that can be said for them being that they were akin to the would-be orator's speeches, for "when he went hoam they pleased hissen".

In the same sylvan retreat, quite naturally, he renewed an early acquaintance with Bacchus, and fixed the habit of consuming more liquor than was consistent with strict sobriety, though within the limits of the good fellowship he loved.

Not that there was any vice about him, merely weakness. Enthusiast by temperament, he firmly believed that this was the royal road to the favours of the goddess he wished to woo; and a very pleasant one he found it.

With fatal inconsequence, the native shrewdness so conspicuous in his business dealings seemed suddenly to desert him.

One day in a characteristic spirit of optimism he threw up his position at the mill, and shortly after started for Paris (he had heard vaguely somewhere that there was the happy hunting-ground he sought), bearing a leather bag containing fifty golden sovereigns, and inspired by the fixed intention of learning to draw in three months!

After that, he felt satisfied, all must be plain sailing. Knowing nothing of the French language—without any prior arrangements of what he was going to do on his arrival in Paris—armed with a piece of paper inscribed with the two words "Académie Julian", he was perfectly and serenely happy.

Fortunately, on board the boat he fell in with a painter named Strickland, on his way to Venice, and the acquaintance ripened in the train over the contents of a fat flask in Strickland's possession.

"Is that right?" said the latter, for the second time pouring out a stiff three fingers and adding a little soda from a bottle he had with him in his bag.

"Well," replied Gibbon, rolling a beady eye, round which the little wrinkles puckered with a critical satisfaction, "I think it's joust a wee thing drouned", and a "wee thing drouned" the drink remained until the flask was dry.

In the interval Strickland rapidly acquired a fairly complete history of this odd companion and his intentions. So, wondering at the audacity of the creature, he half humorously took pity on his helplessness and saw him safely into a cheap hotel in the Quartier Latin, with his rent paid for a month.

Being pressed for time, he next showed his *protégé* the way across the Pont des Arts through the courtyard of the Louvre to the Rue de Rivoli and then left him, hurrying off to catch the express for Venice.

By his own account, Gibbon promenaded the Rue de Rivoli for three days "waiting for a word of English".

How he failed to satisfy his longing it is beyond me to imagine. To put the matter plainly, how anyone of his pronouncedly British appearance escaped the sharks, pseudo-guides and photo-vendors who haunt that long arcade the Fates alone can reveal.

It is just possible that a powerful physique and accent rendered him forbidding, but as he said himself, "he never had a chance of speaking to anyone in even broken English".

When he felt hungry, he walked into a restaurant, placed his finger at hazard on the menu, and took what came, with amazing results to everyone concerned. When he had finished he always paid in gold, and his collection of change was extraordinary.

From a later detailed examination it proved to consist of doubtful coins of all the treaty Powers, besides strange specimens from the mints of remote Republics known and unknown.

On the eve of the third day of misery, "desperate" fails to describe the condition of this essentially gregarious person: he was ready to perform any penance, to go to prison if necessary, provided only that he heard his native tongue again.

Quite reckless, he marched into a *brasserie*, attracted thereto by the bock-drinkers outside, and in a terrific voice shouted one word: "Beer!"

Everyone, inside and out, was startled; then, seeing that he was sober and not dangerously mad, the French audience shrugged its shoulders and went on with its dominoes. The waiter whispered something with the "patron", retired for a space to return with an enormous jug containing somewhere about two gallons of beer; this he set on a stone table before his redoubtable-looking customer.

Gibbon seated himself, for a moment abashed at the result of his daring.

Then, glaring fiercely round on the "frog-eating crowd", for the honour of old England, as he afterwards explained, he set himself to finish the lot.

When about half-way through, as the result of a course of steady drinking, a small dark-bearded Frenchman rose and, advancing carefully, said diffidently: "You aire an Engleeshman?"

Gibbon looked as if some beatific vision were vouchsafed him, but in actual fact nearly fell over the man in his excitement.

"For t'luv ov 'Eaven man," he gasped, "shaw me an Englishman."

A few minutes' eager conversation, and both went forth into the night, Gibbon holding on fast to his heaven-sent pilot.

Ten minutes later they were seated in a café, the rendezvous of all the painters in the Quartier; then, with a glass of hot grog before him, our friend—his troubles past—as happy as a king, was relating with great gusto to a laughing circle of English and Americans the adventures and miseries of his first three days in Paris.

Things were now comparatively easy for him, and contrary

to expectation he was quite a success with the French element at Julian's, where he had been duly inducted.

During the autumn and winter months there were usually several hundred students of all ages, nationalities and conditions gathered there, the whole going to make up such a very free republic that it remained constantly on the borders of anarchy.

The internal politics of this body were entirely in its own hands, authority being vested in four "massiers" elected by ballot, who besides collecting the "masse"—a sum of money paid by each "nouveau" for his first-footing—were generally responsible for order; their decision being final in all disputes, which were not infrequent.

To return to Gibbon. Shyness was not likely to raise any preliminary stumbling-block on his part, far from it. The novelty of everything amused him immensely, and out of its exuberance his amusement seemed to infect others as readily as if it were German measles or any other childish ailment.

When spoken to in French, though not understanding a word addressed to him, he always replied as he thought fit in the most vigorous English at his command. "It's cheery-like, ye see", he explained, beaming pleasantly on his foreign acquaintance.

So popular did he become in his own particular "atelier", with his comic songs and ways, that the practical jokers left him alone, and at one time it seemed possible that he might achieve the acme of fame by supplanting the French "massier" and, following in the same ingenious footsteps, live for the remainder of his life on the proceeds of the "masse" itself.

However, the Fates decided otherwise. Of course, adventures of a characteristic sort were not long in coming to him. While quite a "nouveau", burning with curiosity and heedless of danger, he ventured into an adjoining atelier, to the occupants of which he was practically unknown, his hat thrust well on the back of his head as usual.

"Chapeau! Chapeau!!" a perfect pandemonium of shouts burst about him, till, gathering what was wanted, he smilingly removed the offensive covering and leisurely continued his voyage of exploration towards an Englishman he had recognized at work in a far corner.

"What be yon long-beaked beggar sayin' reet noo?" said he, referring to a big dark man who still kept on a running fire of remarks in French, clearly aimed at Gibbon and in tones unmistakably hostile.

"Oh, it's Jacquet you mean. Why, he's asking if you think this is a stable, and says that if he had his way he'd soon see that such louts were kept chained up, and a few other choice remarks meant to be funny, I suppose."

Without further say, Gibbon walked over to his enemy and, laying a great paw on his shoulder, said hoarsely: "Tha' spake American, ba gum I 'ave heard ye, and why the hell can tha' not spake it naw?"

With that he turned on his heel and went out, leaving the tormentor speechless and the whole place laughing at his impotence to find a ready retort.

The man came from California, half French, half Mexican and a noted bully: hence the success of Gibbon's first effort to assert himself—the beginning of a notoriety which had otherwise been roughly checked in a "nouveau".

For the future the word "chapeau" was added to his vocabulary, and that and one other word "m—", common but unprintable, completed his whole memory of the French language on his return home.

His second experience was humiliating and for a moment it appeared that it was to be an eye-opener, but his self-confidence took the upper hand at once, only to urge him more strenuously on in the pursuit of his chimera.

He had arrived at the atelier one morning rather late, to find a placard inscribed "Le professeur est là" hanging on the handle of the door; as he entered, the unusually decorous silence and air of business for a moment chilled his ardour; but hurrying to his place on the very outskirts of the crowd about the model, he seated himself on a high stool and, whistling, commenced work at a small canvas on which some reckless splashes pretended to represent a human head. A hissing "assez!" and a very distinctly whispered "shut up!" from near at hand cut short his little tune, when, looking down with an injured air, he saw at his elbow a short, bald-headed man with an immense moustache and imperial.

"Another puzzle-whiskered joker!" thought Gibbon, turning carelessly aside.

But the little man was not to be disposed of so easily, for, blowing out his lips with a sort of splutter, he asked sharply in French: "Where is the interpreter?"

An Englishman stepped up, to whom he continued: "Kindly tell this gentleman that it is necessary for him to make a beginning from the cast", and so passed on.

"What for! what the hell be t'business at yon?" says Gibbon, when the sentence had been translated. "A'll see him damned first!"

"Confound it, man, that's the professor", said the interpreter: "and to the cast, or out of this studio you go."

Gibbon was stupefied. "Gosh, Peter, is that a fact?" was all he could find to say at the moment, and, seemingly quite subdued, took his place humbly beside some boys who were making a beginning on casts of legs and arms close by the door of the atelier. For the rest of the day he seemed rather depressed and that night bought a bottle of rum to take home with him. Next morning he was argumentative again, and when a few weeks later he was permitted to return to the "life" unchecked, cheerfully accepted what most knew to proclaim that he was classed as "hopeless" as the sign of his rapid progress.

He had just reached that stage when the power to retain a caricature likeness of the model, often found in beginners without any correctness of drawing, had passed, and had now arrived at the creation of monsters all bearing a family resemblance to himself.

And the worst of it was, there appeared no signs of his emerging from this second state.

His insatiable curiosity ended by landing him in the Police Court. Eager to put in practice the lessons acquired in the atelier, with eyes now opened to the study of character about him, he sought out some spahis he saw in the street. Enthralled by their picturesque robes and magnificent bearing, in company with a couple of English friends he followed them into a dingy little café where they were accustomed to foregather.

Then, having taken up a conspicuous position facing his victims, he essayed to make a sketch, in spite of their obvious annoyance at his intentions.

For a moment trouble threatened, because he resolutely refused to understand their objections, when by accident it was discovered that one of them spoke a little English. Then a few coins passed, and the matter was righted, not without some difficulty; but Gibbon with his usual facility succeeded in amusing the Arabs with his buffoonery and finally overcame their native scruples on the subject of picture-making, or perhaps, having seen what he was doing, they were satisfied that there was nothing in it.

As he left the café, however, a more serious incident took place. Gibbon rightly or wrongly believed that the "patron" was trying to cheat him over the bill, and his companions being neither of them good enough linguists to understand the dispute —indeed they were as new to Paris as himself—he refused to pay the sum demanded.

Matters had come to a complete deadlock, when someone behind the bar snatched the hat off one of the friends.

Gibbon's first inclination was to retaliate by hitting the man in the eye, when, catching sight of a gendarme just outside the glass door, his face brightened with a happy thought.

"All reet, me lads", said he cheerfully. "A'll jist buck out and bring t'gendarme, and we'll soon hav' yon blackguardly thieves toasting their taters in gaol."

At the same time he made a move towards the door, when the "garçon", concluding that he was about to make a bolt, suddenly closed with him and snatched his hat off. There was a scuffle for a moment and the waiter was flung headlong, with an awful crash, through the glass door into the street, while Gibbon followed wildly into the arms of the very policeman he sought.

By great good luck he made no resistance to the Law, being indeed too astonished to think of flight. His volubility, however, returned quickly, but his explanations were of course useless, merely adding a harsh bass to the hullabaloo in French that followed. The three friends were conducted to the Station by half-a-dozen policemen and followed by the "patron", the waiter and an excited crowd of witnesses.

Here good luck still attended him, for he blundered out of the scrape without serious harm. A French friend from the studio who chanced to pass at the time came to his rescue. Being known to those in authority, he got the friends off lightly on payment of 100 francs damages, with a further 10 francs as a salve for the waiter's feelings, that person having been more frightened than hurt.

Such experiences, however, were obviously costly, and the fifty sovereigns were melting away too fast even for Gibbon's optimism.

About this time he must have felt his first real qualms about the successful issue of his artistic efforts.

Certainly some of the difficulties in his path at length seemed to be revealed to him, and the future now looked hazy, rather than rosy as before. After having made a critical tour of all the best work in the atelier during a rest, he would return to his own place and remain silent and brooding for half an hour or so —till his own abortion of a drawing again resumed possession of his eye, when his spirits once more rose rapidly.

"Never was I beat yet", he kept on muttering to himself fiercely after each such tour, "and it's not like I'm goan to start naw", he would finish up, almost triumphantly.

Nevertheless, the former buoyancy of his spirits was affected, and I fear that more and more frequently at night comfort and courage were sought from the bottle of rum kept in his little garret.

Whether owing to the same cause, or merely the old one—"familiarity"—his exceeding popularity with the French element, too, showed signs of waning; but the real cause of its destruction, ridiculous as it may appear, was a rabbit.

It came about this way.

For nearly a fortnight a discussion had been going on in the Académie. A great buck nigger, one of the models then posing, had offered, for a consideration, to eat a rabbit alive. The dispute was whether the feat were possible or no. It was decided that it was to be attempted at any rate, but the English and Americans wished to have the rabbit killed first, while the foreign element held that "alive" would provide the more interesting sight, at the same time vigorously denying the probable cruelty.

The great day arrived. Bambulo, the nigger, brought his rabbit and hid it in a box under the throne on which he was posing until the "second rest", when everyone was to gather into that particular studio to witness the spectacle. As the time drew near, some four hundred students crowded in, standing tier above tier on stools of various heights ranged in a circle round the throne, where Bambulo was appealing for silence to put to the vote the question as to whether the rabbit was to be killed first or no.

A hundred voices were yelling various instructions in different languages, when Gibbon, sneaking down, stole the rabbit from under the throne, passed it on to some accomplices and slipped out by the door near him for a moment almost unnoticed.

Bambulo, turning, just caught sight of his rabbit lifted high in triumph and disappearing from the room. With a savage yell, and seeming to turn a dirty grey with rage, he made a leap towards the door, but by that time a shouting, fighting, stumbling mob blocked the way between him and his prey.

Gibbon and his friends had retreated to the next studio, where they barricaded the door, swearing that they would never give up the rabbit alive.

Something very like a riot threatened, when the Clerk sent for the redoubtable Julian himself, who in a stentorian voice, having called for silence, deposed all the "massiers".

This proved quite a masterly move, for it changed the point at issue, for the time at least.

A clamour now arose as to Julian's rights in the matter.

The "massiers" were sacred. They might not be deposed except by the votes of all the ateliers—such interference with established custom had never been heard of before—the rights of the Académie must be asserted and at once.

An election was held and all four "massiers" re-elected.

In the meantime the Clerk had removed the rabbit from the building. Someone shouted out the "il est l'heure" and Bambulo had to take his place on the throne again; in any case another rabbit could not be got that day. But Gibbon had irretrievably compromised his position—that a mere "nouveau" of two months' standing should take such liberties was not to be endured.

Things were made very uncomfortable for him.

Bambulo was thirsting for his blood and for nearly a week Gibbon went about with the hilt of a large knife sticking out of his waistcoat, ready to defend his life if need be.

His spirits, however, never recovered from the loss of his popularity. From that day he became a sot.

True, the English-speaking element in the ateliers stood by him boldly, and so defended and supported him that in a short time his outward status in the Académie seemed much as before his day of indiscretion. Occasionally a gleam of his old boisterous humour would return and light up the place with a laugh, for the French have short memories and in any case are far from being laggards in the enjoyment of any fun going. But these moments became more and more rare. He seemed, too, to have lost all heart in his work. He was frequently absent for days at a time, reappearing a perfect wreck and showing a nasty temper, quite a new and unsuspected trait.

Still, it was fated that things could not happen to him as to ordinary beings, for the end came with another upheaval.

He had returned after one of these bouts of drinking in an exceptionally irritable mood.

"Hullo, Gibbon!" began an English acquaintance called Richards, hoping to get a rise out of him. "What's up now? Haven't seen you for days! By the way, I met a man last night who said to me: 'Do you know Gibbon? he's become one of the most infernally cantankerous argumentative brutes you ever met.'"

"Did he?" roared Gibbon, with a flash of his old spirit. "Ba gum, that's queer, for I was with a fellow last night and he says to me, he says: 'D'ye knaw Richards? he's the d—est liar that ever walked.'"

He relapsed into gloom and went off to work for that week in another atelier which was mainly occupied by Frenchmen.

There, it seems, the first hour or so was spent in annoying the few English working with them by howling, whistling and other objectionable interruptions; more particularly Gibbon, whose irritability of course made him excellent "sport", and the only wonder is that he did not break out into open violence.

Towards the end of the second hour they had quieted down, more or less tired out by their own efforts.

Gibbon evidently thought that his time had now come, so he proceeded to take revenge by whistling deliberately out of tune in a peculiarly piercing and disturbing manner of which he was a past-master.

Soon nearly everyone in the place was shouting "Assez", and the "massier", being appealed to, had ordered him to stop; but he paid no attention unless it were to try to execute some yet more excruciating cadence.

Without warning, four powerful Frenchmen made a rush, seizing him hand and foot, while a hoarse yell went up from fifty throats: "A l'échelle! à l'échelle!! crucify him! crucify him!!"

Resistance was hopeless; borne on the crest of a surging human wave, Gibbon, nearly senseless with fear, was flung against the studio ladder while the raging crowd leapt up around him, tearing at him like wild beasts.

The first intimation that the rest of us had of the row was the crash of easels falling and the scuffling of many feet, as if the whole Académie were rushing out of doors at once.

Then an American with a face as pale as death put his head into the door, shouting: "They are ill-treating an American", and vanished as suddenly as he had come.

Everyone started up, seizing the first thing handy for a weapon, at the same time crowding to the door.

A frightful scene of confusion greeted our arrival on the field of action.

Gibbon was crucified: that is, he had been tied, hands and feet spread wide apart, to a large ladder used for getting canvasses down from the racks overhead. The ladder had then been turned over so that the whole weight of the victim now hung suspended from his wrists and ankles.

From his face he seemed to be in a sort of fit from exhaustion; for a very few minutes of this treatment will make a strong man faint.

Half-a-dozen English who had fought their way to the ladder were trying to cut him down.

In the immediate foreground was a struggling heap of heads, legs and arms in inextricable confusion, presumably French and English fighting furiously, and farther off an American steadily firing shots from a revolver into the air and threatening to shoot the first man who touched him.

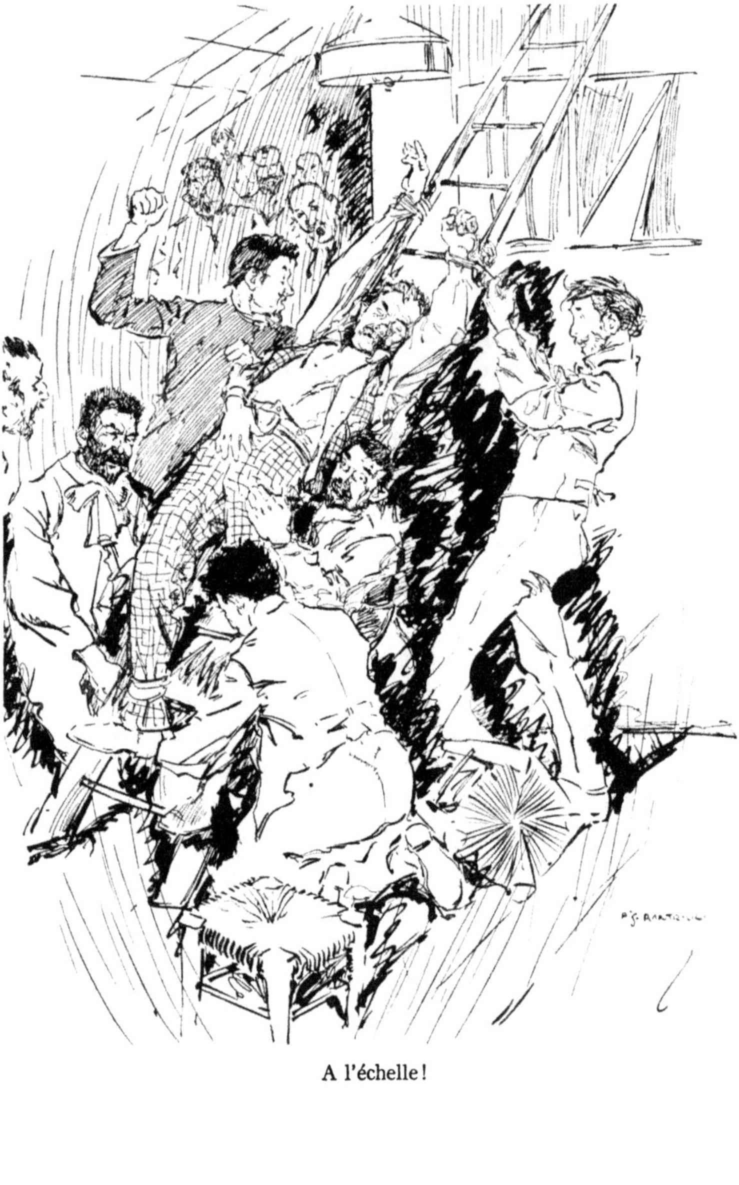

A l'échelle !

All the while there went up a most unholy din, chiefly from those not actually engaged.

The police were at last called in and, coming in force, after arresting some twenty of the combatants, soon restored order of a kind.

After this the Académie Julian was closed for a fortnight, for alterations and repairs all round.

Gibbon returned to England as soon as he was able to travel, and Paris knew him no more.

The goddess, if she were ever near, had passed him by.

When I last saw him, he was back again in Talybont in that sylvan retreat of his holidays, a broken man, still making sticky-looking little landscapes and muttering over his inseparable glass of gin and water: "A' never was beat yet."

CHAPTER III

PAUL GAUGUIN

In the company of several friends, whom I had met at Julian's, I decided to spend my first summer painting in France in Lower Brittany. Pont-Aven, a well-known resort of artists, was the centre to which fate guided me. I was fortunate indeed, but unconscious that I was about to make acquaintance with one of the men who were destined definitely to alter the history of art in Europe within the next twenty years. The death of Bastien Lepage, at the fatal age, for artists, of thirty-six, together with the posthumous exhibition of his work recently in Paris, had profoundly affected most of the younger painters in Europe. In every country the most promising youths were frankly imitating his work, with its ideals of exact representation of nature as seen out of doors, everything being painted on the spot in a grey light, in order that there might be as little change in the effect as possible while the artist was at work. In England Walter Sickert, then an enthusiastic admirer, had translated or was translating the latest life of the genius into English. In all the art schools at home or abroad it was solemnly debated as to whether he painted with large or small brushes. Alexander Harrison, an American painter who had gone into the country where Lepage was working in order to acquire the latest "tips" on the subject, inquired on this matter of the master personally.

Lepage, who had been painting with small brushes, immediately turned out with brushes two inches in width and with them produced results equally fascinating for his admirers. I believe this was the origin of what came to be known as the "square-brush act". Stanhope Forbes introduced it here, where it became the hall-mark of the Newlyn School. It has long died the death of the overdone, but for a period it was believed to be the last word of mastery in modern painting.

Lepage certainly was an artist of real ability, but I fancy his work has failed to last, because, as Samuel Butler has pointed out in the case of many genuine talents belonging to all schools, his skill was in advance of his judgment—in other words the work is too facile, therefore we tire of it. Yet I hold that his talent is one that cannot be ignored permanently. In the National Portrait Gallery there is a portrait of Henry Irving, bequeathed by Ellen Terry, which is a little masterpiece of its kind of painting as well as the best likeness of that actor that I know. Lepage also by some obscure chance painted a small portrait, in the manner of Holbein, of King Edward VII, when Prince of Wales, which is almost certainly the finest work of art of all the portraits of that monarch. It might well have been shown again in the French Exhibition at Burlington House.

Such being the atmosphere of the day, most of the young men at Pont-Aven were striving rather ineffectually to imitate this master. Details of their doings would probably not be of sufficient interest to record, so I go straight to my recollections of Paul Gauguin.

No one who ever saw Gauguin in his prime is likely to forget him. More than once I have been asked to describe my personal recollections of this formidable though creative personality; so here they are, inadequate though they may be.

I never knew him in the way I came to know Van Gogh, and doubt, after considering the man, if that would have been possible.

To begin with, I was but a somewhat green youth, an art student and a foreigner, while he was a man of the world, nearly forty years of age, the first time I saw him in Pont-Aven during the summer of 1886. Why Pont-Aven became a great resort of painters I cannot say. The landscape round about the village is not very attractive or varied. But Le Pouldu, at the mouth of the Quimper river, about fifteen miles away, where Gauguin went after his return from Martinique, is another story.

For dramatic strangeness, that was a wonder of a place; at any rate, such is the impression of it that remains with me of those days before the hotel was built, and before it had become famous among artists.

Imagine a country of gigantic sand dunes, like the mountainous waves of a solid sea, between which appeared glimpses of the Bay of Biscay and the Atlantic rollers. All this, peopled by a savage-looking race, who seemed to do nothing but search for driftwood, or to collect seaweed, with strange sledges drawn by shaggy ponies; and with women in black dresses, who wore the great black "coif" (like a huge black sun-bonnet). Gauguin has given us the exact spirit of the place in that strange picture he called "Le Calvaire"; a carved group of primitive nun-like women (probably the three Maries) supporting the figure of Christ beneath the cross; in the foreground a Breton woman in black with a black sheep; behind, the mountainous sand hills and a peep of the bay beyond.

In this picture of 1888 or 1889 all the characteristics of his later Tahiti pictures are already worked out, and good-bye said to realism and impressionism as we knew it.

Although, as I have said, I never knew Gauguin intimately, I saw him daily at the Auberge Gloanec for three or four months, and heard him talk. At the same time, I knew fairly well Charles Laval, the man who went with him to Martinique in 1887, and also P., a young Frenchman of means who became his pupil.

From these two I gathered, vicariously, perhaps more about him than I should probably have arrived at on my own.

For one thing I learnt, what may now be considered strange, that in spite of his later reputation for amorous adventures, Gauguin's one cry then was "pas de femmes", and I well remember how sardonic and sarcastic he could be about some transitory attachments of the kind which were noticeable at the time. For instance, when he described the fatter mistress of a fat painter as his "slop-bucket".

I doubt myself if women, certainly no educated women, ever got on well with him. In his *Intimate Journals* (called *Avant et Après* in French) he himself says definitely on this subject: "As you perceive, I do not know love. To say 'I love you' would break all my teeth...women, who are shrewd, divine this, and for this reason I repel them."

Tall, dark-haired and swarthy of skin, heavy of eyelid and with handsome features, all combined with a powerful figure, Gauguin at this time was indeed a fine figure of a man. Later on, his low forehead, with its suggestion of a *crétin*, was a source of grave disappointment for Van Gogh, to Gauguin's vast amusement! He dressed like a Breton fisherman in a blue jersey, and wore a beret jauntily on the side of his head. His general appearance, walk and all, was rather that of a well-to-do Biscayan skipper of a coasting schooner; nothing could be farther from madness or decadence.

In a manner he was self-contained and confident, silent and almost dour, though he could unbend and be quite charming when he liked.

I can well believe what his son writes of him: "All his life my father shocked smugly respectable people deliberately, and for the same impish reason that impelled him to hang on his wall that obscene picturê he tells about in these journals." Most people were rather afraid of him, and the most reckless took no liberties with his person. "C'est un malin", was the sort of general verdict.

He was distinctly athletic in his tastes and had the reputation for being a formidable swordsman. I believe it was truly earned; anyway it added to the caution with which he was usually approached, for he was treated as a person to be placated rather than aroused.

Perhaps the most vivid memory I have of him is of a blazing hot day when I was painting, some distance down the river

Rance, and I saw a boat rowed by two Bretons coming slowly up the river; it contained his pupil P., Madame X., her five small children with their *bonne*, and, just astern, Gauguin, naked save for a pair of slips, holding on to a rope, was being towed along on his back, like a dead porpoise, but evidently enjoying himself hugely. He passed about ten feet below me and about fifteen yards away.

At this time he was still painting under the influence of Pissarro, or perhaps rather experimenting with the colour theories of Monet or even of Seurat and Signac. I remember he painted a panel for the dining-room of the auberge, an autumn landscape, which appeared to most of us who fed there as being very extreme in its crude exaggeration of purple and gold, though of course it was nothing compared with that to which we were soon to become accustomed.

I well recall, too, the attack made on him by V., a Dutch painter, who, on the strength of a medal in the Salon, was more or less cock-of-the-walk among the painters then in Pont-Aven. He swaggered about the village, with long carroty locks, on the top of which was set a green velvet cap of Rembrandt pattern, and laid down the law on everything to everybody. Gauguin, shortly after his arrival, a stranger to most, came back for déjeuner one day and passed through the crowd at the door of the auberge. He was carrying a canvas on which he had been painting some boys bathing on a weir, painted brilliantly with spots of pure colour in the usual impressionist manner.

V. started by asking, in the rudest way, what game was this he was playing, going on to quote Rembrandt, Bastien-Lepage and himself as witnesses of its futility, while the majority crowded round to enjoy the fun of the newcomer being baited. Gauguin, however, only smiled grimly, and elbowing his way through went about his business without explanation or retort.

The sequel to all this was really funny. Within a fortnight V.'s special pupil, P., went off to Gauguin for instruction, leaving V. altogether. He invited his new master to share a

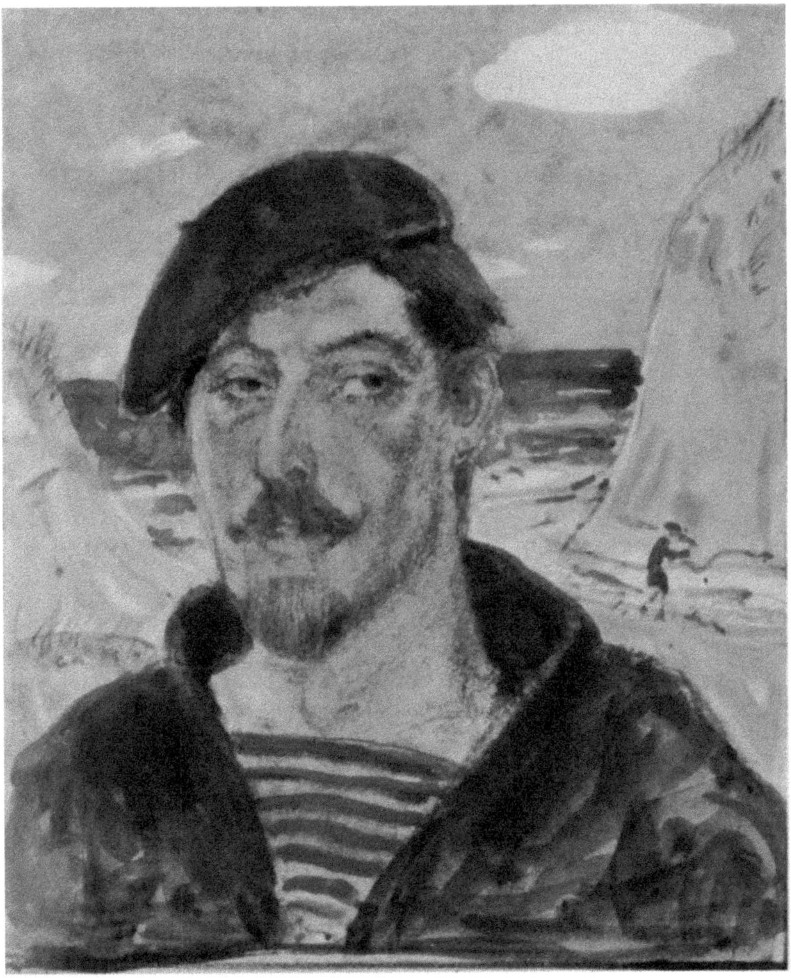

Paul Gauguin

Drawing in red and black chalks with water colour

studio he had taken at les Avens, and there Gauguin worked in comfort for the rest of his time at Pont-Aven.

Within a month V. was secretly consulting his former pupil on Gauguin's methods and theories; finally, he went over a large picture he had just completed, taking out the blacks in the shadows and substituting spots of pure colour in their place.

Six months later he wrote to Cormon, whose pupil he had been, bumptiously congratulating his master that he, the pupil, had been awarded a gold medal for this picture at Amsterdam, and also announcing that he had turned "intransigeant", as the "spot" painters at that time were labelled. I heard Cormon himself tell the story to his pupils at the studio. He spoke with much amusement and some contempt. Yet Gauguin did nothing in the matter himself; though I fancy he knew all about it, and enjoyed the situation in his silent way.

One final coincidence that is decidedly odd. This same painter, V., later went to America and there married the Princess X., daughter of the last King of Hawaii; Fate thus bringing his life into touch with the Pacific and its peoples from quite another angle!

In art, Gauguin's greatest contempt was reserved for the schools and academic art generally. This, of course, is now all "vieux jeu". But I had one conversation with him, illustrating this side of him in a very unexpected way.

He had been making some drawings of geese which he showed me. He then produced one of Caldecott's coloured books, in which some geese were depicted in that artist's very characteristic way. These he praised, almost extravagantly as it seemed to me then. "That", he said, "was the true spirit of drawing."

Gauguin would never allow that he owed anything in art, or anything at all for that matter, to anybody but himself. Self-determination was his god.

This spirit in later years led to much bitterness and recrimination with his early friends—Bernard especially, but there were others—as to who should be called the founder of the New School.

Personally, I believe that Gauguin had by far the best brains of them all. Like everybody of sense, he took much from what was going on round about him, but in my opinion the crucial change in his style came out of his study of stained glass. At Le Pouldu, he was in touch with Maurice Denis and others who were specially interested in Church art and symbolism, though the latter was a phase he rather despised.

Round about 1888, too, quite a number of artists in France were painting the glass in the interiors of Chartres and other cathedrals. In 1889, I know that Gauguin, who noted everything, was in the Clichy quarter of Paris experimenting with glass design and pottery.

So it was from thirteenth and fourteenth-century glass, I believe, that he got an idea of design and colour which exactly suited him; and he then proceeded to translate it into an art of his own, using oil paint as a vehicle. The result was something as near originality as anyone is likely to get. Perhaps the most striking piece of evidence in this direction will be found in his celebrated picture called "The Yellow Christ".

To paint a "Christ" chrome yellow appears on the face of it a deliberate eccentricity, or worse; but when one remembers the magnificent effects obtained by the use of yellow stain in early glass in precisely similar subjects, the matter no longer appears so very arbitrary provided that one has the wit to see it. Gauguin noted the facts and promptly made use of them for his own purposes.

To Cézanne, too, he must be said to be indebted—indeed, Cézanne complained "il a chipé ma petite sensation". And we do know that he owned pictures by that painter at the time he himself was an amateur, and that a still life was one of the most precious of his possessions and the last to be parted with in evil times. It will be found painted in the background of one of his pictures of 1890—a portrait of a young woman. Indeed, he was one of the first to appreciate the significance of Cézanne's aims in art.

In the last phase of all, however, Gauguin had worked round the full circle, and, in spite of his protest against the perfection of Greek art, his design especially is static and leans heavily towards the methods of the primitive Greek rather than the Gothic.

Degas was perhaps the only artist among his contemporaries whom he allowed to be "hors concours", and Gauguin's appreciation of the man and his work is one of the finest and most whole-hearted of all his writings on art.

In the final time of exile and sickness in the Marquesas, he delighted to think that Degas was reported to compete for his work at auction.

He was especially amused and flattered, too, I think, with the story of how Degas, asked by the young sons of Rouart, the picture collector, what was the position of the painting of Gauguin as compared with official art, recited to them La Fontaine's fable of the Wolf and the Sheep-dog, which he finished by saying: "And mark you, Gauguin is the Wolf."

For those who have forgotten it, I would recall how in this fable the sheep-dog, fat and sleek, advises the starving wolf to leave the forest and a life of hardships and to do as he does for a living.

"And what may that be?" asked the wolf, touched by the sheep-dog's solicitude. "Why, consider, you have only to wear a collar as I do, and do as your master tells you", was the reply. "Never", said the wolf with a snarl, and fled back into the forest.

Degas was right: no one could ever "put the collar on" Gauguin.

Though still "high" in the sale rooms—and that in spite of fiction or philosophy remains the ultimate test—Gauguin's stock is rather down in the lists of the prophets of the latest fads in painting and his "soyez mysterieuse" is received with sniffs by the abstractionists, I have no doubt that his reputation will survive this kind of rebuff. I have a memory of going round the

Gauguin Exhibition at the Leicester Galleries in 1924 with Sir George Clausen, a painter who knows all that is to be known of his craft, and a critic with a mind open to novelty, wherever it may come from in sincerity. A remark that he made at the end remains with me vividly to this day: "Why, the man can do everything!" We had finished with the paintings and were examining a head in marble, a portrait of Gauguin's wife by himself done with all the skill and delicacy of a Mercié, as compared with a realistic, even brutal, carving in wood of a girl's head, and these were contrasted with some quite convincing Tahitan idols also in wood; in each case the standard aimed at had not been let down—each was convincing of its kind and not a mere "pastiche". Yes, that was the way with Gauguin: what he took he made his own, whether it was an idea or a studio on loan. Here is his creed in a little song he made:

L'art pour l'art?—Pourquois pas?
L'art pour vivre?—Pourquois pas?
L'art pour plaire?—Pourquois pas?
Qu'importe, si c'est de l'art?

Let me now offer a few more quotations from his artistic creed as written down by himself. I quote from his *Intimate Journals*.

Always use colours of the same origin. Indigo makes the best base, it becomes yellow when treated with spirit of nitre, red in vinegar; keep to these three colours: with patience you will get all the tones from them. Get light from your paper ground, but never leave it quite naked.

Here I will say that I cannot guarantee his chemistry; and I know from his letters to De Montfried that his palette when painting was very different from this; but I can affirm that with a blue, a yellow and a red ink anyone can get all the tones necessary for work out of doors, as Gauguin says here. To continue:

Avoid black and the mixture of black and white called grey... nothing is black...nothing is grey. It is well for young painters to have a model, but let them draw a curtain over it when painting it. It is better to paint from memory, then your work will be your own property....Who said you should seek contrast in colour? If this were so, you ought not to put two flowers of the same colour into a bouquet. Seek harmony not contrast. Go from light to dark, not from dark to light; your work is never light enough. The eye seeks refreshment in painting; give it joy, not mourning.

If you repeat what another has done, you will only make a wretched mixture; it will blunt your sensibility, and it kills fresh colour.

All you do should breathe repose of the soul. Avoid animated attitudes....Let every one of your figures be perfectly statical...give everything a distinct outline.

Avoid overfinish; an impression is not so robust but that its first impression may be lost if we try to strengthen it with minute details.... Would you turn hot blood into a stone? Even were the stone a ruby cast it from you, etc.

Again he says: "In art there are only revolutionaries and plagiarists." And, finally, let me give his most famous aphorism in his own words: "Il n'y a rien qui ressemble tant à un croûte qu'un chef-d'œuvre": a saying which lets light in on the mystery of the bankruptcy of many masters, from Rembrandt downwards. And here is his effort at self-analysis:

I am on the ground, but I am not beaten. The Indian who smiles as he is tortured is not conquered.

You are mistaken, if you meant that I am wrong in calling myself a savage. I AM a savage, and the civilized feel this, for there is nothing in my work which could produce bewilderment save the savage strain, for which I am not responsible.

Every human work is a revelation of the individual. Hence there are two kinds of beauty: one comes from instinct, the other from labour. The union of the two, with modification resulting therefrom, produces great and very complicated riches.

Raphael's great science does not prevent me from discovering that the instinct of the beautiful in him is the essential quality. Raphael was born with beauty. All the rest of him is modification.

It is true I know little, but what I know is my own.

Everyone must allow that those are the notes of a man who sought for himself and also found—no charlatan or poseur could produce them. To me they mean that he had to go back to the beginnings to find an expression that was not banal, and from them he hoped to reach a new and touching beauty that would explain him to his fellow-men.

All the mere imitation and copying of nature is labour, and unless touched with emotion is as dull to the onlooker as it was to the artist producing it; hence Gauguin's insistent command, "Soyez mystérieuse".

CHAPTER IV

VINCENT VAN GOGH

My return to Paris, after the summer at Pont-Aven, was delayed till some time in November. I remember this because, when I left, the leaves had not all fallen from the trees. Pont-Aven was vivid with colour; no longer grey in the Lepage manner, and every painter remaining in the place was feverishly recording the autumn tints to the limits of his palette. Certainly my experiences there had extended my artistic horizon; though I doubt whether I yet had properly realized that there were other sides to painting than were to be found in Julian's and the annual Salon. I had heard of the Impressionists, and through Gauguin seen something of what they were after. I had seen a Salon, and a Salon des Refusés also, where the works were all hung without any selection by a jury—the most tiring and depressing exhibition of pictures I can remember, acres of "dud" paintings, hardly one of which could be remembered separately or deserved to be. Patient search discovered a few oases to surprise one, with strangely coloured work from artists like Signac and Seurat and their followers. My memory recalls, too, some life-sized nudes executed with a mock Van Eyck sort of skill, but more terrifying in their realism and ugliness than anyone could imagine possible, done by some forgotten artist. The result was, I decided not to go back to Julian's. Some time before this, I had made the acquaintance of J. P. Russell, a big Australian, who had become notable among art students in Paris by his athletic prowess in a boxing club he had formed. He was the son of a great Australian engineer, who founded a school of engineering in Sydney University; he was a man of means, but had quarrelled with his people in Australia, married an Italian model and was living permanently in Paris. He had been working for some time in the Atelier Cormon, which was situated in the Clichy quarter, where, I learnt, were the homes of the painters with new ideas. Russell also had his studio in the neighbourhood.

Here it was, then, that guided by pure chance I first set eyes on Van Gogh, or "Vincent" as he was generally known and signed himself in Paris, because the French could not pronounce Van Gogh. It so happened that he, too, had been working *chez* Cormon, up to the summer of 1886, when that atelier was suddenly closed down by Cormon himself on account of a disturbance among the pupils there. In spite of certain quite erroneous theories, which appeared in the press when his work was first exhibited in this country, that Van Gogh was of robust appearance (to fit the fury of his painting, no doubt), I can affirm that to my eye Van Gogh was a rather weedy little man, with pinched features, red hair and beard, and a light blue eye. He had an extraordinary way of pouring out sentences, if he got started, in Dutch, English and French, then glancing back at you over his shoulder, and hissing through his teeth. In fact, when thus excited, he looked more than a little mad; at other times he was apt to be morose, as if suspicious. To tell the truth, I fancy the French were civil to him largely because his brother Theodore was employed by Goupil and Company and so bought pictures.

A very different person this from Gauguin. The only characteristic they had in common, beside the fact that they were both born artists, was that neither of them came to painting professionally until they were of mature age, with considerable experience of life behind them—Van Gogh at the age of twenty-eight, when he could hardly make sixpence at any work—while Gauguin gave up stockbroking on the Bourse in Paris when he was thirty-five, and with it an income he was making of about £2000 a year, though a wife and family were dependent on him.

Van Gogh's life has been told in detail by many hands and best in his own letters, so I will only attempt a short summary here. The son of a Dutch Lutheran parson, Van Gogh had relatives in the picture-dealing trade—indeed, an uncle, also Vincent Van Gogh, was a partner in the great firm of Goupil and Company, with showrooms in Paris, London, New York and Amsterdam, in fact, in all the great cities of the world. So Vincent began work in the London galleries of Goupil and Company about the age of sixteen. At first all went well; then, after a disappointing love affair with his landlady's daughter, which led to his throwing up Goupil and suffering a desperate experience teaching French in poverty-stricken schools at Ramsgate and at Isleworth, he was moved by his relatives to the Paris house of Goupil. From there he was dismissed because he could not handle customers with tact, but insisted on imposing his own opinions on them, to their disgust and rage. Parisian ladies complained of the manners of "ce Hollandais rustre", who dared to question their taste. He returned to his father's parsonage and then decided that he had a call for the Church himself; so he was sent to Amsterdam to live with an uncle—an Admiral—that he might study theology. He had an attack of brain fever and failed at his examinations. Once more he was returned to his father's house for an unsatisfactory period, during which he fell violently in love with a cousin, a widow, who, terrified, repulsed him and his advances. Nothing seemed to go right for Vincent. After a period of extreme self-denial as a sort of missionary among the coal-miners of Brabant, he was again rejected by his superiors. Then, supported only by a small allowance from his young brother Theodore, who was now a picture-dealer in the firm of Goupil, he decided to go in for art entirely, living at the Hague. All the rest of his family had repudiated him, so he took in a prostitute off the streets, using her as a model; but even she decided that he was useless. He stayed for a time in the Academy in Antwerp, where Verlat enraged him by sending him back from "life" to draw "antique", as it is called in schools. Without warning, he left Antwerp and, unannounced, descended on his brother in

Paris. Soon after this he entered the Atelier Cormon, most probably because it was near his brother's flat in the rue Lepic. He was now about thirty-three years of age, and though he had had no success in selling any of his work, there is no doubt he had at last come to an environment in which he could expand. I saw him first in Russell's studio in the Impasse Hélène, Clichy quarter. Russell had just painted that portrait of him in a striped blue suit, looking over his shoulder, which is now, I believe, in the Modern Gallery of Amsterdam, together with the Van Gogh Collection there. It was an admirable likeness, more so than any of those by himself or Gauguin. I am told it has darkened very much. Formerly it was catalogued as by an American—Australia being a *terra incognita* in art.

In the summer of 1886, Anquetin, Cormon's best pupil, who had painted and had on the walls some very powerful studies, rather in the manner of Courbet, quite orthodox academics, which would have won medals in any school, turned "intransigeant"; that is, he went over to the advanced section of the "pointellists" led by Signac and Seurat and carried most of the studio with him. Among those working in the studio was a young man called Bernard, about eighteen years of age, in whom Cormon took an interest. Cormon came round one morning, as usual, to find Bernard painting the old brown sail that served for a background to the model, in alternate streaks of vermilion and vert veronese. On asking the youth what he was doing, Bernard replied, "that he saw it that way". Thereupon Cormon announced that if that was the case he had better go and see things that way somewhere else. In the light of later experiences this action was not so outrageous as might appear to the uninitiated. It was quite a common thing in the studio to make a flesh-grey by mixing these two colours together on the palette; very bad chemically, no doubt. Bernard was religiously carrying out this experiment on the theory that, put down side by side in spots or streaks, these colours at a distance would combine and make a grey to the eye. But immediately "the fat was in the fire". Someone, I forget whom, told Cormon he was an old Academician, hidebound with prejudice, and that he was interfering with genius in the bud. In short, there was a great uproar about little—a disturbance of the sort that could only happen in a studio in Paris. Cormon closed down the studio at once for some months, and all the more aggressive students were sent away. During this period, the story goes that Vincent, full of indignation, took this interference with the free expression of the artist so much to heart that he went round with a pistol to shoot Cormon, but, fortunately, did not find him in.

Bernard later became a pupil of Gauguin, and, being a person of intelligence and adaptability in many directions, helped by his writings to spread abroad the theories of the master. I have heard that Bernard walked all the way from Paris to Pont-Aven, where Gauguin had formed a sort of school, and had paid his way by painting portraits of innkeepers or of anyone who would help him with money, food or lodging. When first he arrived, Gauguin refused to have anything to do with him, but seeing his fervour, graciously received him as a "disciple". Later there was a quarrel, because Bernard, after a few years, claimed to be the founder of the School of Pont-Aven, or something like it. Gauguin was not the man to stand this, from a disciple, for one moment. There was a bitter quarrel, and this time a final dismissal and parting.

In later years Bernard, by his writings, became one of the chief historians of the lives of Gauguin, Van Gogh and Cézanne, but for himself he abandoned his earlier theories, and I am told that he now paints on traditional lines, with under-painting in dead colour and glazes to finish.

At this time, Van Gogh was making his first pictures with the division of tones, painting still-life, flowers and landscapes of Montmartre. There is no doubt that this plunge into pure colour stimulated him violently, and he piled the oil paint on in a way that was astonishing and decidedly shocking to the innocent eye as well as to that of the more sophisticated, but he had not yet mastered his materials in the way that came to him soon after his arrival in Arles.

Although he was using impressionist theories of the division of tones, I do not think he was ever a scientific painter in the sense that Seurat and Lautrec became in dealing with complementary colours; but he was particularly pleased with a theory that the eye carried a portion of the last sensation it had enjoyed into the next, so that something of both must be included in every picture made. The difficulty was to decide what were the proper sensations so coloured to combine together.

An obvious instance of this sort of idea will be found in the fact that the entering of a lamplit room out of the night increases the orange effect of the light, and in the contrary case, the blue. Hence to depict it properly, according to theory, it was necessary in the former case to include some blue in the picture and in the latter some orange. Van Gogh would roll his eyes and hiss through his teeth with gusto, as he brought out the words "blue", "orange"—complementary colours of course.

But the interesting point to me is that he brought a native Dutch instinct for handling paint fearlessly and added to it these colour theories in such a way that, I believe, he is the most original painter of this period, in that he departed from all traditional rules more violently than any other, yet made the result convincing, even in the end to the man in the street. Now this is precisely what genius alone can do. The fact is that whatever Van Gogh got he took from nature; like a hound on the scent of a trail, he was guided by a sure instinct to the capture of the immediate sensation. In spite of much that he has written in the letters to his brother, he would certainly, when I knew him, have repudiated any ethical bias whatever; and though there was no striving for an imitation of nature in the sense of ordinary still-life painting, there was a fierce effort to give the feeling of brightness, or blackness, or dullness, or whatever was the chief characteristic of the object he wished to depict.

Lewis Hind used to tell a story of a lady friend looking at one of the "sunflower" pictures in the first post-impressionist show at the Grafton Galleries. "It is horrible. It has no beauty. It gives me merely the sensation of the rank glare of a sunflower", she said.

"Madame," he replied, "that is precisely what Van Gogh desired to express."

I believe he was exactly right. This is the sort of sensation Van Gogh would often desire to express—you may not like it, but it gives you the feeling of a sunflower raised to the *n*th power, and so attracts people who otherwise would pass it by; later they will find that it has other and more enduring qualities. This seems certainly to be proved to-day, when reproductions of his pictures in every size and quality are to be seen on all hands and sell freely. From what I remember, as well as from recent examination, I am certain that time has toned down the fierceness of his pictures very considerably, and many who accept them now for their undoubtedly fine colour would have been scared of them when freshly painted. At the same time there are pictures painted by him rather later than this, such as some of the orchard pictures and the picture called the "Garden of Daubigny" painted at Auvers just before he died, which are simply tender, beautiful landscapes, not to be surpassed in these respects by any painter at all. I have also seen magnificent pen drawings by him, so large in style that they might have been signed by Titian. In some aspects Van Gogh was personally as simple as a child, expressing pleasure and pain loudly in a child-like manner. The direct way he showed his likes and dislikes was sometimes very disconcerting, but without malice or conscious knowledge that he was giving offence. When in Paris he did not appear so poverty-stricken to me as one would suppose from the various tales written of him. He dressed quite well and in an ordinary way, better than many in the atelier. I have been to the flat where he was living with his brother Theodore, 54 rue Lepic. It was quite a comfortable one, even rather cluttered up with all sorts of furniture and works of art. On an easel was the yellow picture called "Romans Parisiens", the first of a series of yellow pictures. Then he drew my attention specially to a number of what he called "crêpes", i.e. Japanese prints printed on crinkled paper like crêpe. It was clear they interested him greatly, and I am convinced, from the way he talked, that what he was aiming at in his own painting was to get a similar effect of little cast shadows in oil paint from roughness of surface, and this he finally achieved. He showed me some etchings given him by Matthew Maris (Tyse Maris as he called him), an old friend evidently, also a bundle of lithographs by himself of Dutch peasant women working in the fields, and among them a proof of that terrible litho he called "Sorrow" done from the woman he lived with in Amsterdam: naked, pregnant and starving. When I admired some of these he offered me the bundle, but I, perhaps foolishly, refused to deprive him, as he was apt to act thus impulsively if anyone praised his work. But, while in Paris for a week to see the Salons in the year after his death, I made a far more serious mistake. Outside a shop in the Clichy quarter, probably that of Portier or of Tanguy, I saw four large still-life paintings by "Vincent", each marked "2 francs" with white chalk in one corner. One of them, a few green apples in a basket, attracted me especially. I noted that he appeared to have squeezed out a whole tube of vert veronese in streaks for each apple, just touched it with a few flicks of the brush, and lo, there were the most wonderful green apples I have ever seen! My hotel was far away on the other side of the river and I was seeing sights with E. J. Sullivan; the trouble of carrying a canvas of that size, so loaded with paint that it could not be rolled, was too much for me; I hesitated, and was lost. So vanished my one chance of owning a masterpiece. I must make this confession, too, which will prove that Gauguin certainly at that time had made the deeper impression on me; that if the canvases had been signed "Gauguin", I would have carried them off even if it had finished me for the day! Weakness of the flesh, the critical will say, is no excuse for weakness of the head! Others were a little, but only a little, wiser. Joseph Pennell, a few days later, from the same shop, I believe, persuaded Fisher Unwin, the publisher, to buy a flower-piece signed "Vincent" for 25 francs, but this was dearer because framed! It used to hang at the top of the staircase outside the door to Unwin's flat in the Adelphi, "beyond the pale" and obviously reckoned of little account, until about ten years ago he sold it for £1200, as I am informed. Not a bad unearned increment on one pound after about thirty years.

As a matter of fact, Van Gogh could not sell any of his work at this time. He used to rage from time to time that, though he was closely connected with the picture-trade, no one would buy anything he had done. He actually told me that he had never had more than 10 francs for a picture. Tanguy used, I believe, to let him have colours sometimes in exchange. Of recent years I have known several priced £5000 and one at £13,000! When he was lying dead at Auvers, a picture, sent by his brother to a show in Brussels, was sold to a lady for 400 francs.

While I knew him, I don't think anybody in Paris called him mad; but I frankly confess that neither myself, nor any of those I remember of his friends, foresaw that Van Gogh would be talked of specially and considered a great genius in the future. We thought him "cracked" but harmless, perhaps not interesting enough to bother much about. Though he was always an artist in temperament, we considered his work too unskilful in handling to make an appeal to the student mind; for there were many who could surpass him from that point of view, and, as I have said, I think the French generally rather tolerated him on account of his brother Theodore's position in Goupil's.

Russell had kindly offered to sponsor my entry into the Atelier Cormon. I had taken some of my work to show the great man at his private studio; he had been interested and accepted me as a pupil—quite a feather in my cap, I thought, because Cormon's studio at that time was small and select, not more than thirty to thirty-five pupils all told, of whom few were foreigners. Indeed English and Americans rarely got into it.

The studio had just been reopened after the row in the summer, and some of the former pupils had been permitted to return. Among them, Toulouse Lautrec may be mentioned especially, as Coquiot says Cormon turned him out with Vincent; in fact, I had a photograph of him, with others in the studio, taken some months later while I was there. At the same time, Russell, who was going to Sicily with his wife and child for the winter and spring, let part of his house to Henry Ryland (a follower of Burne-Jones) and myself; a very convenient arrangement this for me working at Cormon's, in the rue Constance, and also for Ryland, who was working in Benjamin Constant's studio.

Cormon was a sharp-featured little man, dark-haired, with the quick movements of a small bird, which he somehow resembled. He painted enormous pictures of prehistoric man, with titles such as "Le chasse de l'Ours, l'âge de pierre" or "La famille de Caïn" fleeing through a wilderness: the latter is, or was, in the Luxembourg Gallery. In spite of the abuse which has been showered on him for failing to recognize genius in his studio—a failing common to his contemporaries—I should say that he had excellent brains, was an admirable teacher, more sympathetic to novelties than most of his kind. No doubt he was particular about drawing, and especially construction, as a true Frenchman and member of the Institute. In my time he was respected as an artist and as a teacher. I believe even Gauguin spoke of him with regard and worked for a short time in his atelier when in Montmartre in 1889. The crown of his reputation in the studio, however, was that he kept three mistresses at one time! He was unmarried at this period and was accustomed to receive any of his pupils, who wished to go, at his private studio on Sundays, when he would look at and criticize any work, even a sketch-book, that might be brought to him. There were several former pupils, grown men and quite well-known artists, who used to consult him freely; or before the Salon he would

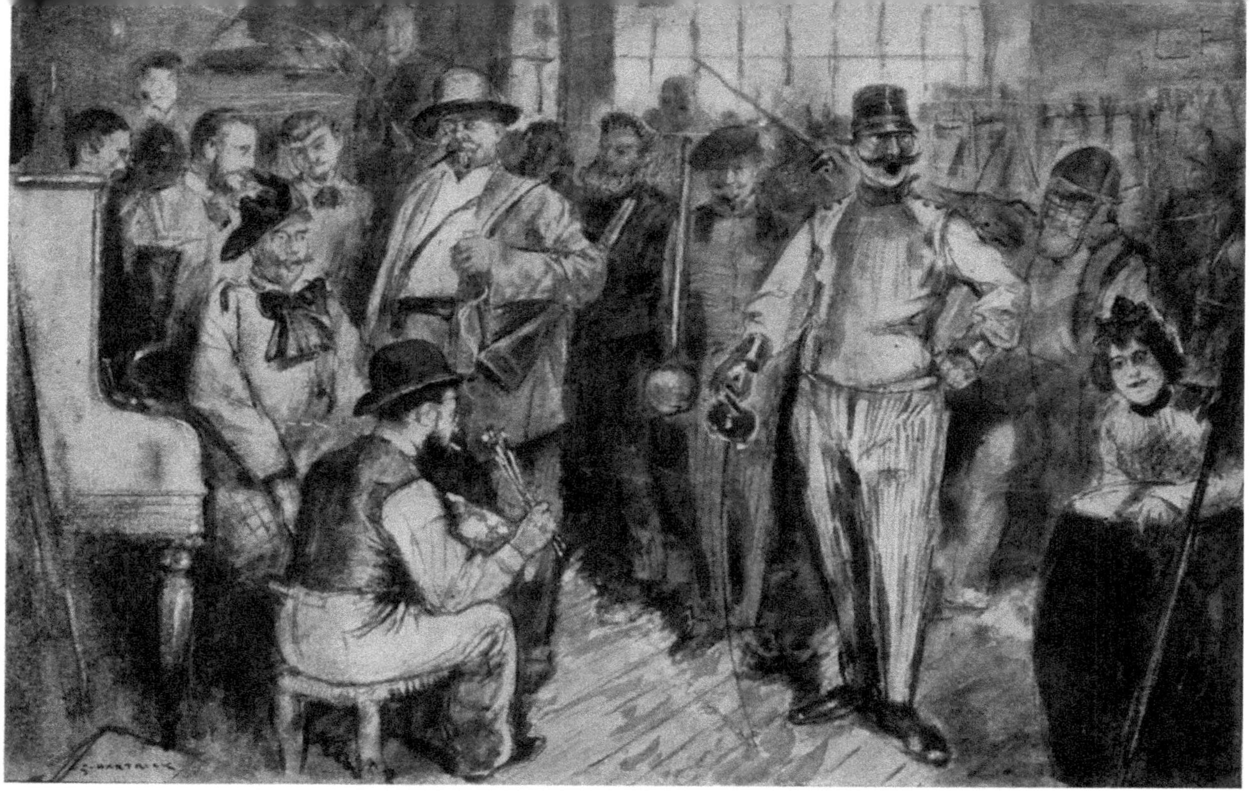

The Atelier Cormon

Drawing based on contemporary photograph. Toulouse Lautrec is seated on tabouret in front

go to see their work in their own studios without any pose at all.

In company with several others of the atelier, I once saw him in the Salon looking at everything with a solicitude that surprised us who, student-like, were dismissing most things there with a glance. His atelier was managed rather differently from Julian's, though there also was a "massier" who collected money, and whose verdict in all disputes was final. To begin with it was very French, and the foreigner was kept rather apart. Thanks to the kind offices of Russell, who had been popular, I got on very well after the first few days, during which I was put through the ritual of induction by paying for drinks, singing a song, etc. Someone even offered to sing for me, I remember. It was much like being a fag at school again; my chief duty as a "nouveau" was to see that the stove was lit and properly stoked; no nonsense was allowed about doing this properly. The man who immediately followed me, a young Frenchman who had been in the Navy, was decidedly fractious. He let the stove go out several times and showed fight when rated for it, but there was no mercy for him; he had to give in or go. Finally he went, but not before he had been put "à la brosse". This means that he was trussed like a fowl, with a long pole run through at the back of his knees and his hands tied in front of them. He was then placed on the throne, or some place raised from the floor, from which he was bound to fall if he tried to move. Having deliberately let the stove go out for the fourth or fifth time, he was suddenly seized by half a dozen men and, in spite of his struggles, soon trussed up on the pole kept in the atelier. Next, he was carried on the pole, surrounded by the whole class, outside across the road to a *brasserie*. As one of the latest "nouveaux", it was my duty, together with three others, to carry the pole with the dissenter suspended from it. One man was told off to turn the victim upright from time to time, before the blood had gone too much to his head. In the *brasserie* he had to stand drinks all round, after which he was escorted solemnly back as before, by which time he was half insensible with hysteria and rage. What surprised me was that nobody took the slightest notice of what we were doing, either in the street or *brasserie*; it appeared to be accepted as just a students' "rag".

Theodore Van Gogh's gallery was in the Boulevard Montmartre, quite separate from the main galleries of the house of Goupil, or rather Boussod, Valadon et Cie, as it was beginning to be known. Here, rather against the instincts of his superiors in the firm, Theodore was being allowed to try to work up a business in the work of the great impressionists, Manet, Renoir, Monet, etc., with Degas a lone figure rather apart. On the quiet he was also seeking to find buyers for the latest experiments by the "intransigeants", as they were named—Signac, Seurat, Lautrec, Gauguin and even by Vincent himself. There, in his brother's shop, Van Gogh at last met and made contact with the artists, whose experiments with pure colour were to open his eyes and to create a new art of his own. Though I cannot remember seeing Lautrec in the company of Vincent, I know they foregathered, and about this time Lautrec made his well-known Pastel Portrait of "Vincent", which is a good likeness and very characteristic of its author as well.

A man I did see going about with him was Alexander Reid, the Glasgow picture-dealer, who later was the first to introduce impressionist pictures to collectors in Scotland. As my home was in the west of Scotland, I also foregathered with him. Reid had tried some painting himself not very successfully, but enough to enable him to understand and become enthusiastic about new movements. His father and principals in Glasgow were interested in the Barbizon School; Corot, Millet, and Daubigny were the artists he had been sent to France to study and acquire.

He was a young man then, younger, I fancy, than Van Gogh, but physically remarkably like him, so that certain portraits Vincent made of him were for long believed to be self-portraits. The likeness was so marked that they might have been twins. I have often hesitated, until I got close, as to which of them I was meeting. They even dressed somewhat similarly, though I doubt if Vincent ever possessed anything like the Harris tweeds Reid usually wore. Reid got into serious trouble with his father for acquiring or investing in some of Van Gogh's work, but I cannot believe he gave much money for them or I should have heard about it from the painter! It was the contact with such atrocities, as they seemed, that roused the ire of the parent; for, in the view of the elder picture-dealer, Reid was destroying his taste for what was saleable.

All through the early part of 1887, Vincent frequently came to see me in the Impasse Hélène, to the horror of poor Ryland, who, having hung up a set of weak water-colours of the "La belle dame sans merci" type, found himself unmercifully attacked by the free tongue of Van Gogh, who promptly told him that they were anaemic and useless reflections of Pre-Raphaelites—a kind of artist that he mostly despised. I would return, from going up and down in Paris, to find Ryland, who suffered from sick headaches, with his head wrapped in a towel soaked in vinegar and looking a sickly yellow, while he wailed: "Where have you been? That terrible man has been here for two hours waiting for you and I can't stand it any more."

On another occasion I would be in to greet him. Now Vincent had a habit of carrying a thick stick of red and one of blue chalk in each pocket of his coat. With these he used to illustrate his latest impressions or theories of art. As he would start work on the wall or anything that was handy, I immediately placed a newspaper or two on the table, where he would at once begin to set out his latest "motif" in lines a quarter to half an inch thick. I recall the set-out of one such, depicting the scene in a restaurant he favoured at that time. It was a long narrow room, with a narrow table, and seats against the wall, a tall window filling the end. In the foreground he showed some overcoats hanging up, then a line of eaters in perspective. Through the window, as he eagerly informed me, was a dung-heap and on it "un petit bonhomme qui pisse". "Voilà!" he said. The design was certainly striking and, again, I wish I had kept it.

During the summer, Vincent kept going out to paint the river at Surennes or Bougival, carrying his painting traps with him and usually covering himself and others with paint from his canvas when his work was complete!

Russell, whose child had died while away, came back suddenly from Sicily, so I had to move out and go to an hotel for the remainder of my time in Paris, and with this move I lost touch with Vincent. In February of the year 1888, he went off to Arles, seeking the sun, he said. There at last he was to find himself as a painter, but to break down finally in health.

After a quarrel with Gauguin, whom he had invited to spend the winter with him in the South, he became insane, cutting off his own ear in remorse, and was confined in an asylum, though he had lucid intervals, during which he worked furiously. Finally he left the Asylum St Paul at Saint Remy, returning to his brother, who had lately married, in Paris; but life was becoming too much for further endurance. On feeling the return of another paroxysm he shot himself, at the age of thirty-seven, at Auvers, where he had gone to submit his case to a Doctor Gachet.

"Assurément c'est la peinture d'un fou" was Cézanne's comment, on seeing his work: but a madman of genius is the verdict of to-day.

The two volumes of letters from Vincent to Theòdore, the brother who believed in him when all others failed, without whose practical aid we should possess no paintings by Van Gogh at all, make one of the most pathetically moving records that have been published in modern times. It is also a mine that will richly repay working by young artists or any who wish to understand the forces behind the modern movement in art.

Van Gogh was no critic, but he can reveal certain hidden depths in art in a way no critic has ever done. I never heard him speak on the ethical side, but always on the technical, but Meier Graefe quotes one of these letters which reveals Vincent's conception of art. "Christ", he says, "was the greatest of all artists because He made Immortal Man, and not works of art. His words, which He, a grand Seigneur, disdained to set down in writing, were mightier in their power than marbles and pictures, because He knew they would endure, when the forms of the world in which He lived had long passed away." Here, says Graefe, we have the whole of Van Gogh, the man who believed, even more fervently than in art, in a tremendous creative power given to men to make others happy. It depressed him to think "that life is created with less effort than art".

In another of these letters he points out that British art is distinct from that of the Continent, and for this reason it is necessary for a foreigner to grow accustomed to it, and not to turn it down at once, because he does not understand it, as is often the case, like a peasant with a new dish, the flavour of which is unfamiliar. Now this seems to me really interesting. May it not be that in this way certain national characteristics are present in our art similar to those which render our general attitude to life incomprehensible to foreigners?

CHAPTER V

THE GLASGOW SCHOOL

It was to Rhu on the Gareloch, one of the many beautiful inlets of the Firth of Clyde, that I returned from Paris towards the end of 1887. My mother had owned a house there since my father's death in 1872. Glasgow, going through a prosperous trade boom, was only about twenty miles away by rail. Through my stepfather, Dr Blatherwick, I soon got into touch with most of the younger artists there. These were the men who within the next few years were to become known here and on the Continent as the "Glasgow School". The characteristic of this school was that its inspiration and methods came from the Continent and chiefly from France. Pictures of the Barbizon and Dutch schools were conspicuous in the shops of all the picture-dealers in Glasgow at that time. Most of these young painters, like myself, had been to Paris to study for some period at least.

Conditions were ripe for the birth of a new movement in Scotland, which would discard the traditional thin and hot-coloured methods of the local artists—whose taste did not go much farther than to make it evident that there were mountains in Scotland and that the heather was in blossom on them.

"Aye! yon's the man that's put up the price of Purrple", was the sort of criticism offered by the new school of the old.

Guthrie (later Sir James, P.R.S.A.), Lavery (later Sir John, R.A.), E. A. Walton, George Henry and Hornel, together with Alexander Roche, were the principal names in the School, and already all of them were known as coming men in Scotland, though as yet unacknowledged, even rather slighted by the national institution at the Royal Scottish Academy. But, in the mere matter of patronage, it may be mentioned that, at that time, the Glasgow Institute was selling three pictures to one sold at Edinburgh.

The first great success of the School came a little later at an international exhibition, a full dress affair, at Munich. There, the Glasgow School first showed as a body, and burst in full bloom on an unsuspecting world, which knew not Scotland, in a way that spread its fame all over Europe. Several members received medals, and one large picture of "A Tennis Match" by Lavery was bought by the Modern Gallery in Munich. It appeared that the fortunes of the School were soon to be made. Reproductions of the principal pictures, with notes on the artists and their works, were published widely in all the art magazines, both here and abroad. This, by the way, was the exhibition at which Whistler was awarded a *second-class* medal for his painting of Thomas Carlyle, and replied that he thanked the "jury" for a second-class compliment.

To return to my personal experiences, Guthrie was the first of these painters that I came to know intimately, because, while I was still at the Slade, my stepfather took me on a sketching expedition to Cockburnspath, a village in Berwickshire, where Guthrie was living with his mother. He had already painted his "Highland Funeral" and the "Goose Girl", both of which had been exhibited at the Royal Academy in London. But by this time, like most young painters of the period, he had been attracted by the work of Bastien Lepage and was at work on a large picture of three children going to school, which afterwards was purchased for the Gallery at Ghent in Belgium. This picture showed the influence of Lepage distinctly.

My return also coincided with turmoil in the art world of Scotland. The new artists were assaulting the fortress of the Royal Scottish Academy, which like academies everywhere was defending its privileges with stubborn vigour. One member, however, William MacTaggart, R.S.A., a born impressionist and the most original painter that Scotland has ever produced, who will in the end, I like to believe, be rated as the greatest painter of the sea who has ever lived, was taking the side of these young painters. Later he even went so far as to withdraw for a time from the exhibitions of the Royal Scottish Academy, to mark his dissatisfaction with the general policy of the Academy in regard to this matter. Long afterwards I learnt that MacTaggart had tried to hang my picture "The Son of the Prodigal", painted at this time, on the line at the Royal Scottish Academy, but had been overruled. No doubt there is an instinctive bond between artists whose work appeals to one another. I never met MacTaggart personally.

Macaulay Stevenson, a painter of dim and misty landscapes, also belonging to Glasgow, armed with a very voluminous pen, was conducting a furious attack on the Royal Scottish Academy and all its works in a Dundee newspaper. The fight went on fast and furious, if intermittently, in the *Glasgow Herald* and the *Scotsman* for months. It is all forgotten to-day, and the leader of the School, Guthrie, did not take part in these literary excursions. The son of a Presbyterian minister of the Established Kirk, he was originally intended to follow in his father's footsteps, and with that in view had taken his degree at Glasgow University; so in the conventional sense he was more highly educated and better fitted for leadership than most of the others. A charming man, if a little prim from his upbringing, with knowledge and wide sympathies, he found the call of art was stronger for him than that of the Church. His natural abilities as an artist were outstanding; from the first he was marked by the initiated as likely to prove the most gifted painter (especially of portraits) in Scotland since Raeburn. He was ambitious and all his work was large.

One of the first things he confided to me was that he had deliberately thus concentrated on large work, in which he could put all he knew; and as he possessed some private means, he was able to do it without the struggle to live that is often the tragedy of those not so supported. If he does not now quite hold the position his friends at that time hoped for him, I sometimes wonder, had he been satisfied to work out his own salvation entirely alone like MacTaggart, might he not have been a larger figure to-day? He had the kind of ability to do it, but Guthrie could never let himself go. I believe that the restrictive character of his early training was against it.

His first picture, "A Highland Funeral", had original potentialities in the way of vision of character and of its expression in terms of paint, but these he deliberately put aside for what I fear were passing phases—first Lepage; then the influence of Whistler, subtle and elusive; but these forces did not provide the soil in which his talent could best expand. At a much later date I heard him speak of those paintings by Hals at Haarlem—especially that of the old women known as "The Regents of the Almshouses"—in such an illuminating way that I have often thought that, if as a young man he had come to this sort of thing coupled with a year or two of hard drawing in Paris, he might have climbed higher on that difficult peak where he might have been set beside Raeburn. Yet he was always a severe critic of himself and never satisfied. He often painted out and altered his work in rather a reckless fashion from the point of view of craftsmanship, and not always for the better.

To my mind one of the finest portraits he ever painted—perhaps the only one in which he never hesitated once—was that of a sister of Jo Crawhall, to whom at one time he was engaged to be married. She jilted him, it was said; so he painted out the head, and tried to substitute another.

Whistler did just the same thing with that portrait of Lady Eden which caused the celebrated lawsuit with "The Baronet". The result in each case was the same—the picture from being a masterpiece became a ruin.

Jo Crawhall was a great friend of Guthrie's, and, though a Newcastle man, has become closely attached to the Glasgow School.

He was an animal painter in the main, and a genius in the sense that he did everything in his own way, and one that no one else could follow. He worked mostly in water-colours, and he looked and rode like a jockey. I first met him in Paris, where he was living at the same hotel as myself. He never went to work in any atelier there that I can remember, though he had entered one under Aimé Morot, the painter of horses and battle pictures; but wandered about les Halles, the great market there, where he found subjects that suited him. I think he only completed one drawing in Paris—that of a bull—but he was always tearing up what he had done if it did not achieve what he was after. It is a curious fact, I remember, that his favourite work in the Louvre was Courbet's "Man with a Leathern Belt".

At this time he worked in pure water-colours on paper; later he used linen and painted with body-colours. Everything was done by him from memory or a few notes, after intense watching on the spot. The Japanese undoubtedly were his masters in a sense; but his results were his own. When working in pure water-colour (in which I now believe his best work was done) he had a habit of putting the drawing under the tap with the water running, watching it till it came to the state he sought for; then, laying it flat, he would finish it with a few bold touches of sharp drawing or strong colour which brought out the character and life to perfection.

But the two members of the Glasgow School I saw most of were E. A. Hornel and Alexander Roche, who later was to be struck down by paralysis: a real tragedy, just as he was getting a reputation as the best painter of ladies' portraits in Scotland.

Hornel was born in Australia of Scotch parents, but was brought back by them to Galloway as a child. It is impossible to think of Hornel apart from Kirkcudbright, as he lived there nearly all his life and bought up much of the town in the days of his prosperity, in the hopeless attempt to save it from change.

He was a fine-looking man of strong character and stronger language, which got him a reputation for being much rougher

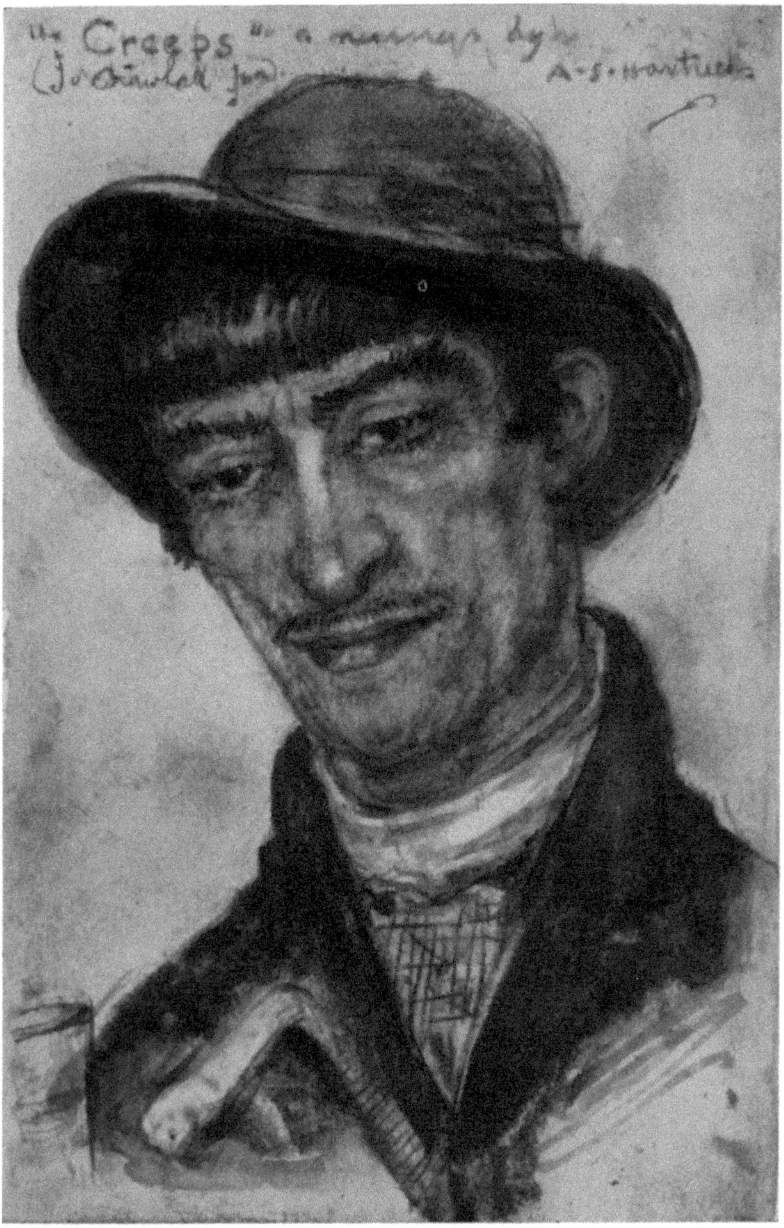

Joe Crawhall

Drawing in red and black chalks

than he really was: just as was the case with Cézanne as a young man.

When he came to Glasgow, he shared a studio with George Henry, a wit who was reputed to know everything that Glasgow concealed.

In the Art Club Hornel was the leader of a band of fighters who called themselves "Poverty and Progress" while they cursed the rest of the Club as "The Glue Pot School". These two bodies occupied opposite sides of the fireplace and never mixed.

Pittendrigh MacGillivray, R.S.A., the sculptor, summed up the situation in a set of verses entitled "Hornel Triumphant to his Goat on the Galloway Hills" that used to be sung or quoted widely, and that W. E. Henley is reputed to have admired. It is lurid and forcible in its language, but I fear unprintable, except its refrain "'Y're richt!' said the goat". Now Hornel had a hobby which has a verse to itself in this poem: at times it was almost an obsession. It began with the discovery of certain "cup-and-ring" markings, as they are called. They are found engraved on the rocks, though mostly half-covered with turf, all over Kirkcudbrightshire. Who made them and what they mean are still a puzzle for the learned in such matters. In the British Museum there are casts of some of the most characteristic. They are usually believed to have religious significance and to have been made by a race that lived before the time of the Druids. Hornel would go any distance to examine a new specimen. On one such occasion he took me and another friend with him to visit a local character named Sinclair, who was reputed to have some special knowledge of them.

This Sinclair, an old man with a head that would have served as a model for the prophet Ezekiel, was reputed to have gone to China from these parts fifty years before with Sir Halliday Macartney, and to have passed at least part of his youth as a pirate in the China Seas. Later he became janitor at Yale University in America. From this last service he enjoyed a pension on which he now lived in a cottage not far from the gates of a large house belonging to the Dowager Countess of Selkirk, one of the few people he permitted to cross his threshold. He was always difficult to approach but, armed with a bottle of whisky as a propitiatory offering, Hornel drove us out to this cottage, which was set down at Balmae by the mouth of the Dee, not far from Dirk Hatterick's cave (the holt of the smuggler in *Guy Mannering*). It looks straight out into the Atlantic, past the Little Ross lighthouse. We were received quite graciously, the whisky being accepted with thanks. That he had been a sailor was obvious, for everything about the place was trim and shipshape. At the end of the garden, reached by a neatly gravelled path, was a sort of summer-house with a large telescope on a stand to sweep the horizon. Round about it were a number of beautifully kept beehives. Beekeeping was his hobby, and the honey in those parts is noted for its quality. When we had seen everything outside, we were invited into the cottage. From the front door we had to descend some steps into what was clearly the chief living-room. In the middle was a table and a wooden chair to which was attached a lead with a collar to it. This, Sinclair explained, was designed to restrain his cat, a tortoise-shell, which we had noticed outside heavy with the promise of a new family, but all to no purpose. "Ah! Nancy, ye ould whoore, th'ere nae sooner oot o' ye than the're intil ye again. And yonder!" he went on, pointing to a black monster on a distant wall, "is the faither o' them. Leopold, King o' the Belgians, I ca' him." After a little refreshment from the whisky bottle, Hornel began to approach him about the cup-and-ring markings. Without more ado he went for a bucket of water and a clout, then led us to some rocks not far off, which had recently been laid bare. Wiping them over with the clout the markings showed up perfectly. After a little further talk we returned to the cottage, when, going into his bedroom, he took from a shelf a small china bowl in which was a small bluish stone like a bean. Holding this in his hand, in a few minutes he seemed to go off in a sort of trance, and then began to describe, like a wireless announcer of to-day, a vision of a procession of priests with sacred instruments and cattle which somehow were connected with the cup-and-ring markings. I cannot remember the details of it; all I can say is that the vision appeared to be genuine, and that he was not drunk. After a time he became normal again, but would not talk any more on the subject.

Henry and Hornel were always spoken of together and, some years later on, they went to Japan together, financed by an enterprising dealer. They remained there for a year or more, and returned separately, when they maintained to all inquirers as to how they fared in Japan, that they had not spoken to one another all the time they were there; and they never spoke to one another afterwards—for some reason never revealed.

Henry once told me that he always regretted that he had not got off and stayed in China, as he thought it more picturesque; but he added that you could smell China far out at sea, and he feared he could not stick it.

Nevertheless both held exhibitions in Glasgow of the work they brought back with them and both exhibitions were successful.

I knew Hornel pretty well in the after years when he developed a style as strong and individual as himself. He had a picture bought by the Liverpool Corporation which caused quite as much commotion in the Walker Art Gallery as did Van Gogh's first appearance in the Tate. It now excites no comment whatever!

Henry has become a full R.A., but he made his reputation by painting a picture he called "A Galloway Landscape" (a very good picture too) that came to be known as the "spear head" of the Glasgow School.

I have seen the spot where it was painted, a very ordinary field with a hill in it; but Henry introduced a blue burn, painted with a palette knife, around it; then put a stain over all, and it became an object of derision for the man in the street as well as for the Glue Pot School, but an ineffaceable memory for any artist who has ever seen it.

Before I leave this record of the Glasgow School, which gradually disintegrated and dispersed in terms of that French proverb—"Tout lasse, tout casse, tout passe"—I must tell a story that E. A. Hornel told me about W. Y. MacGregor, another Glasgow painter. A picture by him will be found in the Tate Gallery.

MacGregor, a man of some means and rather older than most of the members of the School, was a landscape painter of ability with a very bold method of handling oil paint.

At the period of gradual breaking up of the School, he met Hornel in Glasgow and asked him to dine with him. Now Hornel's weakness at one time was that he took too much whisky: later, fearing it affected his sight, he broke the habit off completely and became a strict teetotaller. MacGregor probably knew the first fact; anyway he took him to a Temperance Hotel, where they had a meal washed down with lemonade and ginger-beer! As they were coming away Hornel said to MacGregor: "After all! W. Y., you were the origin of the Glasgow School", when his companion with a scarlet face, almost weeping with emotion, cried out: "Man Hornel! if ye had said that to me before, we'd hae gone to the Royal, and had champagne!!"

CHAPTER VI

'THE GRAPHIC' AND 'THE DAILY GRAPHIC'

Leaving the Glasgow School and the West of Scotland to take care of itself, for more than a year I had been living near Largo in Fife with Frank Dean, the little Yorkshireman who had accompanied me to Paris from the Slade. We lodged at Lundin Links, in the cottage of an elderly salmon-fisher and his wife, named Rogers; a couple representing a fine type of the Scottish peasant, which I fear has almost ceased to exist to-day, so I would turn aside for a little space in order to recall the environment. He rented the fishing-rights of a set of salmon nets, of a kind erected on posts at intervals all along the shores of the Firth of Forth.

These nets he visited at every low tide to remove any fish that had been entangled on their way to fresh water higher up; they were then packed in ice and sent off by train to Edinburgh and other large towns. A magnificent figure of a man, grave, thrifty and independent, he was an elder of the Kirk and greatly respected. With his garden and his cottage and the nets he counted himself his own master; but unfortunately the salmon were growing scarcer, even looked like failing altogether, so his wife added to their income by taking in lodgers. Their only son was a cork-cutter, married and living away.

Nowadays, Lundin Links is a well-known golf course: and I am told there are many houses for summer visitors together with all the regulation holiday attractions. In my time it was still primitive, with one village shop which sold everything that was wanted from hair-brushes to bait-tins. It was presided over by a greybeard named Forgan. Now St Monance, a fishing village a few miles away, possessed a little minister, who must have escaped out of the previous century. Clean shaven, with long white locks, he dressed all in black in a pernickety way with knee-breeches, after the fashion of the eighteenth century: wore lawn bands every day, and even, I think, a three-cornered hat. His church, a well-known landmark from the sea, looked like a small fortress guarding its grim religion.

Entering Forgan's store one morning this anachronism of a man asked for a tooth-brush. "Wa's that?" inquired the proprietor, and when this had been explained, he cried out in contempt: "Gosh man! it's a Roman Catholic priest ye'll be askin' for next"—that being the limit of outrage his mind could conceive.

Painting landscape or even figures in such surroundings was an amusing but hardly a profitable occupation even in those days. An advertisement in *The Graphic* stopped all such activities.

Early in 1889 W. L. Thomas, the founder and creator of *The Graphic* newspaper, the most successful illustrated weekly of that day—paying over 100 per cent in dividends annually to its original shareholders—decided that the moment was ripe for a daily illustrated paper to be published in London: its name was to be *The Daily Graphic*, to extend the fame of its successful parent, and to be financed out of its surplus. This was not the first "daily illustrated" in the world; the experiment of producing a "daily illustrated" had already been tried in New York, but it languished. The cynics were active, and hinted that Thomas was spurred on to action by the fact that he was the father of ten full-grown sons, for whom provision must be made; and that this was his solution of the problem.

A tall big man with a shrewd eye and a long beard, he had an intimate knowledge of the illustration of the period, consequent on the fact that he had started life as a wood-engraver and now controlled a school of them.

The Franco-Prussian War of 1870 had revealed to his acute sense of business the opening for a new illustrated weekly in addition to *The Illustrated London News*, the oldest illustrated paper in London—with which too he had had connections as a wood-engraver earlier in his career.

Equipped with this experience, he quickly enrolled on the staff of *The Graphic*—his new paper—what was probably the ablest band of young illustrators who have ever been brought together in one such enterprise in England. Nearly every one of them made a reputation for himself and the paper within the next few years, not to mention a fortune for its directors.

Luke Fildes, E. J. Gregory, Holl and Herkomer did much of their best work for the paper. Later all became members of the Royal Academy, a great asset in those times.

So now, twenty years after, richer in pocket and experience, Thomas decided to tempt Fortune again in the same direction, but alas! times were different; it was not so easy to capture success without the excitement of a war to sustain curiosity, or to entice even pennies from the pockets of a fickle public. Next, photo-engraving was being perfected and was soon to kill wood-engraving; with it came rapid printing on rotary machines instead of the solid "flat". The machine was preparing to take over charge from the crafts.

As a preliminary, Thomas advertised for "black and white" artists, stating that there was a good opening for young men to make an income of from £400 to £2000 per annum in this way.

This was the advertisement which started me on the move in pursuit of Eldorado. I made a selection of drawings done in Paris, together with a few illustrations to some articles my stepfather had written in *Good Words*; sent them to *The Graphic* and after a time was informed that I had been accepted on trial, and was to hold myself ready to go to London for a real test some time in June. Dean then followed my lead and was asked to do likewise.

This was the year also of the Great International Exhibition of 1889 in Paris—the one that gave the world the Eiffel Tower. In it a magnificent effort was made by the French to display to the world their recovery from the disasters of 1870.

General Boulanger and his march were there to raise the national spirits on the military plane, and on the art side was collected what was probably the last and finest collection of paintings, as understood by the "traditionalists" of the Academy, that has ever been got together.

Dean and I determined to go to see it before entering into bondage with *The Graphic.* No modern experiments later than Manet were shown. Degas had been invited, but refused to exhibit unless he were given a room to himself. Corot, Courbet and the Barbizon School with J. F. Millet, were splendidly displayed. There was an excellent choice of all the phases of the art of Bastien Lepage, of special interest for most young painters of the time. Cazin and the Belgian Alfred Stevens I remember, too, were given space.

Gauguin and some of the younger painters, more or less his followers, also organized an exhibition at a restaurant just outside the Exhibition, but I doubt if it attracted attention from any but the curious.

Immediately on our return to London Dean and I had one unforgettable experience. The Parnell Commission had just begun to sit at the Law Courts on Mr Parnell's case against *The Times,* wherein he sought to prove that certain letters that paper had published as by him were forgeries.

Never since can I remember so many police precautions in evidence everywhere. In the British Museum a pathway was roped off from which no one might stray. The gallery with the Elgin Marbles was closed to all but ticket-holders. As Dean and I still possessed student tickets, we tried them at the door, and to our surprise were admitted without trouble. But inside the whole place was deserted, except for the attendants. Wandering through the galleries with the intention of emerging by the door in the long gallery where the "Discobolus" was placed we suddenly came on one Hitchcock, a humorist we had known at the Slade. While there he distinguished himself by writing and illustrating a ballad he called "The Bishop Q of Wangaloo", which recounted the adventures of a missionary bishop who washed a black man white with soap. This he illustrated himself, and sold to the proprietors of Pears' Soap. It was the first advertisement of its kind, I believe, and a huge success.

At the moment Hitchcock was making a caricature of a small statue of Hercules in the gallery. While we stood talking with him, Dean noticed a wax match on the floor and put his foot on it, whereupon it exploded with what seemed a terrifying bang. Immediately the attendant, who had been dozing on a chair at the end of the gallery, started to life and bore down on us with wand and gown in menacing fashion, saying: "I must make a report of this, I must make a report of this!" "D-d-d-don't you think it has made a report of itself?" stuttered Hitchcock. The official glared—and, speechless, hurried out of the door from the gallery. Immediately all three of us bolted back to the door in the Elgin gallery and out of the Museum as quickly as our feet could take us. To be arrested as suspected dynamiters was not the sort of publicity we were seeking.

We had found rooms at 18 Fitzroy Street, a house occupied by a German called Lesner, a political refugee and a friend of Karl Marx. Lesner, an old man, seemed colourless, but his wife and daughters let lodgings to pay for his opinions, whatever they were.

On arrival at *The Graphic* offices we were interviewed separately by W. L. Thomas himself, for he was thorough in all he undertook. We were then drafted into what we later called "the Studio", at the back of *The Graphic* buildings in the Strand. Here we found gathered half a dozen like ourselves brought in from different parts of the country: all keen enough, but without experience in drawing for reproduction. An elderly Frenchman, Godfroi Durand, who was permanently on the paper to do hack-work, was set over us as instructor or adviser. G. K. Jones, a London youth of about our own age, who was already established as toucher-up of photographs and general utility man, was also there to show us the ropes of the place. E. J. Sullivan, just nineteen, was a new arrival; he came from Hastings, where his father was art master. To Dean and myself, fresh from Paris, his experience seemed more limited than our own, for it appeared to be bounded by Baxter in *Ally Sloper's Half-Holiday* on one hand, with G. F. Watts on the other as the ideal of what high art should be. We chummed up immediately and within a week Sullivan had joined us in Fitzroy Street.

By way of instruction, most of us were sent out each day to sketch in the streets and on return were expected to make drawings in pen and ink from what we had seen. This drawing with a pen in black ink was a highly skilled matter, and we were expected to learn to do it in such a manner that the drawings could be reproduced by direct photo-engraving and printed clearly on the sort of paper in use for printing daily newspapers. This sort of reproduction was then a novelty, and the zinc-engravers wanted a drawing with cast-iron looking lines to etch.

Up till recently all the illustrations in *The Graphic* had been wood-engravings, either in facsimile, as in those of the sixties, made famous by Fred Walker, Pinwell, Houghton and a host of others, or more commonly in *The Graphic* engraved in tones to represent the washes in which the original drawing had been made. When the engraving was completed on the wood an impression was taken from it in wax, which again was electrotyped in a bath of acid with copper in solution; this in turn was backed with lead and mounted again on wood from which to print. The original wood was rarely printed from, but kept in reserve. A method, too, had been discovered by which a drawing could be photographed on to the wood block, so that drawings were now made on paper, and no longer need be cut away on the block. All this was an expensive process; for the engraver was often paid more than the artist designer. As a result there was friction between the two; sometimes bitter enmity, when the artist considered the engraver had scamped or spoilt his work. A classic incident used to be quoted about an artist who had designed a *field with flowers* in it which the engraver coolly cut to represent a *running river*, and so saved himself the labour of rendering all the detail of the original.

In dealing with news work, such as was frequently needed on *The Graphic*, a way had been devised by which the whole-page or double-page block was divided into a number of blocks each about two inches square. These could be bolted together by brass rods. For engraving, the foreman would run through all the joins on the block with a graver, showing the directions all engraved lines must follow. Then the block was unlocked and the two-inch squares divided among a number of engravers—the most skilful of whom would get the heads, and the less skilful the other parts. In the end all the pieces were joined together again in their proper places and the block locked into one whole, from which an electro was taken. It was marvellous how accurately all this was done, so that none but an expert could detect the joins.

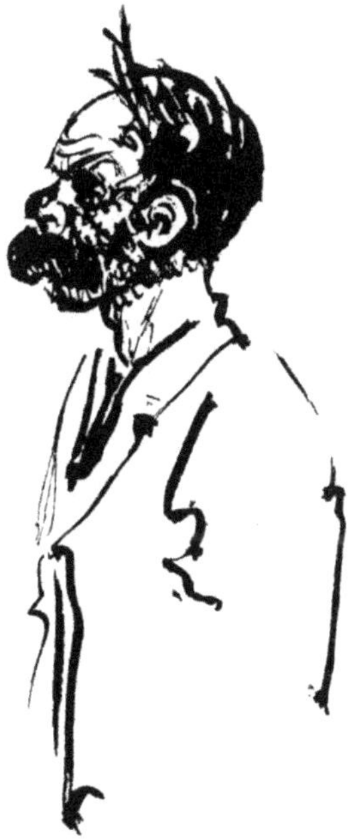

At the Parnell Commission

"I was of Good Templars, Sor"

As already mentioned, the Parnell Commission was in full swing at the Law Courts. Sidney P. Hall, one of the most famous of *The Graphic* Special Correspondents, was employed in making sketches of witnesses and scenes in Court. He could not be in Court all the time, so I was one of those selected to keep his place and incidentally to supply a sketch if some witness of news interest happened to be called

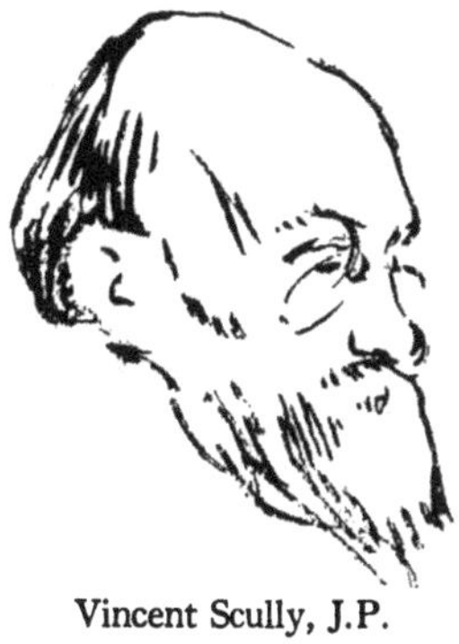

Vincent Scully, J.P.

while Sidney Hall was absent. This was excellent practice, and I quickly became fairly expert at sketching portraits, an important point in my future training.

There were many dramatic scenes in Court, and Sir Charles Russell, Parnell's counsel, was not the man to lose anything of

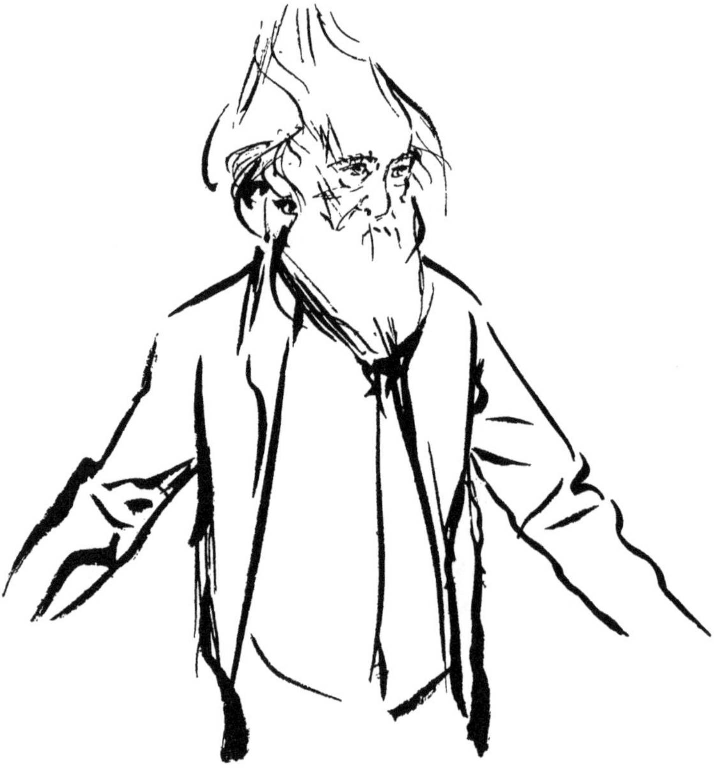

At the Parnell Commission

"*I'm here to answer any question I am asked*"

them. Nevertheless, some of the most amusing incidents occurred when an apparently ignorant Irish peasant bamboozled an important Q.C. who was trying to catch him out or compel his evidence to be contradictory or damaging to his victim's political interests. Time and again the peasant scored a victory.

My work at *The Daily Graphic* was interesting to me from the first, and was to become more so as time went on, because I had the good fortune to be chosen to do special correspondence for the paper. At first my duty was only to make drawings of current events, but soon I had to combine drawing with a written account of what I had just seen or heard, much to the disapproval of the sub-editor!

In those days the Special Correspondent was a more privileged person on the big newspapers than he is to-day—certainly the War Correspondent was. Frederick Villiers had been retained in that capacity for *The Graphic*. His portrait had been exhibited in the Royal Academy, in uniform hung about with revolvers, in his hand the flaming scarlet envelope in which despatches for *The Graphic* might be franked without waiting for tiresome delays at post offices or such-like formalities. By this time he was getting past such strenuous work and it was whispered that his nerve had failed, but little Fripp, one of his understudies, was still active. His nerve was reputed to be iron and indestructible.

I have handled volumes of sketches done by him during the Zulu War, which were ideal to work from. Some sketches made by him at the battle of Ulundi, drawn with a pen as he lay on the leather roof of a waggon, with Zulus charging close up armed with both assegais and rifles, were set out with full topographical details, as if executed in a chair at home.

He was a little terrier of a man, of whom a characteristic story was told that he fought Lord William Beresford because he ordered him out of the water, when bathing in a river in Zululand. This he was doing in defiance of regulations issued from headquarters on account of the danger from lurking Zulus. He died of hardships endured somewhere in Manchuria, in Arctic weather, during the Sino-Japanese War.

No one had yet been appointed War Correspondent for *The Daily Graphic*.

There was no war during the time that I was working for the Press, but I was sent to army and naval manœuvres, and attended military ceremonies, doubtless to train me for war occasions if they should arise. My reason for suspecting this was confirmed later, when W. L. Thomas became very angry with me because I resigned from my position on the paper after two years. He then told me I was a fool, as he had intended to use me as a War Correspondent of the paper on the first occasion that might arise.

Certainly such an opportunity would be most valuable from the point of view of my future success, but the fact remained that I really wished to be a painter, and therefore needed time and opportunity to develop what talents I possessed in that direction.

I do not regret my decision to-day. Though I have not made much of a success of my life as an artist, I am thankful to have been able to make enough money for my needs in doing what I enjoyed doing; the more that in doing so I have retained the respect of my brother artists.

As a Correspondent, I had several interesting experiences, all helping to complete my education as an observer.

One such was a tour round the Mediterranean in a large yacht. This was the beginning of those holiday cruises in great liners which have now become so popular. I was sent to record and advertise this adventure, and was away journeying for a number of weeks. The yacht, however, was hardly large enough to enable me to work in comfort on board. Therefore during the early part of the cruise I had to work hard in an hotel whenever we went ashore in order to get some work completed to be sent off to the paper from each port of call. In doing so I missed some of the organized expeditions from the ship. One that I particularly regret was a visit to the Alhambra before that fire which greatly damaged it, early in the nineties.

Soon I discovered I must make a point of seizing my chance at the moment, for opportunities rarely recur. "Now or never" is the only sure rule in life for mortals. I had to learn also that a Correspondent cannot afford to neglect the smallest chance that fortune may offer.

I have had my return tickets to Monte Carlo—supplied by the paper—stolen, through surrendering to a lady in trouble, in the middle of the night, a porter I had somehow managed to secure. I never saw the porter or my tickets again and new ones had to be purchased.

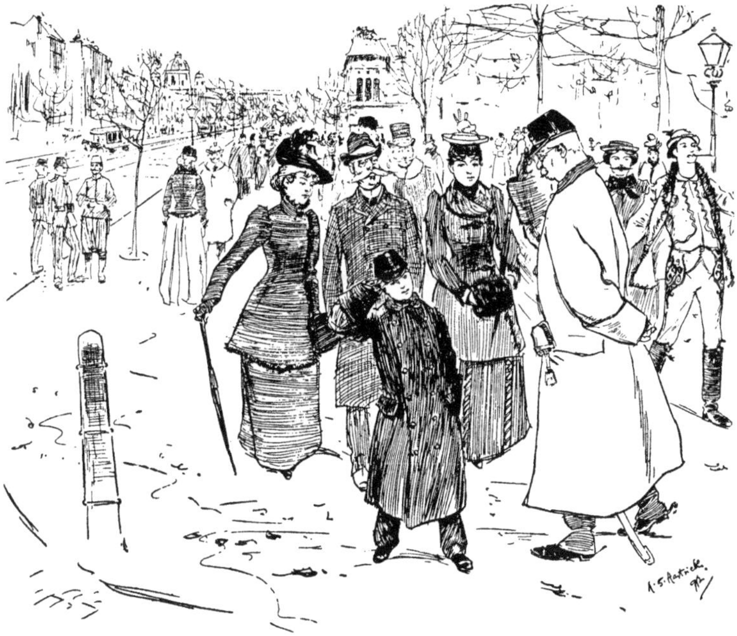

Vienna in 1892

On another occasion I was sent on naval manœuvres when a fleet under Admiral Culme-Seymour, secretly accompanied by colliers, coaled in the calm belt above the Equator, a feat never accomplished before or since. We were away for six weeks, during which time another fleet under Admiral Tryon was unsuccessfully looking for us in the Bay of Biscay. From the newspaper point of view the manœuvres were a fiasco. This was the Admiral Tryon who a year later went down in his flagship H.M.S. *Victoria* with 338 officers and men, after she had been rammed by H.M.S. *Camperdown* at manœuvres off Tripoli in the Mediterranean.

A cousin of my own, who had been acting signal-midshipman to Admiral Tryon on the *Victoria* only a fortnight before the disaster, used to say that Tryon's eyesight was bad, and that was the secret behind the tragedy, as well as obstinacy in refusing to recognize danger. My cousin escaped through being down with a bout of fever in a hospital ship, but was a witness of the disaster. He was killed in the Boer War.

Among the friends I made in these directions were Bennett Burleigh, War Correspondent of *The Daily Telegraph*, and Pearse, who represented *The Daily News*. Both were kind to a beginner. Burleigh in particular was a man of intense energy—worming his way into dangerous situations where he was not wanted, and somehow emerging unscathed. He had a particularly exciting time in Madagascar during the occupation of that island by the French: for he was hunted by the French troops there for months, with the certainty of being shot at sight if caught, on the charge of encouraging the natives to resist in arms.

These were the ways and triumphs of the old War Correspondents, but their days were already numbered. Ten years later, when Kitchener was making his first advance on Dongola, Burleigh, who had bought a small yacht at Cairo, thought he could manage to bluff and wangle it through the rapids above Assouan in disregard of orders from those in authority. He did succeed in getting his yacht lashed to a barge that was being towed through the rapids by some army organization; but then the Fates interfered, the yacht touched a rock in the struggle, and went to the bottom with all Burleigh's equipment but not himself. He was too wily to be there. Then his perspicacity failed him, for he started to make a row at army headquarters and claimed damages for his loss. This proved to be his undoing; he was brought before General Rendle, in charge of the operations, who cut short his bluff at once with the statement: "That the event as it turned out was fortunate for him, because if the yacht had got through he would have sent Burleigh back to the base and refused him further passage to the front"—the end of all things for a Correspondent. So it was a chastened Burleigh who turned up in the Special Correspondents' Mess at the front, without any equipment of his own, and obliged to borrow from others. Not till the Russo-Japanese War, however, was Burleigh really finished—no bluffing proved of any use there and the "old war-horse", as he called himself, returned to England in disgust. Burleigh had another characteristic of his own at that period. Whenever there was a general election or a vacancy, he stood as a Labour candidate for the Camlachie Division of Glasgow. I have been told that, as he was always abroad for his paper at such times, he never personally addressed his constituents. But as a result of this political attachment, I suppose, he and Pearse proposed me as a member of the Social Democratic Club, which had recently moved from a cellar in Chancery Lane to superior premises in Essex Street, Strand. This was quite near to Milford Lane and *The Daily Graphic*, so I used often to go there for a cheap lunch.

Keir Hardie, then a new type of Labour member, had just been elected to Parliament, where he created something of a sensation, in what was mainly a top-hatted body, by appearing in a deer-stalker cap. With this head-dress he became famous in the news of the day. He, too, was a member of the Club and there, I believe, I drew for *The Daily Graphic* the first portrait of him to be published in London, cap and all.

I can remember being struck by his extreme "reserve and canniness". He could not be persuaded to commit himself on any subject whatever: far different from John Burns or Ben Tillett.

One day I happened to be seated next to him at lunch when he fell foul of some Scotch-broth, the vegetables in which were not cooked to his liking. With a gesture of disgust he pushed his plate away into the middle of the table. Just on his other hand was a big dark-haired Scotsman, young and but lately come from his native glen. For some minutes he eyed the discarded plate —then stretching out a hand pulled it to himself and taking a spoon lapped it up eagerly, saying sheepishly, "After-r the M.P." I wonder who he was?

Again, as Correspondent, it was my business to attend several "great strikes". One, of "Cotton Spinners", to which I was sent in Lancashire, with Harold Cox to write it up, remains impressed on my mind by the ability of the strike leaders; they could discuss fractions on equal terms with the masters; and, as a matter of fact, I was told that most of the latter had begun life as operatives themselves.

Oldham on this occasion was our centre, and everybody on both sides was friendly, but I felt there was an element of suspicion attaching to us as journalists from London; the sentiment that Burns has crystallized in the lines—

> A chiel's amang you takin' notes,
> And, faith! he'll prent it

—that might mean trouble.

One evening I was being shown round the sights by a strike leader; we entered a large underground bodega or wine shop where in spite of the strike hundreds of operatives, men and women, were congregated drinking glasses of port at tables that either were or looked like wine barrels. I had found a quiet corner and was sketching the scene to get types and such like, rather from the humorous point of view, when someone shouted out: "There's some b— takin' notes, and he's goin' to show us up!" Everybody got on their feet in a threatening way and the culprit was sought for, so I was hustled out through a back way by the strike leader and implored by the manager then and by letter later to publish no sketch of that incident.

The hardest twenty-four hours I ever worked on end are recalled to me by incidents in another strike. This time it was a strike of miners in the Durham coalfield, then one of the richest in the country. I had been sent off early one Friday morning from London with instructions to go to Newcastle, interview Mr Joseph Cowan, a northern celebrity and a Liberal politician who owned and edited *The Newcastle Chronicle*, and be guided by his instructions where to go.

On my arrival, I left my Gladstone-bag at the Station Hotel and immediately got in touch with *The Chronicle*. Mr Cowan was not there, but I made an appointment to see him at 10.30 next morning.

No mines were working in Durham, but a suggestion was made by someone at the office that I should go at once over the border into Northumberland, where all the mines were working double shifts because of the strike, and immediate arrangements were made for me to go down a pit at Morpeth with the night shift.

Every young miner in Durham who was free had crossed the border, where there was plenty of work and extra pay; but all full-timers and married men had to remain away on strike by the orders of their Union.

As far as I remember, the origin of the strike was a dispute over the time to be worked by men and boys. All the men in the field had got an eight-hour day, but the boys did ten from bank to bank. When it was proposed to take one hour off the boys' and add half an hour or so to the men's time, the whole field came out. Their logic was that, as boys, all the men had done ten hours, and they would be d—d if they would see the boys let off anything and the time made up by the men. No doubt it is all quite different now, but that, roughly, was the position as explained to me.

Having got some dinner at the hotel, I set off for Morpeth and the mine I was to visit. A night shift was going down and with it I went too. It was not a very deep mine, fortunately for me. As a "nouveau" I was let down in the cage very fast just to test my nerve: it felt as if my stomach were mounting into my mouth, but the ordeal did not last long and I survived the test.

Everyone was most friendly when I got to the bottom. I was shown the ponies in their stables and drawing cars along rails to and from the face of the coal; then, the men working at a four or five-foot seam, earning good money with comparative ease by cutting away the coal underneath and bringing it down in masses, as well as others in a two-foot seam, lying half-naked on their sides. Here it was hard work to make 30*s*. to £2 a week, with water dripping on one all the time. My recollection is that these positions were decided by lot every week.

I remained underground making very rough sketches until about 4 a.m., then returned to the Newcastle hotel for a couple of hours' sleep. After breakfast I set off to interview Mr Joseph Cowan, of whom I drew a portrait at his editorial desk, the while he gave me his views about the strike and entertained me with Rabelaisian stories of "Geordie", as the miner is called in these parts. When this was over he sent a reporter with me to show me the strikers "at play", killing time with rabbit-coursing and other sports. Here was quite interesting material for sketches—the men cheerful, and the sport cruel, for the rabbits let out of bags were coursed by whippets and had no chance of escape.

By this time it was one o'clock, so I returned to the hotel intending to lunch before working up the sketches and material I had got, ready to be sent to the paper by the night mail. Fate, however, had not done with me yet. I found a telegram from my Editor ordering me to go at once to Hepburn, where there had been serious rioting at a pit and the military had been called out to assist the police. It was only about twenty miles away, so having paid the bill and collected my bag, I made a hurried lunch in the bar on a few sandwiches and a pint of beer and caught the next train for Hepburn. It was a bleak day in March, and when I got there, a little before 4 p.m., snow was falling; I at once made for the station hotel, but all rooms had been booked for officers and I had no encouragement as to finding accommodation elsewhere. I went out with my bag wondering what to do next. I turned in at a small public house to try to get my bearings. The landlord, it turned out, was a

Scotsman; after hearing my tale and finding that I was a "brither Scot", he said he would take me in, and, further, get out his horse and trap to drive me to the mine, the scene of the riot, which was about two miles away. Within a quarter of an hour we were off, and though the light was fast going when we reached the mine, and there was little to see but a soldier or two on guard and the head workings of the pit, I made the necessary sketches.

On the way back, while passing through a village belonging to the pit, we were stoned by some strikers, but arrived home safely about six o'clock. The mine in question was an old one with much water in it: if the pumping ceased, the mine would quickly flood, in which case it would become too costly to pump it clear again; then it would go derelict, and about 300 men would be thrown out of work permanently. Everybody knew these facts, yet the riot had started in order to force the engine-men, who worked the pumps, to come out with the strikers.

My friend the keeper of the "pub" himself was in bad odour with the miners; his offence being that, for weeks, he had been feeding children of the chemical workers, who had been thrown out because their works had been shut down from want of coal; these people were much poorer than the miners, but their lot did not trouble the strikers. Such is the perversity and selfishness of men when excited in mass.

After a cup of tea and some buttered toast I settled down by the fire in an upstairs room to write out my interview with Joseph Cowan, the best parts of which I omitted as unprintable.

I also wrote out a few notes on my experiences in the pit and with the strikers "rabbit coursing", but first of all I put my sketches in order to make them more intelligible, as they would have to be re-drawn in pen and ink next day by somebody in *The Daily Graphic* studio before they would be fit for reproduction in the paper.

There was a clock on the mantelpiece of the room, which marked about 9.30 p.m. when I had finished; at 10 p.m. I knew the last train for Newcastle departed. With everything packed safely in that large scarlet envelope of *The Graphic*, marked "*Urgent—Deliver Immediately*", at a quarter to ten, relieved and feeling virtuous, I strolled over to the railway station to deliver this packet to the guard of the Newcastle train—it had just left!

That infernal clock was a quarter of an hour slow. I felt faint and was nearly sick on the spot, but was too empty of everything. The only way left to me, that I saw, was to drive the twenty miles to Newcastle before midnight, and it was still snowing. On account of the soldiers being called out everybody in Hepburn was thoroughly roused and ready to help.

After a little time the station master remembered that a goods train for Newcastle would soon be passing through his station. He agreed to stop it and to hand over my precious envelope to the guard, who would deliver it to the guard of the midnight mail at Newcastle. This was finally accomplished.

I felt I was saved from disaster. Most of what I sent appeared in *The Daily Graphic* of Monday—the paper had not been let down, and that was the vital matter.

In spite of the excitement I slept soundly that night in my friendly "pub" and the strike petered out a day or two after.

One more incident that belongs to this period seems to demand some record. I mean the Great Dock Strike of 1889, in which the larger issues of Trade Unionism in this country were made manifest, and John Burns, the first Labour leader to rise to Cabinet rank, made his reputation. Surely it must also be a unique coincidence, that he together with his two lieutenants, Tom Mann and Ben Tillett, are still alive and in the news to-day, just fifty years after their first success.

Sent by *The Graphic* to collect material for a drawing on that fine Sunday late in August, as if it were yesterday I can still see John Burns, sturdy, black-bearded, wearing a straw hat far back on his head, leading his army of about 100,000 men into Hyde Park, and swinging his columns through the Park gates to positions with a voice like that of Boanerges, Son of Thunder.

There must be something persistent in personal magnetism, because of all that multitude I cannot recall another face.

The strike was for the "Docker's Tanner"—that is for *6d.* an hour for casual labour instead of *5d.*, together with a minimum of *2s.* for the half-day—and it lasted for four weeks. There is no doubt that these men had been shamefully exploited, and to-day the sum in question appears ridiculous: yet there were people who thought the end of the world had come when, with the assistance of Cardinal Manning and the Lord Mayor, the miserable demand was granted. My duties in this matter also took me to the docks, where Tom Mann and Ben Tillett were at work organizing and encouraging the strikers. In addition to some sketches, I brought back with me to *The Graphic* photographs of these two leaders. The instant old Godfroi Durand saw that of Ben Tillett he cried out "Voilà le vrai type révolutionnaire". He had been out himself in the Paris Revolution of 1848, and henceforth considered himself an authority on all such matters. Tillett, I suppose, if he knew, would take Durand's remark as a compliment.

Forty years later my friend Kerr Lawson (the portrait painter) told me that Tillett when in his studio had recently announced as his opinion that "all geniuses should be strangled at birth".

This sort of talk is not new. Envy, hatred and malice were common in the world before Joseph told his dream to his brethren of how their sheaves bowed down to his; nor did the speaker trouble to explain how he would distinguish genius at the breast.

But the idea is not scotched, for I note that Chaliapin in his reminiscences of Soviet Russia, called *Man and Mask*, reports a similar instance of muddled thinking in regard to himself. A Russian communist, in a company of which the singer was one, shouted out that individuals like Chaliapin ought to have their "gullets slit". Somebody asked why. "Because no man should be superior to another. Genius destroys equality", was the naïve reply. I may add that they all had been drinking vodka.

One wonders how such people accept Stakhanovism, the latest fad of the Soviets, where the most vulgar and unpleasant inequalities of men have been exalted for the admiration of all into acts of "gods".

As for Tom Mann, his sincerity impressed me—a little volcanic, round-headed man highly conscious of the wrongs about him, a Christian Socialist, and in deadly earnest. I have never seen him since, and he now has the reputation of being a fire-brand. He was a type outside Durand's experience and his portrait excited no comment from him.

The offices of *The Graphic* at this period were placed on the south side of the Strand opposite to the Church of St Clement Danes: the printing works were in Milford Lane near by. In Milford Lane also was the new building which was to house the whole of *The Daily Graphic* presses as well as the editorial and other departments: all was now nearing completion and there was no longer any pretence of a secret, for the title over the doorway proclaimed it to the world at large. The premises began to be occupied.

About this time most of us in the studio were put on salaries —I will not go into their names. Up till then we had been on trial and paid piece-work for what we did, and the salaries came to considerably less than the piece-work, which is a way they have. Some of our friends disappeared, having been found wanting.

Gilbert Thomas, one of the sons of W. L., was put in charge of the studio, and we all started to work as a staff exactly as if the paper were in running order. Some of us "did" stock, if we were not out sketching (i.e. made drawings that could be used at any moment). Sullivan developed skill in drawing portraits in pen and ink, a difficult job. Being successful with likenesses, presently he was more or less tied to that sort of work, doing portraits for the "graveyard", the section of a newspaper where the biographies of all notabilities are kept in store, in case of sudden death or accident. As a sop to the sceptics who prophesied the failure of the zinc blocks, we were also practised in the handling of small wood blocks about two inches square, and did some stock in this style.

Before the actual start of the new paper on January 1st, 1890, the whole staff was turned on to the production of a trial number to display the exact form the newcomer would assume, with all the novel features accentuated.

Reginald Cleaver, A. S. Boyd and Herbert Johnson, all experienced draughtsmen, took up a position of superiority in the studio in an inner room, together with Adrien Marie, a Frenchman, and "Pal", a Belgian. These latter were to continue to do the important work until the paper was fairly started as a going concern. Just before Christmas a trial was made of the new Marinoni machines. Special invitations were issued for an evening to see "the wheels go round". I was not present at the function, but next morning we of the studio heard weird tales of machines being choked, and papers pulled out by the hundred before the eyes of agonized directors!

Nevertheless, by January 1st everything was in apple-pie order, and the presses delivered the papers printed and folded to schedule. *The Daily Graphic* had started out as a daily paper ready to report news without a hitch like any other newspaper.

Mr J. Heath Joyce, the Editor of *The Graphic*, was the first Editor of *The Daily Graphic*, combining the two; Hammond Hall was Assistant Editor and a little later on took over full control. He was a serious-looking man; but one day he came over to the studio beaming, to tell Gilbert Thomas, who was in charge then, that a boy, a printer's devil with a batch of proofs, had just said to him: "When you have a lucid moment, Mr Hall, will you please look at these?"

CHAPTER VII

RENOUARD, TOULOUSE-LAUTREC, AND OTHERS

By the end of the eighties, the Impressionist Movement, which began in France as a recoil from the Romantic, had arrived at victory and had achieved material success. At the same time in the official Salon the academic painters were turning out vast "machines", executed with great skill, which were becoming more and more without any inspiration beyond the advertisement of their producers. It was obvious that these artists would never fuse with the impressionists—yet some fusion was needed to go forward or for a change. Accordingly in 1890, a new body, including the more liberal-minded members of both schools, was founded. It obtained from the Ministry of Fine Arts the use of the buildings of the Art Pavilion of the International Exhibition of 1889. Meissonier, the "grand old man" of the Société des Artists Français, that is the Old Salon, was captured to make the figure-head of the New, which was named the "Société Nationale des Beaux Arts".

The first exhibition of this Society was a great success; it made a profit of about £8000. This was the beginning of disaster.

Paul Renouard, a member of the jury, told me that at one of the first meetings to consider what should be done about a second exhibition, Meissonier rose, and with impressive gesture began: "Gentlemen, we have this splendid surplus in hand. I propose that we use it to build a magnificent flight of steps up to the Gallery, worthy of the new art era we have inaugurated."

The jury was dumbfounded! for many of them knew that the old man had spent nearly all of the enormous sums he had made by his pictures in building, regardless of expense, first a staircase up to a gallery in his own studio; when the staircase was complete he pulled down the gallery and substituted another to suit the staircase; then he demolished the staircase and built a new one; and then again the gallery—and so *ad infinitum*! His proposal was negatived and the old painter went home to bed and died of chagrin.

This is the true story of the end of the great Meissonier.

My sketchy and slangy knowledge of French was the main factor in my becoming well acquainted with Paul Renouard. He had been sent over to England in the first instance (more or less by a happy accident, he told me) by *The Graphic's* agent in Paris, to make drawings in Ireland during the Land League troubles of a few years before. He was a very able and interesting man, to whose advice I owe much that has been of value to me, both in theory and in practice. He it was who really introduced me to modern French painting and painters, for though attached to no particular clique he was friendly and in sympathy with most of those artists who were to make French art paramount in Europe from this time on. He was the last person in the world to have pretensions as a great artist: his usual attitude about himself was to say "Moi, je suis observateur", and this he was to a superlative degree. But the French, who understand that the painting of large oil canvases does not necessarily make an artist, know also how to value their "dessinateurs". He did not speak English, though I think he understood more than he would allow. But he had a theory that for his work this was an advantage, because he was thus compelled to make his drawings explain themselves entirely to the eye. Certainly no other foreigner has ever expressed in drawing the characters of the people of this country so convincingly and with such understanding. However, he sometimes needed help when he had been sent on expeditions by *The Graphic*, and I was frequently told off to go with him to arrange sittings, for he always used the real people and not professional models.

Everything was drawn by him direct from nature, and he

worked slowly, though the appearance of his work to the lay eye was that it was done rapidly from moving figures, so that it often seemed unfinished.

His beginnings in art had been in straitened circumstances and financial difficulty, aggravated by the fact that he had no facility in drawing. He told me he had been a country postman at one time; but he had character and determination and developed a style that was his own, that both made money and brought him into the first flight of draughtsmen of his day.

One result of this independent training was that he was unusually open-minded and free from the fads of Academies or cliques. Some of his observations on the works of the masters were original and illuminating in directions that seem always to escape the notice of the professional art critic. Every painter knows that Holbein was accustomed to paint his portraits from drawings. But Renouard pointed out that there are certain of them that display signs of direct painting from nature, and these not the least interesting. For instance, the portrait of Erasmus in the Louvre, one of Holbein's masterpieces, is of this kind; if the nose is examined carefully it will be seen how the brush worked tentatively, seeking for the exact form; thereby giving quite a different expression from that of his usual direct method, when he had learnt and made certain of everything he wanted in a drawing before the painting was started. The same tentative touch will be noted all over this portrait, in the features and in the hands especially; the reason being that he was intimate with Erasmus and was able to get him to sit for long periods. The other portraits which display the same qualities are, like those of his own family at Basle, of intimate friends. Important people like Henry VIII and his courtiers were impatient, and possibly dangerously so for a foreign artist; so he invented this method of drawing with red and black chalk so that he could get all the facts he needed quickly and then paint from the drawing quietly in his own time and place. It has been recorded that he could make a drawing of this kind in about one hour and a half.

At other times Renouard could be just as interesting about Velasquez. In this case he pointed out that it seemed probable that the original and finest editions of that master's work, dealing with family portraits, were sent to Vienna; the Emperor was the head of the Hapsburgs, and accordingly Velasquez is superbly represented in the Imperial Gallery there, especially by children's portraits.

Renouard was similarly interesting on other topics; always he had something original and illuminating to say about any works of art, ancient or modern, in which he was interested.

Of the moderns, Degas was his ideal: of him both as man and artist he always spoke with the deepest respect. He knew him well in connection with the Opera House, where he himself also frequented the school of ballet. Once, he described how his self-confidence received a check there, when a girl, whom he had refused to employ, replied: "But I am the model of M. Degas." From that moment he viewed her with new eyes. He spoke also of a portrait of a ballet-master by Degas, done in the school against a whitewashed wall, which he considered the most wonderful painting ever done by the master. I have never heard of it from any other source, nor seen a reproduction; so I sometimes wonder if it belonged to the kind which John Sargent once referred to when he said "Every portrait is another enemy", and whether it has been destroyed because of the vanity of the sitter.

A little bald-headed bearded man, about forty-five years of age, with bulging eyes and a merry laugh, Renouard was a delightful companion: witty, gay and full of the most amusing stories, which he fired off at us boys from time to time.

Sarah Bernhardt, who was starring in London, he had known intimately from the time she was fifteen, so there were tales of her vagaries many and peculiar. Now, Sarah Bernhardt was the greatest actress I have ever seen; it is quite impossible for me to convey her magic in writing. I have seen her often, but only once at her very best; it was in Paris about 1887—the play *La Dame aux Camelias*. She was acting with Damala, a Greek, the only man she ever married—they quarrelled soon after, as might be expected; but he was dying of some incurable disease and had asked her to play through some of their roles together again, before the end. The occasion was one of this series.

Never before or since have I seen a French audience, which is critical first of all, so obviously affected; it was quite broken down. A man near me said to another: "Look! Look at Sarah! it's the real thing, she's not acting now." Certainly it was almost too much to see and listen to. This memory has always recurred to me when I hear the debate as to whether deliberate or emotional acting is the more effective.

And while on this subject, I should like to record one other experience which may prove interesting on this point.

I saw Beerbohm Tree play "Macari" in *Called Back*, long before he was famous. In that play the villain "Macari" stabs the fiancé of the heroine before her eyes: she screams and goes out of her mind as the result. Tree stabbed the man in a particularly vicious and unexpected manner, whereupon the heroine performed her scream with vigour; but just behind me in the pit, some woman let off a *real* scream—there was no doubt about its meaning—it was absolutely bloodcurdling—everybody leapt up and nearly out of their skins at the note it struck. The stage scream was but a mouse squeak beside it.

To return to Sarah Bernhardt, of course she was unconventional. I think it was on her first visit to England as a star that she brought her son Maurice with her, then quite a little boy, whom she introduced in society and everywhere she went as "une petite caprice de ma jeunesse", to the patent discomfort of many lion-hunters of the period.

Ten or more years later, Renouard had another tale of her arrival at Le Havre after a triumphant if stormy visit to America. For days before landing she practised before a looking-glass saying two words, "Mon fils", which were designed to greet this same son, now a young man, on her return to the shores of La Belle France.

But a more intimate tale described a visit to her dressing-room while Renouard was making a series of drawings for *Harper's Magazine* of Sarah rehearsing a play by Sardou.

Here, he said, she was the limit. First she seized hold of her hair and shook it fiercely, saying: "It is all my own this toupet of mine you see", adding, after a pause, "and it has served me well!" Next without warning she indulged in some antics so shameless that even the hardened Paul Renouard was shocked. "C'est le théâtre" was his comment, and he shrugged his shoulders.

One more memory of her, and I have done. I saw Mrs McLure Hamilton one afternoon years ago calling on Mrs Pennell in Buckingham Street, Adelphi. She was in a fury about Sarah. The Hamiltons had let their house in St John's Wood to her for her season in London. What was their horror to discover, on their return, that Sarah had had two cartloads of gravel shot on to the lawn, which was their special care and pride, in order to let her little grand-daughter "Simone", whom she had with her, dig in it. However, she paid up for all this, as well as damage in the house, which looked in parts as if a fury had been loose upon it, Mrs Hamilton said.

A pet story of Renouard's was one he told about Chevreul, the chemist whose theory of colours was taken up and applied to painting by the impressionists in France.

The occasion was his hundredth birthday. Renouard had been sent by *Le Monde Illustre* or some such paper to make drawings of the centenarian. He must have been living somewhere on the outskirts of Paris, because Renouard described how he walked far, and at last came to a gate in a wall. It was unlatched; so he went in, found the house door and rang the bell, but could get no answer. Accordingly he entered, and began opening doors as he found them. The second one revealed what he had come to see. There was Chevreul fast asleep in bed under a *canapé*, on his hundredth birthday! Now Renouard had a peculiar way of carrying his portfolio or sketch-book. He pushed it up underneath his waistcoat and wore it as a breastplate. He said it left his hands free when walking about. Pulling it down, he took a chair, set his chalks in a box beside him, and began to draw the sleeping man without more ado.

After a time, an old *bonne* came along to demand what he was doing there? He told her he had been sent by the papers to make a drawing of her master, and as he could get no answer to his knocking he had just come in. Immediately, she stepped forward and shaking Chevreul cried out: "Hi! here is a gentleman come to take your picture for the papers!"

Chevreul stirred, then looking round at them said: "I was dreaming, dreaming of the guillotine and those times. There was Bouchot the baker and Ponchon the butcher and all the others going along with the crowd", etc. Then, suddenly seeming to wake up to the present, pointing a threatening finger at Renouard, he shouted, "Moi, je ne suis un de ceux qui font descendre l'homme d'un Ouran-Outan"—and at the moment he himself looked exactly like an ape, as Renouard added.

In this wise he made a drawing of him. Presently some officials, accompanied by the son of Chevreul, an old man over seventy, turned up to say that the President of the Republic offered his box at the Opera to the scientist for the Gala to be held in his honour that night. But Chevreul would have none of it. "Mais Papa," said the son, "think of the honour." "What are honours to me?—I'm a hundred years old to-day", was the reply—one in which certainly no signs will be detected of senile decay.

Renouard, too, is now gone to keep company with the scientist, and I wonder whether we shall see again the like of either of them: anyway, each had sampled life to the full and has left a memory that will not easily fade.

Renouard really liked and understood England and the English in a way few Frenchmen ever do. He did not live at an hotel when over here, but liked to find lodgings with some typical English family in Vauxhall or somewhere like that. Once it was at a wigmaker's, I remember, and another time at a pastrycook's. In these surroundings he met the genuine characters whom he enjoyed, though he could hardly speak to them.

No entertainment here delighted him more than a visit to the "Old Mogul"—the Middlesex music-hall as it used to be, in Drury Lane. There he sat rolling with laughter while the tears ran down his cheeks with joy. This was the real English Comedy, he found: and I have heard that Degas has said much the same.

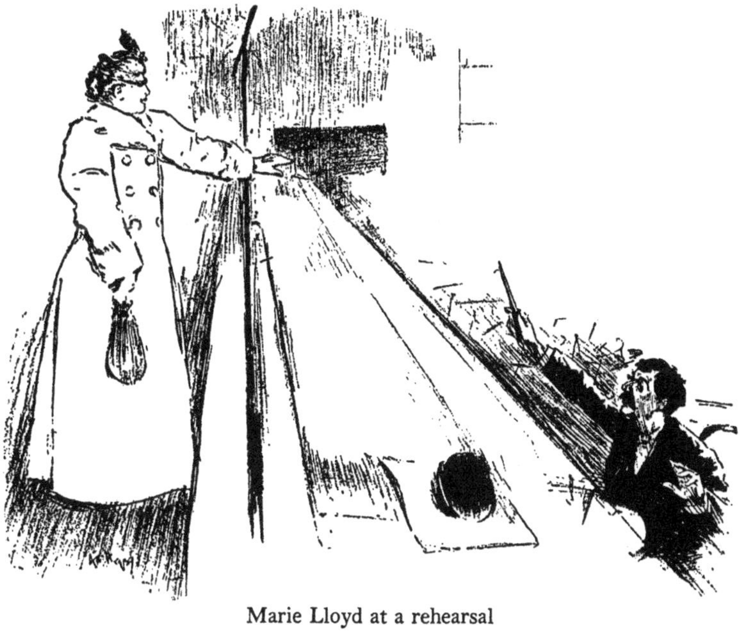

Marie Lloyd at a rehearsal

Rich and fruity! Certainly nobody who has not seen Marie Lloyd and Dan Leno, as he did in that music-hall, with all Drury Lane in its shirt sleeves to applaud, has known the heights that laughter can attain.

It was in the Atelier Cormon I first met Toulouse-Lautrec. Lautrec was an artist of very marked individuality and, I should say, had one of the best artist brains in Paris. He was not mad at all. I can still remember vividly how novel and interesting his work looked to me among those of others in the studio. He was painting in turpentine on cardboard, using a very liney method of drawing, showing the influence of Degas and also of Forain. No one else attempted this method at the time, though many copied it later. Cormon, who was really, in spite of abuse by modern writers, nothing of a fossil but one of the most liberal-minded teachers I have known, was quite interested in what he was doing and left him alone. Lautrec, as Paul Renouard used to say, was "un véritable fin de race". He was a descendant of one of the oldest families in France and the portraits of his ancestors, who were companions and ministers of François I, are to be found among the drawings by both the Clouets in Chantilly and the British Museum.

He was a dwarf; it was said that he had been dropped by a nurse and injured as an infant. Anyway, he looked more like an ape than any man I have ever seen. He said his ambition was to find a woman as ugly or uglier than himself for a mistress, in order to breed a monster. I think he understood Chevreul's theory of colours and the division of tones better than anyone else, as applied to painting, but it was perhaps in his colour lithographs that this scientific side of him was best displayed. He is the only Frenchman I have known who really liked whisky, and he died in an asylum a dipsomaniac. I knew him personally, and his dissipation and bitterness arose largely out of disgust with his deformity. Through all his grotesques and cruelties there persists a strange sense of beauty.

Lastly, in this chapter I must recall a visit to the famous collector, Manzi, the printer to Goupil.

Manzi had what was reputed to be the finest collection of Japanese prints in Europe—it is all dispersed now, but I believe that even so it forms the nucleus of half a dozen of the best collections made since. I had an introduction to him and went to see the prints at one of his houses, for he had several.

John Swan was in the same hotel with me, and, as he was keen on Japanese art, I suggested that I should ask Manzi—with whom I had an appointment *chez* Boussod Valadon, to fix a

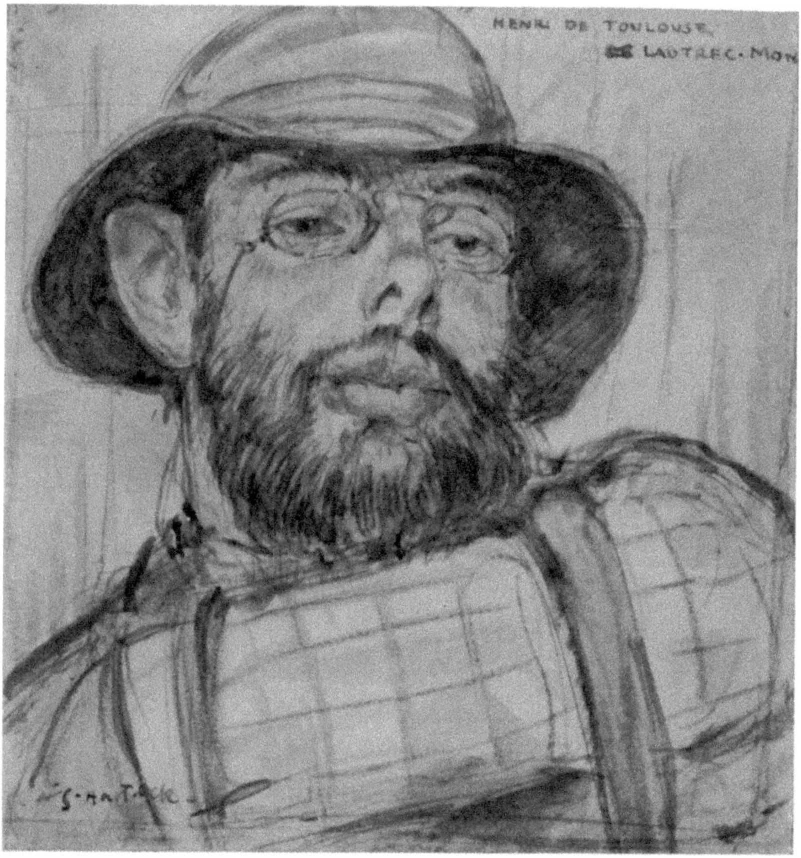

Toulouse-Lautrec

Drawing in pen and chalks

time and day—if Swan might come with me. Arrived there, Manzi, who drove up in a splendid carriage and pair, was quite amiable and agreed that Swan should accompany me. What followed was nearly a catastrophe. Swan had bought a commercial bronze after Barye. He knew that Bonnat had an original proof of the same with the chasing Barye had put on it. So he asked Manzi if he would give him an introduction to Bonnat that he might see the original. Manzi, with a face like a yellow mask, replied dryly, "Peut-être". Swan was furious. He turned his back on Manzi and said to Boussod, who was standing by, "Ah! you can give me one then." "Certainement, Monsieur", says Boussod immediately, in evident alarm at the threatened storm; and I went out with Swan a few minutes later, taking no further notice of Manzi or his carriage and pair. Swan cursed and swore that nothing would induce him to go to see that brute again. He would show him he was no starving artist to come crawling to his carriage door to beg for his support, etc. When he had calmed down, I said: "Well, it was his prints we wanted to see and they are known to be unique and wonderful, so I certainly shall go." Finally, he did come with me next day. The meeting of the two was threatening, and I feared the worst; but the prints were really superb, and under their influence Swan and Manzi became quite civil to one another and even chummy. Manzi brought out a large print, very rare and rather faded but fine, I think by Hokusai. We duly admired. With deliberation he drew from a portfolio another of the same subject, in absolutely perfect condition. It looked as if it had just come fresh from the printer's hands, with a marvellous blue in it like the first sight of a "morning glory". We were now speechless with admiration. Manzi turned and pointing to the first said: "Bing would tell you that is a masterpiece but I know better"—drawing himself up proudly and pointing to the perfect print—"I am a printer, c'est mon métier", he added, slapping himself on his breast.

From this, he went on to show us his most secret treasures,

among them the great pornographic set that Utamaro is said to have done for Chinese merchants. Here again Manzi became exalted, and thrusting his arm into the air he declared: "The Japanese are the only people who have known how to lift 'la pornographie' into a Religion." John Swan leant back like a great bear and shouted, "Ha! ha!! ha!!!" We all left the house delighted with one another.

CHAPTER VIII

SOME BLACK AND WHITE ARTISTS

For me the birth of *The Daily Graphic* will always be associated with the death of Charles Keene of *Punch*, perhaps the most original of all British draughtsmen in black and white, and in his way one of the great artists of the nineteenth century. I had long been an admirer of his work, and, after his death in 1890, I bought a drawing out of his memorial exhibition at the Fine Art Galleries in Bond Street, as well as several sketches and etchings from that Mrs Edwin Edwards, of Golden Square, from whom, for several years, the initiated could buy little masterpieces of drawing by Keene, for from *5s.* to *£5*. This lady was also the source of the supply of paintings by Fantin Latour to the English market. A large painting of herself and her husband by Fantin is now in the National Gallery, Trafalgar Square.

It seems worthy of note that Keene was the last of that brilliant school of illustrators, with Frederick Walker as its head, which sprang up here in the sixties, exploiting a new technique suited to reproduction by facsimile engraving on wood. It is one of my regrets that I never met him, though he was still to be seen at a window, working in a room in the King's Road, Chelsea, when I first passed that way.

Until after his death Keene was known to the public chiefly as a comic draughtsman; rather vulgar in his subjects, with nothing of the refinement and elegance of his opposite number on *Punch*, George Du Maurier. It used to be said by way of distinction between these two "that Keene could not draw a lady". What was more important Keene could draw anything and anybody and make the result a work of art. Du Maurier, a

Frenchman and an artist himself, has emphasized that fact. By use of a technique that cunningly concealed its art, Keene's work no doubt appeared to the uninitiated and popular critics as rough and unfinished. Without the joke it had hardly been tolerated; yet as a draughtsman he had perfected a method of drawing as masterly for its purpose as that of Rembrandt.

His reputation has been increasing with the years, and though his little drawings do not yet command fancy prices in the sale-room, they are steadily sought after and are now hard to find. In the year before he died he received the first public recognition of the true quality of his talent with the award of a gold medal at the International Exhibition in Paris of 1889. Someone at last persuaded him, rather against his will, for he was a modest man, to send them a couple of frames of the originals of his *Punch* drawings, and this was the result.

Whether it was by coincidence, or natural evolution in such matters, almost at this very time there was published in Paris an illustrated edition of an old Spanish book, *Pablo de Segovie*, by Quevedo, illustrated by a living Spanish artist, Daniel Vierge, with pen drawings reproduced by direct photo-engraving on zinc blocks. This is one of the pioneer illustrated books of the world, for it was one of the factors in changes which were to transform the art of illustration as then known, to kill wood-engraving for the purpose of news illustration at any rate, and incidentally to make such publications as *The Daily Graphic* possible. I had seen a few of the trial blocks, printed in *La Vie Moderne*, an illustrated weekly in Paris of 1886 or 1887, so I acquired a copy of the book as soon as it was published. It is now more or less forgotten except by experts, though I believe that young illustrators would do well to look it up again. Nothing better of its kind has been produced since, nor is likely to be now.

In this provisional period, as well as after the paper had actually started, there were many applications for positions on the staff; of these one of the most surprising was that of Aubrey

Beardsley. He sent in a mass of work showing influences of every sort, but mainly of Burne-Jones and the Japanese.

Many of these drawings were reproduced in the article which Joseph Pennell wrote later introducing him to the art world in London through the first number of the *Studio*, which appeared in January 1890.

Obviously his work was unsuitable for a daily newspaper, where the first requirement was not imagination, but a capacity to draw everything in a way that would be clear to everybody.

Nevertheless, Beardsley was a man of his period, and though his equipment as a draughtsman was nothing like so complete as that of E. J. Sullivan, for instance—another tyro of about the same age—his judgment was extraordinary for a youth. Instinctively he seemed to divine just how these new photographic methods and zinc blocks could be used to express what he wanted to say in art.

The result was that within a few years he had made a reputation that reached every place into which printed paper could penetrate. I did not know him intimately, but saw him frequently at work and at play, especially while he was Art Editor of *The Yellow Book*, to which he asked both Sullivan and myself to contribute from the first number. I never knew a young man who understood and accepted his own limitations so completely.

It looked as if, like Keats, he knew his time in the world would be short—he died when only twenty-seven—and therefore decided early to waste no time or energy in any direction he did not feel sure of. Certainly no English artist of his time, or perhaps of any time, has been so well known and imitated and even forged. Critics of his work there were in plenty. It was called affected and degenerate. Unhealthy it may have been, for the man was a victim of consumption, but it was never weak and it possessed a beauty of its own that was original and attractive.

To all who came in contact with him it was soon made clear that he had an uncommon talent and a first-rate brain.

I can recall one occasion when Whistler, in his house in the rue du Bac, Paris, probably annoyed by some extravagance of Beardsley's admirers, spoke rather contemptuously, calling his line "spidery", and waving his hands and fingers about, making grimaces of disgust.

Yet I have also heard Pennell tell of that meeting, a year or two before Beardsley's health finally gave way, when the two met in Pennell's studio in Buckingham Street. Whistler, looking at some of the younger man's more mature work, in which were included a few of those erotic drawings that the artist wished to have destroyed before he died (they would pass as harmless to-day), turned suddenly and said to him, "I was mistaken—you are a great artist", and Beardsley burst into tears. The story may sound fictitious, but I saw the drawings to which reference was made at the time I was told of it. For me the story is equally characteristic of Whistler and Beardsley at their best—their masks were off.

"Harris's Silver Grill" was the name given to a number of popular eating-houses in London of the nineties. One of these, in the Strand, was frequented by Sullivan and myself at lunch-time, for Harris also was a picture collector, and if he sold sausages he invested in Edward Stott and so had acquired grace. There we found a Tory weekly called *The St Stephen's Review*, which introduced to us the then novel and striking drawings of Phil May.

May had recently been appointed cartoonist to that paper and had inaugurated his arrival with a serial called *The Parson and the Painter*, which was really an excuse for a series of articles written by I know not whom, but illustrated by May at his ease, while sampling life both in London and Paris. The extraordinary freshness and brilliance of the drawings, together with their humour, made clear to us that a new star-illustrator had swum into our ken. What specially interested us, however, was the technical side of these drawings, for they were masterpieces of the sort of work that was most suited for reproduction in a daily newspaper.

A few months before this, May had returned to Europe from Australia, where he had been the most important factor in the creation and success of *The Sydney Bulletin*, which was also a weekly paper. No other artist, I have been told, has ever had such a vogue in Australia. Pages from *The Bulletin* were to be found pinned up in shacks at the back of beyond.

Australia of that period knew little and cared less about art, but it took May to its heart for the humanity and humour of his work. J. P. Russell, my Australian friend in Paris, told me that there was no appreciation of painting there, for its inhabitants were at that stage of culture when thirty shillings would be considered a good price for a portrait; therefore he decided not to return to his native land, but abide in France.

I do not think that it was lack of culture that sent May back; he was the sort of artist who took his art with him.

Like the Kingdom of God, art is within you, or not at all. It was in May. All environments were so much material for him, neither more nor less; and he had enjoyed great success in Australia. His own account was that he had never had any opportunity for study in his life; for he had begun life in Leeds by attaching himself to a theatrical travelling company as a boy, and taught himself to draw by doing the posters by hand for the company. This gradually led to small drawings for theatrical papers, which were based on the methods of Linley Sambourne, the *Punch* artist. Realizing his skill in this sort of work, some friend in London got him the job of cartoonist to *The Sydney Bulletin* at twenty pounds a week, and out to Australia he went with his wife, considering his fortune was made. After a few years, having saved a little money or borrowed it, he determined to go to Paris, which he understood was the Mecca of all artists, in order to make a serious effort to study to become a painter!

That no studio or professor there captured him for a pupil is only what might have been expected: May's kind is not to be bound or taught in schools. For a few months he remained in Paris using his eyes and sketching in the streets. Then the necessity of making money drove him back to London with his wife, and the job on *The St Stephen's Review*, if precarious, promised an income of a sort, for both.

Working on *The Sydney Bulletin* May had been accustomed to draw for printing of the most uncertain character, so he had evolved a method of drawing with a pen and a line, which, while retaining some art for those with eyes to see it, was almost fool-proof for the printer.

Sullivan and I, indeed all the younger members of *The Graphic* studio, at once reacted to the methods of this man, who had already solved most of our problems at *The Daily Graphic*.

We had not to wait long to make the acquaintance of this master in person. Perry, the manager of the Art Reproduction Company, who was making blocks for *The St Stephen's Review* and also for *The Daily Graphic*, brought him round to the studio. I can recall that first vision of his slim figure, his smile and his eye that seemed to take in all at once as he passed. Joe Crawhall, the animal painter, had the same power of concentrated gaze. It was a compelling eye; when it looked up from his drawing at his model, it was like a flash and gave one an uncanny feeling of insight.

May was on his way to see W. L. Thomas for a first interview, and no time was wasted there, for he returned quickly with a commission for *The Daily Graphic*. He stayed in the studio on his way back to be introduced to Gilbert Thomas and the rest of us, and we learnt that he had been given a series of snapshot photographs of Hastings or some other watering-place, from which he was instructed to make drawings in pen and ink for the paper.

A few days later he brought the drawings and we had a lesson in the proper way to treat such a commission. The monotony of the snapshots had disappeared, the subjects had become varied and the incidents made clear in line and embellished with humour.

The Fates worked kindly, and it was not long before Sullivan and I began an intimate friendship with May and his wife, which lasted till his death.

As he hated being alone, he often took one or both of us during his peregrinations, when he turned night into day.

Whether he belonged to them or not, he seemed to have the entrée into all the night or supper clubs, as they were then called, in London, and his acquaintance was extensive and peculiar; yet his behaviour and support of the same was mainly one of good fellowship accompanied by drinks: for even if he were fuddled, his wit remained quick. We even took him home with us occasionally when the hour was too far gone in the a.m.'s for him to be anything but a nuisance: and Mrs May forgave us because she knew we were looking after him, and that he would come home sober after breakfast, for we had to be at work at *The Daily Graphic* at nine-thirty. But he was impossible and elusive when it came to something he did not like, such as restraint—though never so cunningly applied—or porridge for breakfast!

One of the strangest of these nocturnal prowlings landed us in the flat occupied by Sandow, the strong man of the period. He was a young Austrian lately arrived in this country, who had cultivated his muscles to an extraordinary extent by methods he claimed to be unique. After some success on the music-hall stage with weight-lifting and such-like acts, he was about to launch a physical culture school to teach the gilded youth about town to become strong men too. He was living with a woman who claimed to have been the *belle amie* of a royal personage, and, to commemorate that dignity, she had embroidered a bedspread with the royal arms. As we sat round for drinks this magnificence displayed its parts to us through an open door!

Sandow was like a child in his vanity about his muscles and insisted on stripping to the waist to show them off. With a strong German accent he would name some special muscle and then with a twist and a flick it would jump up into view, to his evident delight. To the touch he was as hard as a piece of wood all over.

About this time May had gone to live at 9 Holland Park Road in a studio that belonged to a water-colour painter called

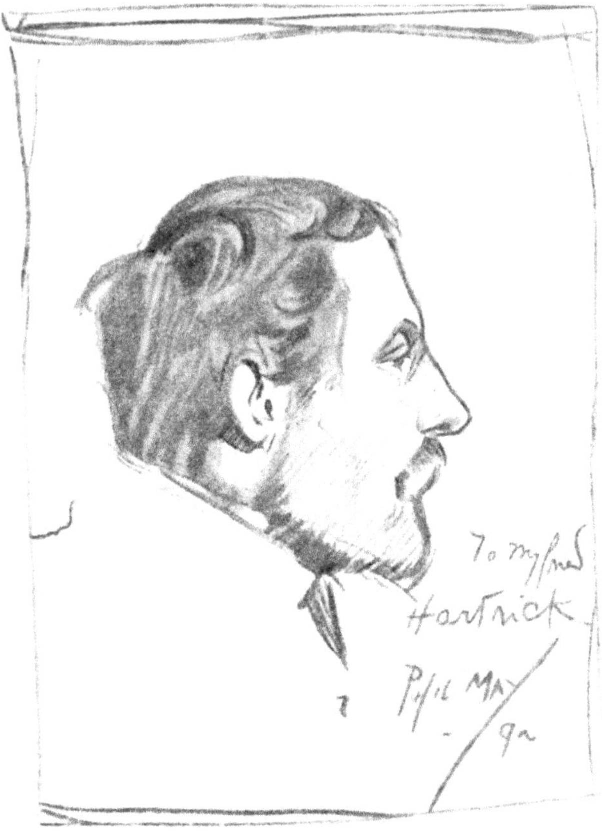

A sketch of the author by Phil May

Tristram Ellis. It consisted of little more than a long narrow studio with a bedroom at one end and a kitchen at the other.

There it was he started his Sunday evenings, which we were to attend regularly for a number of years and thereby meet many men who afterwards became famous.

I will try to introduce perhaps the most remarkable, to me, of all these people, Dr Morrison, celebrated as Morrison of *The Times* and the adviser of Sun Yat Sen.

He was an Australian, tall, spare and quiet in manner, with nothing sensational about him. May had known him when on *The Sydney Bulletin*, where he had given an account of some adventures he had had in the South Sea Islands; from which he had brought away an uncomfortable souvenir in a spear wound that was to give him trouble for years after.

Now he turned up again, as May's friends were always doing.

He had just published a book relating how he had walked through China for two years, unarmed and unharmed, for an expenditure of about £20 in English money. The first Sino-Japanese War was threatening; China was coming into the news.

The book therefore had a certain amount of success and was largely quoted in the press, but Morrison cannot have made much money out of it; perhaps it barely paid for his voyage from Australia, because he certainly was hard up. He was doing all he knew to try to return to China as the Correspondent of some paper here, and May was doing his best to help him.

Obviously he was a most interesting man and full of unusual knowledge. He was a doctor of medicine to begin with, and this had been of value to him on his travels.

I remember asking him why he kept giving interviews to all and sundry when he might have written all the matter himself? But he was not good at exploiting himself, he said, as was obvious.

He was turned down by *The Times* and *The Telegraph* as a Correspondent, and at his wit's end to know what to do next, when suddenly the way was opened and off he went immediately back to China at his own expense.

May's account of this was, that some old gentleman who had read his book had died and left the writer a sum of £3000 in cash. It was a marvellous coincidence. Within three months Morrison was Correspondent of *The Times* in China, sending telegrams that were quoted all over the world, and Lord Curzon complained of his "intelligent anticipation of events".

To return to May himself, his talent was quickly noted by the people that mattered in London; but it must be recorded that at first *Punch* looked at him askance—he was suspected of being vulgar, which of course May never was. *Punch* learnt better, however, and Burnand, the Editor, was very kind to him, turning a lenient eye on his weaknesses.

May was a very lovable man but with a strain of melancholy, which was often his undoing. He was unable to be alone for long; always he seemed compelled to seek company. His wife told me what a great trial it was, that she must never be out when he came in, or he would go out again immediately! She was a very pretty and charming woman with the prettiest laugh imaginable. She had need of courage too, for though she was always a good wife and understood him thoroughly, she had a lot to put up with from "Phil". He knew this quite well, but remained incorrigible.

I painted a little picture of them together in that studio and both liked it; I often wonder what has happened to it, as I never saw it after the death of May himself. While painting it I remember a little incident characteristic of both.

Mrs May suddenly turned from discussing the ravages of time on women to remark: "There are no plain women nowadays." In a second came back the reply from May: "No, they are all coloured."

Certainly that is truer of these days than of forty years ago.

Next she said: "You never pay me any compliments now Phil." "No! but I owe you them", came the reply with a grin, and so he would keep the ball rolling for half an hour with this play.

At one time he was always signing agreements about his work, but it was soon found it was impossible to hold him to them.

The Graphic was willing, indeed anxious, to retain and pay him twenty-five guineas a page, but he felt in bondage to do something remarkable, and worse, had to wait for payment until the end of the month at earliest! He discovered that Clement Shorter of *The Sketch* was willing to pay him five guineas down and to pay that sum on the nail for anything he liked to take in. This suited him better.

I once found him finishing a set of drawings for this paper; he had half a dozen ready and was about to take them down to the Strand, as the house was short of money. Mrs May went out knowing what he had done. The moment she was gone May took out a new sheet of Bristol board, smiled to me as he thought of a joke to suit the occasion, and in half an hour had produced a seventh drawing. Then packing the lot up he went out and, calling a hansom, was off to catch Shorter before he left the office.

Having handed in the work and collected the cash he went off to the Savage or National Sporting Club and probably spent most of it before morning.

All very wrong as well as foolish, no doubt, but when one knew him there was nothing for it but to forgive.

He died when thirty-nine years of age—the dangerous age for artists—of cirrhosis of the liver and tuberculosis. I was living in Gloucestershire, but was in town for a few days at the time. He asked to see me and I am thankful I was able to go. He knew he was at the end, and lying on a sofa said goodbye, with the old smile, adding: "My father was a drunkard, Hartrick, and I am one too!"

In spite of everything he was one of the best and I have not known another like him.

A year or so later Mrs May married again, one John Ross, a wharfinger and member of the National Sporting Club. He was a good fellow and could afford to look after her well, which she surely deserved. When she died, Ross was inconsolable and with tears in his eyes just said to me, "What a companion!" and those three words are her best epitaph.

CHAPTER IX

THE PENNELLS

Any account of the life of Joseph Pennell which did not include that of his wife, Elizabeth, would be woefully imperfect, because, though less conspicuous and effective in public, she was the power behind the throne. Without her good sense and quiet but ceaseless support Pennell would probably have worn himself out fighting shadows, mostly fiends and spectres raised by himself; for, as I have often told him, he was the most quarrelsome Quaker that ever was, and was apt to say things to which the only possible reply was a blow. As he knew I was a friend and meant well, he received my criticism without an explosion —sometimes sadly, for he knew his faults and allowed them with a sort of sheepish shyness which was quite characteristic of the real man, though only exhibited to those he trusted well.

I certainly knew them both under many conditions of life, for I worked with him on all sorts of committees and juries connected with art, as well as socially, and never found either of them, though very human, other than of the very best.

The truth is that Joe Pennell was his own worst enemy. Highly nervous, but of a tireless energy, the pent-up force of generations of repression, he was one of the hardest workers and one of the most astonishing in the results accomplished that I have ever known. If it was not one thing, there was always another. Drawing, writing, committees, quarrelling—each in turn received the utmost attention he had to give. This ceaseless worrying about so many differing interests may have affected his art for the worse, but it was the nature of the man. His talents, brilliant always on the technical side, may have shone most in a journalistic setting, even gaining from his lack of reticence. In this direction he certainly was a genius, which I understand to be one who does those things well which nobody else can do.

He could be outrageously rude, for his Quaker upbringing urged him always to say exactly what he thought of any one and everything. Then he would defend the natural result of such action vigorously, adding insult to injury. Thereby he made many enemies, especially among those with a sense of their own importance: a matter which he could not regard at all. But his reaction to the genuine, both in art and life, was instantaneous and true. At bottom he was as modest and decent a man as one could wish to meet—doing many kindnesses quietly, even on the sly; and in art matters without jealousy, though no doubt he often roused that feeling in others.

When Sullivan and I first knew the Pennells, they had just moved into 14 Buckingham Street, Adelphi, where they had a flat in what had been the house of Pepys, and their dining-room later became the studio of Etty the painter. In the very heart of London, it overlooked one of the finest views of a bend of the river with St Paul's in the centre, together with Waterloo Bridge, and the passing barges for constant change. I believe we first got to know Pennell through an article in which he ridiculed some remarks by W. L. Thomas supporting his new artists on *The Daily Graphic*. Characteristically he abused the make-up of this paper and finished up by saying that Thomas's artists were more often geese than swans! Whether this has proved true or not, neither of us bore him any grudge at the time or since. Pennell, we knew, was a real enthusiast in our job, as well as a most notable exponent of its qualities. Soon we were sufficiently friendly to be invited to those Thursday evenings in Buckingham Street which had become known at that time as one of the best centres in London for meeting people who mattered and for hearing good talk.

The nucleus of these meetings after the Pennells themselves was W. E. Henley and the staff of *The National Observer* (formerly *The Scots Observer*), a weekly which went to press on

Thursday and attracted most of the coming writers who foregathered under the banner of Henley.

W. E. Henley may be but a tradition to the youth of to-day, but it is certainly safe to say that there is no editor now in London who occupies any such position as was his. As autocratic as Mussolini, he was permitted to alter manuscripts of his writers, who included some much more successful than himself, in a way that no one has since ventured to do; so much did his judgment inspire confidence. He has been described a hundred times, and as I am dealing only with what I myself have seen and heard I will confine my notes to a memory of him seated at a table in the middle of the room (the rest are shadows), with a big stick and a drink in front of him. A Viking from the waist upwards, supporting a magnificent bearded head with a shock of red-grey hair brushed up "en brosse"; beneath the table his legs were crippled and nearly useless. Often he sprawled over the table on his stomach, while he laid down the law of Henley in language that was never weak or hesitating. He looked explosive and he certainly was so. Beside him Beardsley, a boy of twenty, so pale and fragile as to seem a wraith, was discussing the erotic writings of the Jesuits in Spain. How Beardsley had acquired knowledge of such matters is surprising, but that Henley was ready to discuss them with this boy was still more so, and evidence that the youth really understood what he was talking about.

One never knew whom one might meet on these Thursday evenings, but in a general way they formed a sort of liaison between what was going on in the art world in England and in that of America; while later to those of *The National Observer* were added members of *The Pall Mall Gazette* staff.

Mrs Pennell was the perfect hostess, and Pennell, as he described it, "jibbered" to such purpose that he managed to bring out the best of talk from anybody who had anything worth saying About this time Pennell frequently went off to the Continent to make illustrations for articles in *The Century* and

Harper's, the two chief illustrated magazines in America, then at their very best. Mrs Pennell kept the home going and held all the strings together in Buckingham Street, so that when the traveller returned, everything was ready for her to take up the writing of a book or help him with journalistic work; for by this time most of the art criticism that Pennell had started in *The Star*, *The Chronicle* and elsewhere, but had abandoned, was in her very capable hands.

At first, all these journeys were made with a push-bike, and Pennell, who never could take a back seat, was soon an important member of the Cyclists' Touring Club—directing policy usefully on the Committee, or quarrelling as he always did.

Although he was anything but an athlete to look at, his energy and staying powers were amazing. His long, thin, typically Yankee body, with spindly legs, that seemed to get twisted up like wires, could perform feats that left professionals gasping. He had begun bicycling in America on an old penny-farthing bike. One of the tallest of his tales told how it had run away with him and he had ridden it through a stone wall, coming off without a scratch! Mrs Pennell at first used to accompany him on a tandem tricycle. Thus it was they made "The Canterbury Pilgrimage". But an early journey through France to Italy on an extraordinary-looking tricycle with wheels about five feet high, which they had had built for them—creating wonder and a sensation wherever they went—was one of their first successes when the story was published with illustrations in *The Century Magazine*.

Now that I am writing of the penny-farthing bicycle, as it is now called, it seems prehistoric to remember that, in the early nineties, I witnessed for *The Daily Graphic* one of the first occasions when the new little pneumatic-tyred and geared machines swept the board of prizes at a race meeting for cyclists here in London. The surprise to an immense crowd was such that it almost led to a riot. The police had to be called in to protect the table with the prizes. There had been the usual betting on the results and the crowd fancied there had been something wrong with the riding, when these insignificant-looking machines simply ran away from the five-foot penny-farthing solid-tyred monsters.

Pennell, of course, had the newest of every kind, so never went anywhere without creating a sensation: he could not help it. He wrote and drew with his left hand: even that attracted attention. Perhaps the most exciting of all was the occasion when he was arrested in Czarist Russia for entering the country without proper papers, in pursuit of some picturesque Jew "motives". They put him in prison and he never forgot it. Old Russia was thorough in her police methods. "God's Country", as he called his native land, as well as embassies and consuls all over the place, were called on to effect his release. He came back voluble, though a little subdued, with a lot of drawings of the Jews in the sort of surroundings in which pogroms took place, and wearing an astonishing fur coat, called a *Shube*, in which Whistler made a lithograph of him later.

From push-bikes he went on to motor cycles; and though a poor mechanic, because of his impatience, he managed safely one of the first, riding the Alps and all over Europe.

To him, as a Quaker, war was, of course, anathema; but when the U.S.A. declared war on Spain over Cuba, he had a wild idea of arming a privateer, manned by volunteer Americans, to ravage the coasts of Spain after the manner of Drake himself. Of course this was foolish as well as fantastic, but I heard him discuss its possibilities in imagination with Thomas Janvier, an American of French descent who could not speak French, but in appearance and manner was so convincingly Gallic that the fact of his not speaking French made one uncomfortable. He was a most delightful man and a writer of short stories. To see him with Augustine, the Pennell's French treasure of a "bonne à tout faire" who spoke no English, was one of the most comic sights I can remember—like the hen with a duckling. Pennell, too, got more riotously excited with Janvier than with anyone else,

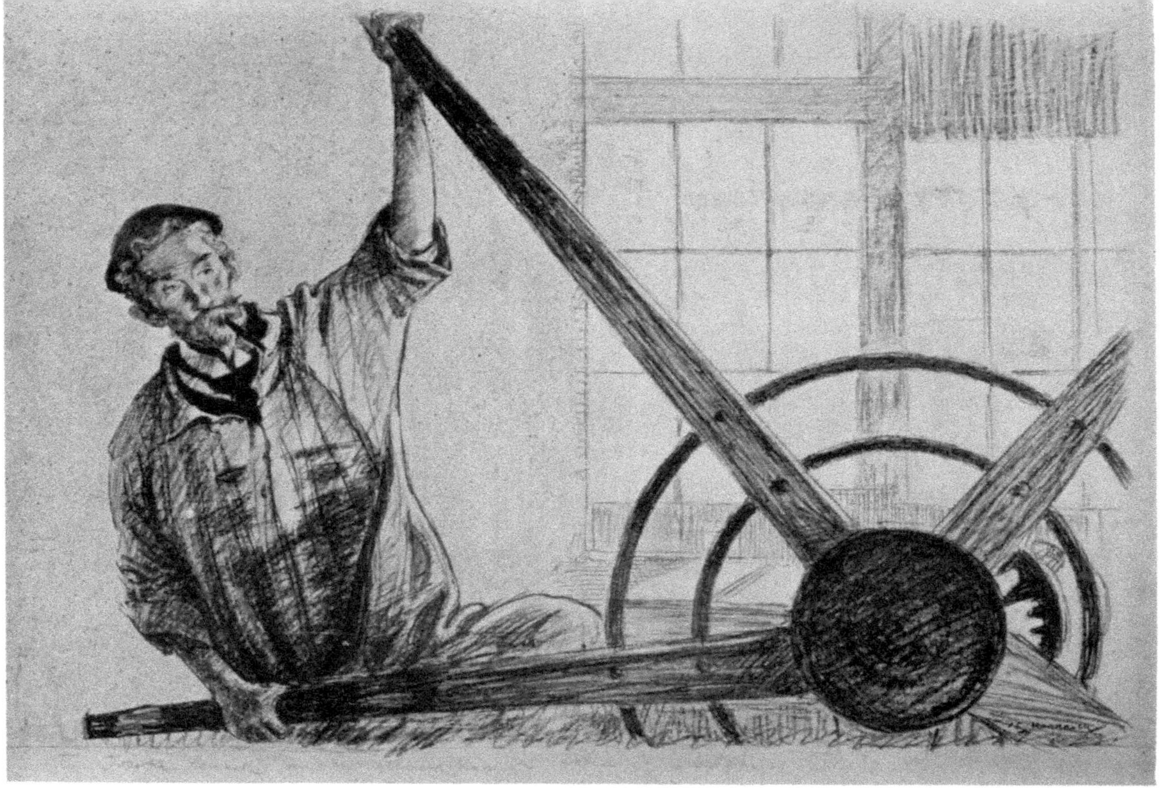

Joseph Pennell

Lithograph

telling tales as wild as Don Quixote's charging at the Windmill, while Janvier's wife, a homely little woman who had been a school-marm in America, looked silent disapproval at the pair of them.

When the Great War came Pennell thought he could ignore it, and got into trouble. As a neutral he fancied he could go anywhere and say what he thought just as before, but the War broke him in the end—he never was the same man afterwards. When he returned to live in the States again, after thirty years in England, it was a tragedy—everything and everybody was different. There was no longer the "God's Country" he had known. He wrote to me: "I am one of the few real Americans left and they are going to put us in the Museums with the Buffaloes and the Injuns."

To return to Buckingham Street. As I have said, the Pennells were hospitable and everybody who arrived in London with something uncommon about him seemed to call on them. I don't know how they stood the interruptions and got their work done. Pennell was an early riser; that, of course, is a most valuable aid in getting work done.

The most important and original personality that I met there was Whistler, then at the height of his fame. Especially after the death of his wife, which he felt dreadfully, Whistler was always at the Pennells, dropping in for dinner unannounced, for Mrs Pennell, I believe, really helped him in his trouble, and Augustine's cooking was to his taste. She could be called on for a special effort at any time and never failed.

Whistler became so much at home that he often slept in his chair for half an hour after dinner, and would wake up suddenly, quite bright and cheery, a relaxation that I am sure he would have permitted himself only where he felt quite safe. I have seen him so on several occasions, always in evening dress, of course, with his white lock dressed to be obvious. Thus at ease he was a different man from the "butterfly" of public debate, simple and unaffected, yet most entertaining, without any of the tricks he used to focus attention on himself in public. For a whole evening I have heard him telling tales of Chelsea in the sixties, mimicking the voices and manners of Rossetti and Swinburne in a way that was very funny.

Frederick Sandys was another he delighted to mimic. It appears that Sandys was always in difficulties about money or women. Whistler described him as a magnificent specimen with curled moustaches and the manners of a guardsman in a Ouida novel. He had asked Whistler round to see him and his work at one of the large houses he was accustomed to hire, living in a few rooms and leaving in a hurry, without warning. On arrival he found Sandys occupied with an old gentleman even more magnificent than himself, though of an earlier period, with flowered waistcoat, strapped trousers and all the rest of it, to whom he was formally introduced: "My father, Mr Whistler."

After an interval of talk on things in general Sandys suddenly began: "What do you say to a little sherry, father?" "Well, Fred," replied the old gentleman, "I could do with a glass of sherry." Sandys went off to rummage about in a cupboard in a corner. Presently he turned round to say in a surprised voice, "It's very queer, but there seems to be no sherry, father". "Never mind then", replied the parent politely. "Perhaps you would like a little whisky, father?" he went on, turning round and searching about lower down. "Certainly, certainly, my dear Fred", was the answer. Again there was delay and more handling of empty bottles. "Most extraordinary—there is no whisky either", went on Sandys. "Could you do with a drop of gin, father?" "All right, Fred, let us have the gin then." More rummaging by Fred. Next, Sandys went to the door and calling to a boy he had about the place, whispered: "Here, go out and bring me in two penny-worth of gin."

In the meantime the old gentleman had taken a large and ornate cigar case from his breast pocket. Opening it, there were two cigars visible. "Will you have a cigar, Mr Whistler?" he said, offering it politely with a bow. "No, thank you, I don't smoke", was the reply. Preparing to close the case again carefully, he went on: "I need not offer you one, Fred." "Oh, yes, I'll have one", said Fred, stretching out a hand with alacrity. "I suppose you know which end to bite off, Fred!" was the parent's final word as he prepared to return the last cigar to his own pocket.

Whistler told us nothing further about the gin, but from this he went on to another tale where Sandys was in trouble, and staying with Rossetti and Swinburne in the Queen's House, Cheyne Walk, Chelsea. George Meredith was there, too, busying himself over getting up a subscription to send Sandys to America. When Sandys was told of this, all he said was: "Splendid, because if you get the money, I need not go!"

On another occasion I was there when Charles Whibley and his first wife were present, as well as Whistler, who was in good form. The Whibleys had just come over from Paris, where they had been living. Whibley was a well-known writer in a high Tory style, who wrote a monthly article for *Blackwoods* for many years, called "Musings without method". He was an obviously English type, and therefore something of a red rag to Whistler. I have suspected, too, that he wished to write the Life of Whistler himself, as his wife was a Miss Philip and a sister to Mrs Whistler. Anyway, the matter of writing the Life arose, and Whistler, who I gathered had put down some notes on paper of his early days, said Mrs Pennell was to have them. "Elizabeth", he said, "is to write my life." He spoke definitely and I remember Mrs Pennell looked pleased and a little confused, for the idea had been mooted and she already had started to make notes of what he said. Almost immediately afterwards the conversation turned on Paris, and Whibley began talking rather loudly about life there, finishing with: "I had become quite a *boulevardier*", when Whistler let off his little scream and laughed, "Ha, ha, ha, the British boulvardeer". Whibley was furious and departed with his wife shortly after.

The history of the Life is another tragedy of human cross-purposes that were probably quite unnecessary. Pennell made it a success by sheer energy and will-power. It is a great mistake to believe that Pennell kow-towed to Whistler and was a mere echo of his opinions. He had a sincere admiration for his talent as an artist and was influenced in his own work by his technique in etching, but he held his own end up always, though I fancy the Quaker in him sometimes was suspicious of the artificiality in the man—Pennell had a conscience, an inconvenience that never troubled Whistler! On the other hand, the fastidious element in the latter shied away from Pennell's methods of expression, and he felt quite rightly that Mrs Pennell had more of the reserve with which he would like to be treated.

An unfortunate characteristic of Whistler's, one that seemed to increase as he grew older, was his habit of demanding that all his enemies or adversaries should become automatically those of his friends and followers. To speak or have any dealings with such was to be cast off instantly if he discovered it. All rather childish and petty, no doubt, but I was to learn for the first time how a friendly circle can be shattered and broken up permanently by the vanity or selfishness of even one man.

The famous quarrel with Sir William Eden over the price of a portrait of his wife, known as the case of the "Baronet and the Butterfly", was the cause. Yet I believe, if by chance Lady Eden had handed that unfortunate cheque to Whistler or Sir William had restrained a facetious pen, we should never have heard a word of the controversy, and the world would have been richer by a little masterpiece—for such it was when I saw it before it was altered. Whistler did not paint out the head but scraped it off, so that if he lost the case it could not be recovered. The Fates were adverse. The quarrel started and all sorts of serio-comic situations arose. George Moore called on the Pennells and just missed, by a few minutes, Whistler, who wanted to challenge him to a duel (to Moore's obvious alarm) for something he had said in Paris about the business.

Walter Sickert, one of Whistler's oldest friends and pupils, was dismissed for consorting with Moore and the baronet, accused of having, "like André, gone over to the enemy with the papers in his boots". The allusion was to Major André, an officer who was shot as a spy in the American War of Independence.

Such was the beginning of the break-up of those delightful Thursday evenings. Everybody even remotely connected, like myself, was somehow drawn in.

Some time about the end of 1893, Pennell conceived the idea of a Society of Illustrators that was to do for its members what the Society of Authors was doing for writers. Thus began for me a long experience of work on committees of different societies with Joseph Pennell, in which I got to know the man well. Sullivan and I had been elected to the Committee of the Society of Illustrators, and after a time I became Chairman, largely because no one else would take on the job. The Society began with a great splash at a meeting of illustrators in the hall of Clifford's Inn with W. L. Thomas in the Chair, and it died after a few years' struggle, so difficult is it to keep artists together. Opinion was divided as to whether the Society should take on the form of an exhibiting one, or be frankly trade unionist. The latter part of its aims have survived to this day in the Imperial Arts League, which has done good work for artists, especially in clarifying the law of copyright.

I have an amusing recollection of the Society in connection with William Small, the most highly paid artist on *The Graphic*. He was a Scotsman. When approached about becoming a member of the Society of Illustrators for mutual protection and defence he refused. "The prices", he said, "are 'fine'", and so they were for him, who was paid sixty guineas for a double page which he would do at the office without a model, between Saturday and Monday morning, with a bottle of whisky beside him. And when he left, he was said to have taken his cheque for work done with him too.

I had bought one of the best drawings he ever did, an illustration to Victor Hugo's *Ninety Three,* which had been published in *The Graphic.* Meeting me shortly after, he stopped me to say very deliberately: "I hear you have paid me a great compliment!" I looked surprised, so he went on: "Ye have bought a drawin' by me; I wouldna' buy a drawin' by annybody!" and he walked away.

Next, the Pennells, having prospered materially, moved into Adelphi Terrace House, not far off in Robert Street. This had formerly been an hotel, but was being changed into flats and offices. Pennell took the top flat and had it arranged to suit him exactly. The situation was nearly perfection for an artist like Pennell, and the views up and down the river could be enjoyed from the studio, where the windows were arranged like those in the stern of an old battleship. There they remained till after the Great War, which has changed everything of the old life and killed old friendships as well as men.

The Pennells returned to America and are now both dead. A memory of them lingers still with their friends about the Adelphi, soon to be utterly destroyed; but their work there will not perish so long as men are interested in London.

Many letters by Joseph Pennell have been published in various places, but I have not seen one by Mrs Pennell. She was a well-known and accomplished writer here and in America, and most of Pennell's books have more than a little by her in them. The following letter explains itself:

449 Park Avenue, New York City.
March 23rd, 1930.

Dear Mr Hartrick,

It was good of you to find time to write me at such length about *The Life and Letters,* and I cannot tell you how glad I am that you like it. You knew Joseph so many years and so well, working with him, that you understand as the casual readers cannot. I was anxious to show him just as he was, for there is no question that he had a vivid personality and was not like anyone else who ever lived. The Quaker in him explains much, as I tried to show. I do not quite see the Quaker in the photograph frontispiece of the first volume. The Quaker face, I have always thought, is a peaceful face—perhaps I know too few Quakers to be an authority. Anyway, that photograph seems to me full of sadness—it is very like him in his last years. I agree with what you say about the energy repressed by generations of Quakers bursting out in him. He had to say what he thought and to say it so it would tell. A more honest man never lived. Most people did not understand, but those who did loved him and he had as many good friends as a man could ask for. The devotion of his students I like to remember—it explains a side few had their chance of knowing. And speaking of his students reminds me that Mrs Lowengrund did not get the Guggenheim Scholarship, or whatever it is called. She asked me to send in a report or recommendation—first she wanted me to propose her but that I would not do, for a man I seconded last year failed in his application. I did not mind, however, writing the report she then asked for. I can't help thinking one must have some special influence to bring it off. When she told me you were writing, I thought she was sure to succeed. What better recommendation could she have? However, I think it is better for the young to work out their own salvation without any such props.

It is too good of you to say what you do of me and of the help you believe I gave to Joseph. I wish I could believe it too.

Mr Wuerlt, who made the Catalogue of the Etchings, is now busy with a Catalogue of the Lithographs, and at the moment I am kept rather busy, for I still have here more of the prints than he can find in any other one collection. Then there is preliminary stuff to write for the publishers—an introduction—and so on. The Benns are to bring out *The Life* in London. I fancy it will be published this spring.

I envy you the great Italian Exhibition. It must have been amazing to have the chance to see and study so historic a collection—though I always think the masterpiece looks best in the place for which it was painted—when it is allowed to stay there. Of course we can have no such exhibition over here, for all the great pictures that have drifted and are drifting into the country. The trouble in N.Y. is that too many shows are given. We have been flooded by the "Moderns", who do not very much appeal to me at their best, and at their worst are only fit to cast into outer darkness. The trick is so easy that too many who know nothing of drawing or paint can bring off a fair imitation. There has been a large—too large, perhaps—and representative memorial exhibition of Arthur Davies at the Metropolitan Museum. Do you know his work? I doubt if he is known in England. Joseph once had one of his pictures sent over to the International but it was not a very good example. He did some very beautiful things, but he seldom varied his subject or motive. The Metropolitan made the mistake of showing too many paintings instead of a very careful selection. The Museum is showing also the pictures left to it by Mrs Haver-Meyer—Old Masters and more recent Masters, Degas, Manet, Cassatt, and so on. One turns to them with relief after the endless display of Matisse and Piccasso and the rest.

And the Hamiltons—are they really getting off this month? This is a poor letter to send you in answer to your last. But this last I do not want to leave unanswered any longer. And this morning I have a vile cold in my head brought on by the return of winter. My love to Mrs Hartrick and yourself—

Your old friend,

Elizabeth R. Pennell.

CHAPTER X

'THE PALL MALL BUDGET'

"All change is for the worse!" as the old Duke of Cambridge complained when he relinquished the post of Commander-in-Chief of the Army. It is a sentiment we are all apt to express when we have passed fifty; for the fact that change in this world is as inevitable as death itself is the one platitude most difficult to grow accustomed to. Memories of the newspaper world are full of it. Who, for instance, in the early nineties, would have imagined that great dailies like *The Standard* and *The Daily News*, as well as well-loved evening papers like *The Pall Mall Gazette*, *The St James* or *The Globe*, not to mention many of the weeklies, monthlies and halfpennies, would be all wiped out in one generation? The list of the survivors would be shorter.

In 1893 William Waldorf Astor, descendant of one of the earliest American millionaires, tired of personalities and attacks in the press of the U.S.A., came to live in England, seeking peace and privacy. With the idea of protecting his interests in this country, which were already considerable in real estate, he purchased *The Pall Mall Gazette*, one of the more intellectual of the evening papers in London of the period, Liberal in its politics and in full working order. Immediately its politics were altered to suit the views of its new proprietor, and from Liberal it became Tory. This meant one of those complete changes of staff which are the curse of a journalist's life, as well as the source of openings for big chances in Fleet Street.

Some months before these events, E. J. Sullivan had been quietly dropped from the staff of *The Daily Graphic*. On his return from his annual holiday to his regular work, as he fondly supposed, W. L. Thomas sent for him. He was told shortly by the great man that in his opinion he would do better for himself elsewhere, and was then given a week's notice to leave, which, as he was paid a weekly salary, was all he was entitled to at the time. This was a shock for both of us—sharing a studio and living together, happy in the belief that we were in permanent employment. The situation was aggravated by the fact that Sullivan had spent all his money on a visit to Bordeaux and its neighbourhood. True, he had been growing sick of drawing portraits in the studio for the "graveyard" of the paper, and a man of his abilities was not long in finding other work. For the time being he found it under John Latey of *The Penny Illustrated*, an offshoot of *The Illustrated London News*, the office of which was almost next door to that of *The Graphic*. But the warning was not wasted, and I began to look about for another string to my bow. This was not easy, because I was tied to a full-time job at *The Daily Graphic* and I had no experience of any other. My first effort was to try to make a new agreement by which I should work only three days a week there, but the authorities did not see things in my way at all; with them it was all or nothing!

Now *The Pall Mall Gazette* published a weekly edition also, illustrated to a small extent, which had been worked up into quite a nice little property by Charles Morley, a nephew of the great John, who had been the first Editor of *The Gazette*. With the change of policy he had been cast out or resigned. Henry Cust, a Tory M.P. and heir to Lord Brownlow, had just been made Editor of the reconstituted *Gazette* and Lewis Hind was appointed Editor of *The Pall Mall Budget*. Both were young and determined to make a splash with the aid of the Astor millions, and they certainly succeeded, particularly Cust, whose ideas, fortified by the experience and advice of W. E. Henley, soon brought many of the best writers in England to his staff.

For Sullivan and myself here was an opportunity to work together again and in circumstances more congenial to our ideas of progress. We both approached Hind, were received favourably and were given places at once on the staff of *The Budget*, which Hind was designing to improve by extending its illustrations to include "news" work; and this would be largely in our hands. Accordingly, I sought an opportunity to see W. L. Thomas to give him notice, having my new agreement with *The Pall Mall Budget* in my pocket. As I have already said, he was much annoyed with me, but having looked at the agreement told me to come back and see him in a year, but by that time I had no desire to return to such close work. I must say, however, that he bore me no grudge, and he offered me several further chances. First I was wired to by *The Daily Graphic* to go to meet Jameson at Las Palmas when he was returning to England after the Raid in the Transvaal, and again in 1897 to go to the Greek War against the Turks as Correspondent for the paper, but these chances did not suit my new arrangements. As things turned out later, I like to fancy that Fate was taking care of me after all, or I had been dead long ago, as Maude is, who took on the job in my place.

To mark the period, I would like to record that one of the first important engagements I had for *The Pall Mall Budget* was to make sketches at the wedding of King George V to Queen Mary. My post was just outside the archway to the Ambassador's Court of St James's Palace. The wedding took place in the Chapel Royal, St James's. As the carriage of Queen Victoria emerged from the archway after the ceremony it stopped for a moment a yard or two from me, so that I had a perfect view of that great Queen. On her cheek there rested one big glistening tear. Tears of joy or laughter—are they not typical of her people, too?

The work on *The Pall Mall Budget* was certainly the most favourable for our development as artists of any I have since known. It was for three days in the week, certain, with the chance of doing more if called on. Best of all, it brought us into contact with most of the new rising artists and writers of the period. H. G. Wells, Arthur Morrison and Pett Ridge had just begun to make their mark as writers of short stories and sketches, which often fell into our hands to illustrate. Some of Morrison's *Tales of Mean Streets* thus came to me, and I have a vivid memory of

Wells in his curious high-pitched voice demanding of me where I had got the type I had used to illustrate a sketch he had written about an old cricketer on a village green. He had taken his father—actually a professional cricketer—as his model, and I had drawn an exact portrait, he said, which he feared his father might recognize. But it was no more than coincidence; I had used a sketch of an old man made when out drawing for a new political stunt with a Liberal van, the year before, in Surrey, and his name was not Wells.

Raven Hill, Greiffenhagen, Phil May and Beardsley were the most important outsiders among the artists, and Sickert made a drawing in pen and ink of George Moore which of its kind was a little masterpiece of portraiture.

George Halkett, afterwards Editor of *The Pall Mall Magazine*, during its best period, did the political cartoons; he was already known widely for his caricatures of Mr Gladstone.

Lewis Hind, the Editor, was an ingenuous young man who was reported to have come to literature from lace-manufacturing. He had been the first Editor of *The Studio*, but had little experience of ordinary journalism, and none of "news" work. This led to friction with the staff, because at first he imagined that all tickets sent to the Editor with invitations to attend periodic events were for his personal use. Soon after we had started work, the "Trooping of the Colour" at the Horse Guards fell due. Sullivan was appointed to make a drawing of it for the paper. A ticket for the ceremony had been applied for, but had not arrived at the office on the day before the event. Therefore Sullivan rose early in order to call at Northumberland Avenue, where the office then was, to get it, if it arrived by the morning post. There was no ticket, so after hanging about till the ceremony was over, Sullivan went out. Just outside the National Gallery he encountered Hind, immaculately dressed. He immediately explained to him why he had not done his work, when Hind with a cheerful smile stuttered: "I-I-I- have just been, t-t-there was n-n-nothing to see. M-m-make a p-page drawing", he added. He had used the ticket himself and left the infuriated Sullivan to make his drawing from *The Daily Graphic* and any old material he could dig up. Hind learned better in time, but to begin with, "news" appeared to him rather vulgar and to prepare for it beforehand superfluous. The challenge of Lord Dunraven with his yacht, the *Valkyrie*, for the America Cup, after a lapse of many years, was the cause of excitement in yachting circles and had spread to the great public. In America defenders had been built and were being tried out one against the other. The race itself was in sight. Although he had been warned in ample time, Hind could not be persuaded that pictures of the yachts and the race itself would become of vital importance to all the illustrated papers, both here and in America. This pigheadedness had of course to be corrected at great expense, but fortunately the proprietor was a millionaire. He paid and Hind learnt wisdom in such matters by experience.

Twenty years later he was more spry. As an art critic, he became one of the chief exponents in the popular press here of the Post-Impressionist Movement in painting. Van Gogh became a sort of god to him, and his appreciation was genuine; though I used to fancy that it was mixed with a notion that thus Lewis Hind himself believed he would have painted if the Fates had been kinder, for he had tried his hand at landscape painting too, but his efforts had all turned out to be *croûtes*. Hind was certainly clever, but a sentimentalist whose nerves too often ran away with his head.

Sullivan's daughter was questioning me lately about one Freese Green, who belongs to this period of my connection with *The Pall Mall Budget*. Her father had often spoken of him to her as a character of whom he was specially curious. Of course I remember him. Green was a photographer in a small way, with a shop in the King's Road, Chelsea. Rather insignificant and colourless-looking at first, he had a sort of Cockney cleverness that attracted both of us. A few years ago the cinema trade gave him a magnificent funeral as the inventor and founder of their business in this country.

When we first knew him, he was trying to synchronize a photographic film with a gramophone, with some success. This was the first of the "talkies". He asked both of us to see it, but somehow I omitted to go. I was more interested in some experiments he was making in colour photography. He showed me a set of test-tubes containing coloured salts with which he was experimenting. He told me further that he had gone back to Goethe's theory of colours (I don't know what that is) because he could get no further with Chevreul's theory, which really has to do with coloured lights, whereas he wanted pigments.

A year or two later than this he started to produce a paper on the lines of *The Sketch* or *The Bystander*, the printing and illustration to be done entirely by photography. Newnes, the publishers, we learnt, had provided some capital for his experiments. For a time, I know, Green went up to town every morning, a rather comic figure in a tall hat and frock coat, like a "pukka" business man of the day, and he was successful in so far that his efforts were threatening big interests in printing. Certainly he gave me some sheets with pictures and type which he had produced. I regret that I have lost them. Anyway, Newnes dropped him and his experiment ended.

Still, his activity was ceaseless. He started writing plays and for a time we were lent some black exercise books containing them. They were not easy to read and my impression now is that they were somewhat of the nature of Shaw's *Back to Methuselah*. Sullivan took them to Frederick Fenn, a friend from *The Graphic*, who was writing plays, but he was not interested and I doubt if he took great trouble with them. As with Van Gogh, I fear his contemporaries did not take Green seriously.

I recall now that our first introduction to him came about because a photograph of Chelsea Pensioners was wanted for *The Budget* and Green supplied it. This led directly to our meeting another character of a different type altogether, for I enlisted a pensioner to come to my studio to sit for a drawing and an interview if possible. This man, a Crimean and Indian Mutiny veteran, was an Ulsterman, but he had served in a Highland regiment and spoke with a Scottish accent. He was a formidable figure to meet, gaunt and bony, clean-shaven, with eyes that glittered from beneath the shaggiest of eyebrows.

There was something fantastic about his dourness at first approach, which he soon started to develop further with a grim tale of the Crimean War. He had been in hospital in Balaclava, he said, and was convalescent when he was reminded of a promise he had given to get a "Roosian" skull for a public-house in London. Mine host there wanted one as an attraction for his house, and had promised a sovereign as a reward for success.

Accordingly our friend, together with a hospital orderly, set out for a battlefield where there were plenty of mounds marking the presence of half-buried "Roosians". They had an axe with them for business, and were searching about for a suitable mound when the Russians opened fire on them with a field-gun, scattering the remains about most effectively. Alarmed, but strictly businesslike, they dropped what they had come for into a sack and returned to the hospital in haste.

Hardly to be commended as an adventure; but it was told with a frankness that was entirely objective and inoffensive. It might have been a cannon-ball they had collected—no sign of nerves, just a job well done and the money earned.

How callous and brutal, the righteous will say, but where, may I ask, does it morally differ from the rifling of tombs in the name of science which we read of without a qualm? The only difference lies in the element of danger those old soldiers accepted.

From this narrative, prompted by some liquid refreshment, he passed to memories of the Mutiny. So startling a change came over him as he described what he had seen of the Massacre of Cawnpore, that we were made to understand the horror of the reality. His jaws became set in a grin, with the teeth bared, and his eyes fixed like those of a fanatic. "The sword of the Lord and of Gideon" was in his hand. He was Vengeance, and we knew instinctively it was something that would not be stayed in the way of judgment this side of death itself. In the click of a camera, as it were, again his mood had changed; he came back to the studio and was blinking rather foolishly over his glass. I made a drawing, but the moment had passed.

To return to *The Pall Mall Budget*. Its end was another journalistic tragedy. Astor had given the paper to his wife. When she died suddenly, the bereaved husband decided to bury the paper with her. There was consternation at the office, of course. Hind had been told to leave the mourner undisturbed, but insisted on going to see Mr Astor to protest against the execution of the paper. We were informed that he then inflicted a two-hour oration on his victim with the not surprising result that when he had finished Mr Astor rang the bell for Mr Adams, his business manager, to say to him "Give Mr Hind notice at once!"

Contracts for about £30,000 were broken and paid for over this trouble. Harry Furniss, who had resigned from *Punch*, tried to save something from the wreck by continuing the paper as *The New Budget* under his own editorship, but Harry Furniss, in spite of his "bounce", which was boundless, was not equal to the occasion; the paper went under, and Sullivan and I became free-lances again; that is, chiefly "free" to wonder where the next job will come from!

The beginnings of the "Carmencita" episode are hazy, but the incidents of the drama connected with it are clear enough, being of the kind that are unforgettable.

Carmencita was that famous Spanish dancer whose portrait by John Sargent for long was one of the attractions of the Luxembourg Galleries in Paris. As a young girl, Sargent had helped her to make her reputation in New York by giving a reception at which she danced. All I have to tell happened years after her debut, at a time when her reputation as a dancer was world-wide and she had come to London as a special attraction to dance to the tune of £300 a night, or some such extravagant sum, at the Palace Theatre, which had not long been open as a music hall, after having proved a failure as an opera house.

On the staff of *The Pall Mall Gazette* was a theatrical critic, one Jack Stuart, whom Sullivan and I knew well. Carmencita's manager was a little Australian, who had been intimate with Phil May during his time on *The Sydney Bulletin*, and wished to renew his associations. Stuart had often heard our talk of May's Sunday evenings, where all sorts of people used to be gathered from the ends of the earth for mutual entertainment.

He was proposing to give a dinner to Carmencita, her husband, a guitarist named Echeparay, and the manager on a Sunday, so asked me if I could arrange with Mrs May and May that he might bring them all on to the studio in Holland Park Road afterwards. This was easily arranged to everybody's satisfaction.

What happened next is not so clear, but I believe Sullivan, Charles Sheldon, the American War Correspondent of *Black and White*, and myself joined the company at Stuart's rooms after the dinner, and the next thing I distinctly recall is that we went to Carmencita's lodgings to see the sketch which Sargent had given her in memory of her debut in New York. There we were shown into two immense rooms with folding doors between them. They were hardly furnished at all: but conspicuous was a huge brass bedstead completely furnished with sheets and pillows of chocolate coloured silk, over which was a lace bed-spread. The fireplace was filled with pots and pans, where Carmencita evidently did the cooking for her husband and herself. This was a surprise, when one considered what her income must have been. On an easel beyond the folding doors was the painting of "Carmencita" which we had come to see—a charming sketch done from her at her best some years before, apparently singing to the playing of a guitar—which was her husband's job—and keeping time by clapping her hands.

Carmencita herself was a big, handsome, good-natured specimen of a Spanish peasant girl, already beginning to put on weight.

After a round of drinks the important members of the company set out for May's studio in hansoms. I expect Sullivan, Sheldon and I followed by bus or underground, for my next memory is of being outside High Street Station. Certainly we all foregathered and were most cordially received by the Mays at the studio, where about a dozen others had already arrived. After a little time Carmencita danced to the accompaniment of Echeparay's guitar. The effect of her dancing thus at close quarters was superb.

Most of those present sat on the floor, and as the studio was large there was plenty of room.

Drinks as usual at May's flowed freely, but Carmencita herself refused to touch anything. Her manager, who had no such scruples, was renewing memories of Australia with May, while the latter, glass in hand, kept circling round the dancer, who was now enthroned in a yellow leather arm-chair with a very tall back, saying softly from time to time "Have a drink!"

Suddenly a disturbance arose between the manager and Echeparay—angry voices startled the company. Carmencita, like an angry queen, turned in her chair from time to time to throw in a word or two in Spanish. May continued to circle round and round with an inane smile on his face repeating his refrain "Have a drink!" Furious, the dancer rose up from the chair and marching over to the two men cried out to the manager: "What for you spik my 'usband so? Get out!!" and she smacked his face hard. The next moment the two men were at each other's throats. Those of us who were nearest rushed to separate the fighters, both mad drunk, and struggling in the arms of their restrainers to get at each other again. Carmencita was in hysterics in her chair, round which May still circled. The studio was at the top of a narrow flight of stairs, so while Echeparay was detained above, Sheldon and I dragged the manager downstairs and shut him in the dining-room, where he marched round the table, shouting from time to time, "It's an outrage, so help me God!" Then he would bolt to the door and shout something at Echeparay in Spanish. Each would make a dash for the stairs, but were again pulled back by the guardians of the peace. It was now about 2.30 a.m. With much persuasion Sheldon and I at length got our man into his overcoat and out by the front door to the street. There we thought he would be safe, so we walked on either side of him towards the entrance to Melbury Road and High Street, Kensington. From time to time he would run forward a few steps to stand in the gutter; then, taking off his tall hat and turning up his eyes to Heaven, he would affirm: "It's an outrage, so help me God!" Going on thirty or forty yards he would repeat the same. Just as we had got him into High Street a hansom came along from behind us. We looked, and to our horror saw it contained Carmencita and her husband. At the same moment the cab turned round and drove back rapidly from whence it had come. Our man started in pursuit, but we restrained him and finally got him as far as High Street Station, where we found a hansom in which we took him home.

Next day I went along to Mrs May to make apologies and discover further what had happened. The meaning of the turning back of Carmencita's hansom was explained. She had left her bag with £20,000 worth of diamonds in the bedroom and when she returned accused Mrs May of having concealed it. Mrs May was furious with everybody and I was instructed to get apologies from all parties concerned.

The sequel was that Carmencita was absent from the Palace "indisposed" for three days and her Manager was dismissed.

I attended a performance some days later at which it had been arranged I was to see Carmencita and receive from her a written apology for Mrs May. All of which I accomplished safely.

When she received me in her dressing-room after her performance I was astonished to see the sweat standing on her face from her exertions in the dance. She indignantly explained that some lashing out with legs and suggestive waving of petticoats after the manner of Otero, another dancer, was not her style but had been forced on her by the Management.

"It is not gut, I know my bisiness!!"—for her dance was classic without such barbarisms, she explained.

She gave me a note for Mrs May amiably: beside her was the bag for the diamonds, which she was in the act of taking off. Chirgwin, the white-eyed Kaffir, who had followed her turn, came along with a diamond he had picked up on the stage and presented it to her with a quip about "Getting rich quickly".

CHAPTER XI

THE CHELSEA ARTS CLUB

It is not my intention to attempt a history of the Chelsea Arts Club, or to record the names and deeds of those to whom it is most indebted: there must still be someone better qualified to deal with such facts in detail, and with the accuracy to which I cannot pretend. My effort will be to give some sort of sketch of how the Club and various members of it impinged on my own life, just as memory happens to record them. Chelsea of to-day may regard them as myths if it ever hears of them: nevertheless I witnessed the beginning of the Chelsea Arts Club practically from its conception.

The Chelsea of the early nineties of last century was far different from that of to-day. True, artists had begun to settle there because the scene by the river was still picturesque, though the Embankment had been made and Old Battersea Bridge had been destroyed. There were old houses which could be acquired in whole or in part with gardens, and the rents, most important, were moderate. Whistler and Rossetti had given it an artistic "cachet", and the name and appearance of Carlyle as the Sage of Chelsea had not been forgotten in the shops, but there was nowhere a café in which a stranger could get light refreshments or an artist could be certain of a drink and a meal that he did not cook himself, or, most important, a room in which to meet his fellows after dark, not to mention a lavatory, one of the most difficult places to find in London of those days. There was, of course, for those who knew, the old "Six Bells" with its skittle alley, and there some friends used to meet regularly.

About this time James Christie, a Scottish artist of ability and wit, held the lease of the house at 181 King's Road. He was finding it a bit too large for him, so he decided to let part of it.

From this the happy thought arose: why not start a club to supply the growing number of artists with a meeting-place where they could also get meals at prices suited to their pockets? 181 King's Road was well situated for this purpose.

A meeting was called in Christie's studio, to which all known artists of Chelsea were invited; the proposal was considered and unanimously approved. All present signed their names in an old exercise book, a chairman and committee were elected on the spot: so the Chelsea Arts Club was born, and those who signed were the foundation members. I know not if this book still exists, but I have seen and handled it.

Sullivan and I had recently come to live in Chelsea and were sharing number 6 Trafalgar Studios in Manresa Road. We had been invited to the inaugural meeting, but, artist-like, failed to attend. A place in which we could get our meals was one of our problems; so we quickly made it our business to inquire all about this new club, with the result that Sullivan's name and my own were the first two names entered for election in the Club book of members.

The Club premises at that time consisted of the ground floor and a basement, which contained the kitchen quarters; the dining and billiard rooms were entered down a flight of stairs in Christie's studio, which had been built out over a back yard.

The first person we saw in the Club—though I don't think he ever became a member—was Walter Greaves. He was seated in the Clubroom upstairs, wearing a flat-brimmed top hat and a flowing French tie, waiting possibly for Whistler, for whom we at first mistook him. Our impression was that he was very shabby and dirty-looking for such a celebrity, whom we had never seen up to that time. A lonely figure, he sat in silence, while we in truth were too shy to speak to him, imagining ourselves in the presence of a famous man. The fact was that Walter Greaves imitated Whistler to the extent of dressing as nearly like him as he could. He died, a brother of the Charterhouse, in comfort; something of a mystery, but a genuine artist to the end.

I do not write thus with the wish to belittle Greaves or his art, for I consider that he was one of the most naturally gifted and distinguished of British artists of his time. His picture of "The Boat Race at Hammersmith Bridge", as well as many others, seem to me more accomplished works of art than anything by the *douanier* Rousseau, his opposite number in France, which have been much more advertised and written about. I saw the exhibition of his work at the Goupil Gallery about which Pennell made trouble, because he thought that Greaves's pictures were being used to attack the reputation of Whistler, an impossibility to anyone with eyes to see. My own opinion is that there were then three kinds of pictures shown. First and most numerous were Greaves, pure and simple; then some Greaves over Whistler and a few Whistler over Greaves.

Greaves was Whistler's jack-of-all-trades for years and had the run of his studio, preparing canvases and painting there himself. He thus got hold of many discarded canvases on which he himself painted innocently, and there were also some on which Whistler had painted to show Greaves how something should be done. I have been shown a picture by Walter Sickert in which he pointed out how Whistler had painted a curtain exquisitely in it for him. The Master was always ready to help a friend genuinely in a difficulty. Once on a time both the brothers Greaves, as housepainters, decorated Streatham Hall. I never saw it; but on one occasion Henry Greaves showed me over his house in Lindsey Row which had been decorated in a scheme of chocolate with pink lines by both brothers. It was Whistlerian in taste and quite successful. I fancy Streatham must have been treated in this way.

For years the brothers were Whistler's shadows. Christie used to tell an amusing story about them and their attendance at a life-class, which had been started by a Frenchman called Barthe, a dealer in old costumes and antiques. Whistler, with other Chelsea artists, attended this class in the evening, and "Ze brothers Greaves", as Barthe called them, always sat behind "the Master" doing whatever he did. From time to time

Barthe would produce a piece of blue china, a costume, or an old plate. Whistler, interested, would admire it and say to Barthe, "Very nice! Send it round to me." Which of course was done. This went on for some time, but no cash came back in return. Barthe began to get anxious, so he consulted Christie, a large and hearty person who inspired confidence. "Vill he pay?" was his cry. "Certainly, my dear Barthe, certainly", was Christie's consolation.

One night after the class, in desperation, Barthe again approached Christie on the subject: "Ah! Zat Vistlaire! Vill he pay?" was his refrain, so Christie at last said, "Why not go and ask him for it at his studio?" "Thank you, my dear Christie, assurement I go", says Barthe, and off he went.

According to his own report afterwards, he rang the bell, which was answered by Walter Greaves, who showed him into the studio, where Whistler was working on a picture while Henry held a candle. As soon as he saw Barthe, Whistler cried out: "Ah, my dear Barthe! Glad to see you! Hold a candle", and he gave him a candle too. Then according to Barthe "he paint and paint and paint and we hold candle. When he finish, he say to ze brothers Greaves 'Get a cab', and when they come back he take ze picture and go out into ze cab and he drive away! Ah! Zat Vistlaire, he is terrible! Vill he pay? Vill he pay?"

From the start it was clear that the Club was filling a want; Sullivan and I began to go there for lunch or dinner and sometimes for breakfast. Soon there were a dozen or so regular in attendance at meal-times, and more for company in the evening, when a billiard table had been introduced. There were, however, several failures as stewards, if I recollect aright, before the right man came along; but when he did he was a jewel. Meyers was his name, an Eurasian or someone of that kind, I fancy. He was married to an Englishwoman, who was also a first-rate cook. They were the ideal couple for the position and soon made it manifest that they knew their job. But, as must be expected, there was "a fly in the ointment". They quarrelled like cat and dog or worse, though that did not come out till later.

All went well to begin with. In a short time the whole house was taken over from Christie and the Club dinner on Mondays was a feature that became known in art circles all over London. The fame of Meyers's "Angels on horseback" spread abroad. To be sure of a seat at the Monday dinner, you had to put your name down a week ahead, and the dinner was always crammed to the limit of capacity by members and their guests. An invitation was a thing to be sought for. John Sargent came regularly to lunch for several years, and celebrities used to be brought in frequently. George Moore I remember, particularly after a visit to Bayreuth for a Wagner festival—he was sick of music and wanted to talk painting. A painting by Jordaens in Munich, in which some flesh had been painted pure blue, had attracted his attention. This discovery worried him, and he played about with the idea all through lunch, speculating why, though he found the result magnificent. Of course this is nothing now, when you can colour as you please and call it creative. The moderns of that time already had Besnard's "pink horses" and Gauguin's vermilion dog, which so shocked an English painter that he left the gallery at once; but neither of these would attract any attention to-day—nor the Jordaens either. The Varnishing Day dinner was made an annual event and there were other special occasions for Meyers to show off his skill, as when Whistler gave his "Ten o'clock", an unforgettable experience; and a dinner to Claude Monet—I don't remember exactly why, but he was just emerging into world-wide fame. A big, black-bearded silent man is all the impression that remains with me of him; like Sargent he could not speak to a company, and we had no oration from him.

I think Stirling Lee, a sculptor, was the first Chairman of the Club. He was a man of some means and business capacity, so possibly assisted with money at the start. As a sculptor he was believed to have a future, but I fear he is forgotten. The most innocent and inoffensive of men, he became notorious because of the nude female figure he had introduced in a panel he had been commissioned to do for St George's Hall in Liverpool. Its removal was demanded in the name of social purity by one of those outbursts of Mrs Grundy, not uncommon at this period. The scandal and the worry it caused brought about a nervous breakdown in Lee, from which he never fully recovered. He was a very slow worker, so did not leave much work; but he is represented in the Tate, or was. Tales used to be told of a "Venus" on which he was at work for years, so long that his model married and had a grown-up daughter with the work still incomplete. Finally the clay itself disintegrated and fell down, and that was the end of a masterpiece; it is like a story by Hawthorne. He used to have a studio opposite Trafalgar Studios, where the Public Library and Polytechnic now stand, which was the scene and occasion of one of the strangest jobs I have done in painting.

Lee, always doing good works, had modelled a nose in vulcanite for a patient from the Cancer Hospital. It was attached to the face by a pair of spectacles. He asked me to paint it on the girl—for she was quite young—so as to match her general complexion. It was something of an ordeal for both of us; but at any rate for the time the result was satisfactory.

These memories of Lee recall to me some details of a more famous sculptor and member of the Club, Havard Thomas, for I had something to do with the introduction of his statue of Lycidas (now in the Tate Gallery). This was ten years later than Lee's time in Chelsea, though both of them had worked in Paris together in the eighties.

Thomas had brought the original from Capri modelled in wax —a method which he believed was used by the late Greek sculptors of the Naples Museum for casting by *cire-perdue*. The statue had been begun as a Narcissus, which explains the pose far better than its present title "Lycidas". That title, I believe, was given it by Steer, who thus named it (Narcissus being too hackneyed) as more likely to excite curiosity. And so it turned out, for when the storm arose about the statue on its exhibition at the New Gallery, few people knew who Lycidas was. Instantly those students who still read Milton wrote to the papers to proclaim their faith, or to put the ignorant right. The task of bringing the statue to England, together with the Thomas family, is a chapter by itself, and too long to record here; but the model who came too was the hero of it, though he had never been out of Capri before and spoke no English. Shortly before the sending-in day for the Royal Academy the statue reached Chelsea safely and was set up in Basil Gotto's studio, where it created a sensation among all the members of the Arts Club who had been invited to see it. Nothing like it had been seen there before, so there were conflicting opinions, especially among the sculptors, but the general verdict was that this was the best statue by a British artist for a generation.

At this time I was working for *The Pall Mall Magazine*; George Halkett, the Editor, was away, and Charles Morley, his deputy, was in charge. Now Morley had the making up of the illustrated catalogue of the Royal Academy, called *Pictures of the Year*, published from *The Pall Mall Gazette* office. I told him that he ought certainly to have a picture of this statue in it: also that, as I felt certain that here was something likely to cause a sensation in artistic circles, he ought to give it a page in the *Magazine*. Morley, the weary journalist, wizened by his everlasting cups of tea, was pessimistic of course. "I hate the rich," he said, "and when I go home in the Tube I look at the crowd and think, 'Good God! I have to cater for each one of all those people!' What an existence!"

So he hesitated and demurred, because it was not an art paper, but finally gave in, on condition that I wrote some account of its genesis to go with the picture. *The Pall Mall Magazine* had to go to press a month in advance of publication; therefore all this had to be prepared and printed before the "Lycidas" had been submitted to the selecting jury of the Royal Academy. I accepted this risk in good faith, so the photograph of the statue and my article about it were sent in in good time; and all seemed well so far as publicity could be prepared beforehand.

The "Lycidas" went into Burlington House on the appointed day. About a fortnight later Thomas came round to my studio early with a very long face, to say: "They have rejected my Lycidas." This was a nasty blow and Thomas, after the compliments he had been receiving, seemed stunned by it. Then I had a brain wave. I knew the jury of the International Society of Painters, Sculptors and Gravers were still at work at the New Gallery in Regent Street; also I knew that John Sargent had seen the statue and admired it, for I was present when he saw it. Therefore I suggested to Thomas to go at once to Sargent and ask him to write a letter to the jury of the International, explaining matters, and asking them to find room for the rejected "Lycidas".

Off went Thomas with his request. Sargent, though he hated rows of this kind, liked art better. The cause he considered worthy, and like the good fellow he was, he did all that was wanted. The statue was sent along immediately to the International and was given a place of honour in the Entrance Hall of the New Gallery by the jury. The Private View had been fixed for a few days before that of the Royal Academy.

Never have I known an outburst on art by both press and public to compare with this. Every paper had an article on "Lycidas", demanding why such work had been rejected by the Royal Academy, and columns were filled with similar protests from readers explaining their reaction to this wonderful statue, and also explaining who Lycidas was. Thomas wisely fled to a retreat in the country, refusing all requests for interviews. But he left me a set of snapshots of the statue done in Capri, together with the photograph which had been taken for *The Pall Mall Magazine*. For a week my door-bell was never silent for long; if I went out, on my return a journalist was waiting on the doorstep, wanting a photograph. I doled them out at a guinea each, and gave such details about the statue and its author as I thought fit. To make a long story short, Thomas sold the statue, or rather, was commissioned to have it cast in bronze, which he had been prevented from doing before owing to the expense. It is one of the mysteries of Art why this statue was ever rejected by the Royal Academy, because in the eyes of most artists it fulfilled every condition that academies usually demand.

Nor had I escaped unscathed. Halkett had returned to the office and, when he heard of the rejection, was annoyed with me for getting the photograph of the statue into the *Magazine*. "One of your d—d enthusiasms", he complained to me, but he changed his tune completely when he saw the sensation it was making later. Charles Morley, who knew nothing about art (which Halkett did), was so impressed that for several years after he was careful to inquire if I had another "scoop" of the same sort for the *Pictures of the Year*, and Thomas presented me with a charming drawing by himself as a souvenir of the battle. He was a fat little Welshman with black hair and a fiery temper, who came from Bristol. Though he had no Welsh he usually spoke in a slow, deliberate manner as if translating from the vernacular into English, which used to irritate some people as supposedly "put on".

The Club possessed also a very peppery member, a native of the Potteries. He had been a china-painter there for years, and made money at it, with the fatal result that he came to believe that it was time to become a proper artist and paint pictures. Accordingly he went to study art in Paris, Antwerp and Munich, and returned after about five years poorer in pocket, but a fully fledged artist, only to discover very quickly that he could not make sixpence painting pictures. This was a perpetual source of wonder to him, and the more he considered the facts the more they worried him; it finally upset his temper. His name was Hollins, and as he had a room in the Club he was always about the house. At the same time the Club contained two other members—Rollins and Collins respectively.

After one of his frequent absences Thomas entered one morning to find Hollins idling round with a bad attack of "blues". Thomas began in his most deliberate manner, "I nev-ar can re-mem-bar whethar your name is Collins or Rollins or Hollins". "And I nev-ar can remember whether your name is Thom-as or fat-arse, or jack-ass" was the infuriated reply of the dyspeptic, rubbing the side of his nose with his finger, a trick he had to show contempt for everything in general.

A man of this kind of course had many opportunities to quarrel with Meyers, the steward, one of which ended in the dismissal of that "treasure". I am not sure, but I fancy it was Hollins who came down to breakfast one morning to find Meyers chasing his wife, who, he said, had called him "a d—d nigger", round the table with a knife, and when expostulated with knocked the complainant down for interfering! Such conduct could not be passed over. Meyers and his wife were dismissed. It was a serious blow to the Club too, for with Meyers went its unique character. I certainly have never seen another servant like him.

There is just one more member of whom I would like to attempt a sketch at this time. James Charles, a Yorkshireman from Bradford, was one of the most marked personalities in the Club of the nineties. I first heard of his existence at the International Exhibition in Paris of 1889, when his name was fixed in my mind by the report that Degas had said that a picture of "A Village Christening" by Charles was the best picture in the English section there. To have a work praised by Degas was considered a greater honour among the younger painters in Paris of the period than to receive a gold medal. Degas certainly knew his business as a painter and did not hand out "bouquets" freely. This picture was sold at Christie's from the collection of a Bradford merchant some time after the War. It ought to be in the Tate Gallery, being more representative of the best English work of that time than anything I know of there. Charles was of a cheerful nature, but he did not come often to the Club, because he had a large family and lived in the country. When he did come, for Sending-in or Varnishing Day, his high spirits were the origin of numerous stories—how he would conduct a discussion on art from pavement to pavement across the traffic in the King's Road without ceasing, as far as Sloane Square! or sit down to paint a puddle in the road outside the station at Bosham after a Varnishing Day at the Royal Academy, just to settle some question he had been discussing with his friends there! When called on for a speech at the Varnishing Day dinner of the Club, he stripped off his coat and waistcoat, mounted a chair and announced that "The Royal Academy looked quite different, even a very fine show, when you found yourself hung on the line"—a truth that was very near to those present, though no one before had the frankness to express it. Whistler's "The Academy is an omnibus; you pay your penny and take your ride, if there is room", has more wit, but is less convincing.

I believe I served my time on the Committee of the Club twice at 181, and once after the change to Church Street. It was during this last, and not long before the War, that the occasion I am now about to recall belongs. The Russian ballet had come to London, and proved to be a real novelty and a great artistic success. The money that it made and the fashion for everything Russian that came with it, inspired the Royal Academy of St Petersburg to imagine that it had only to come with its pictures to surprise and conquer likewise. The Academy, or its agent here, leased the Doré Galleries in Bond Street—where Sothebys now is—and sent over to it a collection of works by its members for an Exhibition which was to be opened by the Russian Ambassador at an entertainment to which all London would be invited. About half a dozen Academicians were selected to accompany the pictures. Douglas Macpherson, an old colleague on *The Daily Graphic*, had been to Russia as a Correspondent and had been treated royally while there. Therefore he wrote to ask me if the Chelsea Arts Club could be persuaded to do something to entertain these artists, who knew nobody, while in London. I laid the matter before the Committee, who decided to ask these strangers *en bloc* to the Varnishing Day dinner, which was not far off. An invitation was despatched. No reply was received up till the morning of the day, when a telegram arrived expressing regrets that no one could attend the dinner. I had been in correspondence with a Secretary of the Russian Embassy, a Count P., about the matter, and had invited him to the dinner as my private guest. Nothing more had been heard from the Russians, but after everybody was seated for dinner, the soup finished, and the fish course being served, there was a commotion at the door. Five Russian artists who spoke no language but their own were there. My guest turned to me saying, "That is just like Russians", and with his aid explanations were given and received. Finally places were made for them: no easy matter, for the room was crammed. They drank a good deal, found a little French for speaking, and soon seemed quite happy. Their exhibition proved a fiasco; neither the press nor the public took to it, and truth to tell, it had nothing of the novelty of the ballet; it was simply academic and dull.

My Russian count had an English wife. They invited me to a real Russian dinner at their flat, to which several of the artists were bidden also. One of them, a well-known Russian sculptor, whose name I have forgotten, spoke French and told me that he had recently been staying at Tolstoi's country house in order to model a bust of him. "Il est fou", was his report on him; and he went on to tell me of the strangeness of his household. There was a long table for meals—for he kept open house. At the top end of it sat the Countess, who looked after all normal guests seated at the upper part of the table. At the bottom sat Tolstoi in peasant dress and on his left a favourite daughter, also in peasant costume. These two were also served with rough peasants' food. On Tolstoi's right hand was placed the chief guest or guests, who were given food by the Countess. After a little time Tolstoi began to steal the more delicate food off his guest's plate, and to eat it himself. Altogether he behaved, said the sculptor, as if he were not "all there".

About the end of the nineties I went to live in the country, letting my studio and only coming to it and town at intervals, when business called. So I will leave Chelsea and the Arts Club for a time, as I can write only of my personal experiences, just as they come back to me.

CHAPTER XII

EARLY DAYS AT THE NEW ENGLISH ART CLUB

My first contact with the New English Art Club was through W. J. Laidlay, a Scottish artist and brother of a famous golfer; he it was who first put up £100 to take the gallery for the first Exhibition of the Club in 1885, and was also the first of those with a grievance against it, because of the way he was ignored by those in power after the initial success, and a footing found; but this is a familiar tale of the birth of most societies. He it was, too, who advised me to go to Paris to study rather than Antwerp or Munich, and for this I am grateful. Paris certainly was the centre of the art world of those days, and the best students from all nations tended to gravitate there: for it contained the men with the most vital ideas about art.

The formation of the Club was indeed the practical result of a number of painters in England going abroad to complete their training, and of their being dissatisfied with the teaching in the schools here; this culminated on their return in a series of attacks on the prestige of the Royal Academy and of these attacks the Club was to be a permanent witness.

The current system of teaching drawing in the art schools of this country was dull and uninspired, incapable of producing draughtsmen with any initiative or vitality in their work. I will attempt to describe it. Great care and surface finish were the main qualities demanded for success, so it came about that, among students, the time taken to produce a work was more honoured than the quality of draughtsmanship itself. The British Museum, even more than the Royal College, South Kensington, was the centre in which to study these methods, because there the masterpieces of the system were produced by those who were striving to enter the Royal Academy Schools.

Someone had discovered that by plotting the drawing out into a series of squares, it was easier to measure proportions with accuracy: at the same time the area of each plane could equally well be mapped in the same way by anyone with neatness of hand and an ability to take pains. No effort was made to train the eye to observe the main movement of the rhythm or to capture the character of the line. Only the surface drawing was important and this was made smooth with a stump or stippled with a pointed chalk pencil to a paralysing degree of finish. The cast or statue was examined with field glasses to explore the smallest accidents, which had nothing to do with the form, so that they too might be reproduced. A drawing two feet to a yard high would take anything from three months to a year to complete—and the one which took a year was likely to be considered the masterpiece.

The two figures in the British Museum usually selected for these exercises were the "Faun" and the "Discobolus". These statues at least have all their limbs, so afforded a complete study. The magnificence of the sculptures of the Parthenon and its Frieze was tacitly acknowledged, but not studied; they were incomplete! There was the same lack of comprehension about the painting; a slick surface smoothness was the standard of excellence at the Royal Academy, and this ideal imposed itself on buyers and public, chiefly through the medium of some sentimental story told in paint.

Of course there were artists who knew and understood other ideals, but the Academy was such a magnificent shop that most members soon had their senses blunted to finer issues by the richness of their sales. A standard price to denote a masterpiece, ancient or modern, was fixed at 1400 guineas: it is even so stated in reference books of the period. A successful Academician expected to sell his chief work in Burlington House for about £1000 or he had failed for the year. I can remember a letter from the wife of one, complaining of bad times because sales were confined to two or three unimportant works at £500 each.

These prices have tumbled in the sale rooms for many years now. A work of art has no intrinsic value: it is worth in cash only what it will fetch; but there is also a spiritual value which is the expression of some subconscious human want, and even the Soviets appear to recognize it. Certainly those in power have always gone to art for help for purposes of propaganda and glorification, whether they happened to be Kings or Communists. All the same, it may be argued that fame is controlled by the material value posterity puts on a man's work; and so long as anyone, dealer or critic, can make a living from what is left, it will not be allowed to die. We see the same reactions even in religion. The priest acquires power from his craft and so has made a living, good or bad, in all civilizations, though his livelihood now appears to be challenged by the latest forms of government. So history repeats itself.

Paul Renouard, round about the time of which I write, was making for *The Graphic* a series of drawings of Royal Academicians at work on their annual labour of "hanging" the pictures. He told me that H. T. Wells, R.A., "a monsieur who spoke French perfectly", he explained, came up to him to say: "I want to show you one of the most awful pictures you can ever see", and he took him up to Sargent's "Carnation, Lily, Lily, Rose" then exhibited for the first time. Renouard told me he hardly knew what to say, but did expostulate—when the old gentleman next took him up to a "St. Christopher" by himself. Poor Renouard did not know where to look and stood speechless. The Sargent of Mr Wells's condemnation is that which is now in the Tate Gallery, having been bought by the Chantry Bequest; but the story shows the extraordinary blindness of quite an intelligent man (H. T. Wells was that) when faced with something in art wherewith he was unfamiliar. How can we wonder at the difficulties of the public?

Legros, as Professor, in his teaching at the Slade was the first artist in a position of importance to challenge directly these ideas, and he had been recommended for that position by E. J. Poynter, later P.R.A., who had been Slade Professor before him. Poynter had studied under Baron Leys in Belgium and was familiar with Continental methods and ideals in art.

It is only fair to recall here that Legros was as much opposed to his pupils going to Paris, and so coming under the dangerous and disintegrating influence of the Impressionists, as any of the Academicians, but he was counted here and in France as a sort of living old master, and more or less an anachronism.

There is a note by Leonardo da Vinci in one of his sketch-books referring to the study of light out of doors. He writes of "a woman in white on a grass plot in sunlight", and decides that it is beautiful but beyond painting. This would have been Legros's view also, I feel sure. Now that I am nearing the end of my life as a painter, taking everything into consideration, I am not sure that this view is not the right one. At the same time I am not ashamed to say that I was, and am, a humble follower after the Impressionists and yield to none in thanks and appreciation of the victories of its masters, without which the world would certainly be poorer, even if their brilliance fades and does not last for ever.

The craft of painting has the last word in the end, and it is impossible to deny that those who have observed and obeyed the limits of the craft have reaped their reward also.

The observation and rendering in paint of the effect of light out of doors was therefore the chief preoccupation of the young and most advanced artists in the eighties and nineties of last century, not only in France but all over Europe. Constable at the beginning of the nineteenth century had started a number of French artists in that direction with some pictures he sent to the Salon, and the ultimate result was the Barbizon School. Turner with his later work is said to have affected Claude Monet;

though Vollard certainly reports Renoir to have been contemptuous of later Turner, and called it "patisserie"! French art, moreover, has always stood for a tradition based on sound draughtsmanship, and this persists to this day in spite of the "isms"—most of which have been introduced to Paris by foreigners.

I hope I have now explained the origins of the forces that created the demand for a gallery in England, in which the new ideas could be displayed. In this matter London, as usual in art fashions, was about ten years behind Paris: but in 1885, as I have stated, the nucleus was formed which grew into the New English Art Club. It was Fred Brown, as Professor at the Slade, together with his staff there—Tonks, Steer and Russell—who finally made and fixed its form, with the Slade itself as a permanent source of young and new talent to rely on; but this was later.

In the early nineties I naturally gravitated towards the artists with similar training and ideas to myself. I had already been painting in Fife for two years and, before I left Paris, had exhibited pictures in the Salon. I had also shown the "Son of the Prodigal" in the Royal Scottish Academy and others in the Glasgow Institute and other galleries, including that of the Royal Society of British Artists in what proved to be the last exhibition of Whistler's presidency. Although it was not easy to find time for painting, I desired to hold on to that art as much as possible, so continued to paint. At *The Daily Graphic* they laughed at my ideals, and in a brochure published by the staff to celebrate the first year of the paper, I was reported as saying in the witness box: "I am an artist but I draw for *The Daily Graphic*!"

With this ambition in view, together with E. J. Sullivan, I joined the evening life-class at the Westminster School of Art, then controlled by Fred Brown, soon to be appointed to the Slade Professorship. There I got to know Henry Tonks, at that time lecturer on anatomy at London Hospital, together with W. W. Russell, Ronald Gray, F. Pegram, and others who also were looking towards the New English Art Club as the coming show in which it would be an honour to be included.

The exhibition of the Club by this time had been established in the Dudley Gallery, which consisted of one room on the ground floor in Piccadilly nearly opposite the entrance to Bond Street. La Thangue, Stanhope Forbes and Clausen, some of the earliest names of those prominent in its formation, were giving way to those of Steer, Sickert and Fred Brown. The first two had just advertised in the papers the rejection of their pictures by the Royal Academy, though the first picture I remember by Steer was on the line there and entitled "Fantasy". Steer is the same yesterday, to-day and to-morrow—slow, matter of fact in his opinions, though with a quick taste for collecting Chelsea china and Greek coins—the last person to be suspected of revolutionary ideas. He is also peculiarly susceptible to draughts and does not like thunderstorms.

Sickert, on the other hand, was always something of a chameleon. He had begun as an actor and emerged into a painter of pictures! When I first saw him he sported a large fair moustache like a French cavalryman of the day; since then he has been clean shaven or bearded in many fashions; what he is at the moment I do not know, though I agree "age cannot wither nor custom stale" his activity. Again, he could always be most witty and delightful as a companion in the press or in private. Fred Brown, now become Professor, was of another kind: there lay the power behind all the movements for building up permanence. With greater talents as a painter than he has revealed, selfless in seeking what he believed to be the best for art, he sacrificed his private renown to teaching and the organization of other outlets than the Royal Academy for young and promising painters; D. S. MacColl also championed the cause with his pen.

The Club too was fortunate in finding a man like Francis Bate for its first Secretary. Bate was an extraordinary type for an artist: he could make things pay. One of the first instances by which I became aware of it was the way he took a place in the country with an orchard, and after the first year, as he explained, sat rent free for the future by the marketing and sale of the apples. It was so with everything he undertook. He saw the Club safely through its most difficult days, and then passed on to the County Council of Berkshire, where I am told his talents in matters of agriculture have been appreciated for many years.

First of all I exhibited only drawings at the New English in those days, but soon went on to small pictures. There were two yearly exhibitions, one in spring and one in autumn. Very soon I was elected to the selecting jury, and after a year or two, to the Committee of the Club, which used to meet at Applegarth Studio, Brook Green, where Bate also had a class in which he taught painting. In all I remained a member for about fourteen years, when I left to join the International Society of Painters, Sculptors and Gravers. Neither society liked its members to belong to both and in any case one society was as much as I could supply with decent work. There was another consideration also which should be mentioned. Some years before I left the Club I had written to Bate to point out the weakness in the system of voting both for the jury and for elections to the Club. On the surface it appears as right and fair as possible that the exhibitors should elect by ballot the jury which shall select and hang the works at each exhibition. But when a number of the more important members are teaching in a school, the tendency must be naturally and without conscious bias for these to select and hang the works of their own pupils. In time the aims and teaching of the school, if it is large, must be spread abroad wider and wider, until its virtues become common or diluted, and its vices aggressive. What originally was a strength in supplying new talent becomes a weakness. It is not the fault of the teachers so much as the weakness of human nature. In the early days of the Club the method of selecting the jury was on the whole beneficial. It was the source of constant change, as well as frequent rows, which led to resignations. Youth, as ever, was impatient with age, while there is even such a thing as jealousy of success. The evils which are inseparable from public exhibition were soon at work. Sickert, I believe, has always held that there should be no selection, but everybody's work hung, just as it came to hand, or in alphabetical order; this he would wittily defend. But after having seen one Salon des Indépendants I am satisfied that life is not long enough for such experiments.

On the jury of the N.E.A.C. of those early days Sickert always stopped for further consideration not only those strange works which came up in plush frames, but those weird daubs sent to every exhibition open to all-comers. Sometimes it was in a spirit of *blague*, but also because he had a genuine liking for the naïve. If a picture from the *douanier* Rousseau had turned up, he would have insisted on it being treated with respect. This was all to the good; but sometimes this power was exercised to give a snub or a smack to somebody who was no longer wanted.

Edward Stott was another painter who was constantly on the jury. Very sensitive and artistic in his nature, but limited and egotistical in his outlook, like a severe judge he generally voted against everything not just to his taste. He had a number of imitators: whenever an obvious one came up, there were ironical shouts of "Now Stott!" Sure enough, Stott raised his arm to vote for the work, no matter what anyone else might do.

About 1893 or 1894 two remarkable newcomers appeared from Paris, William Rothenstein and Charles Conder. Sickert, ever on the alert, at once named them "Puffing Billy" and "The Strange Bird".

Rothenstein, small and looking like a Japanese, with his round black head and spectacles peering into everybody's face and mind, was soon in evidence everywhere.

Conder, for me, fulfilled all preconceived ideas of what a genius should look like. He was beautiful to look at, with a head like an antique marble, and a sleepy charm that somehow convinced one that here must be someone unusual. "The Strange Bird" describes exactly the sort of sensation he first aroused. The son of an English official in India, Conder was born in

England. At the age of sixteen he was sent to an uncle in Australia to learn surveying; but a born artist, he soon left his theodolite and chains to begin painting landscapes near Melbourne with Arthur Streaton and Tom Roberts, and migrated thence to Paris after two years' experimenting. In Paris he quickly made a name among artists, but while still almost a stranger was elected a member of the Société National des Beaux Arts—commonly known as the New Salon. There I first saw his painting, which was achieving an immediate success. From a visit to Normandy in the spring, he had brought back a series of landscapes of apple blossom and cliffs by the sea, which, hung in a group together, made the most attractive show by a young man that I ever remember. The delicacy and charm of them is indescribable; I doubt if he ever did any better, and he sold every one of them at once.

This success was the beginning of his ruin, for with the money so made he launched out into a life of dissipation, which he could not otherwise have afforded. With no sense of responsibility he was soon in trouble with drink and women. A challenge to a duel was the immediate cause of his coming back to England. He had made himself so expert with a pistol and was so determined to kill his challenger, that the latter or his friends cried off, and Conder's friends, fearing murder, removed him to London. I saw a good deal of him at one time, but his life for the rest was a tragedy.

One day, some years after his leaving Paris, I met him in Piccadilly; he was then living in Jermyn Street. He looked quite shaky, an old man. I was shocked and asked what was wrong. He replied, confidentially, "I had a man in to lunch and bought a bottle of liqueur brandy at the Café Royal for afterwards. I have just emptied what was left in the bottle down the bath, because I felt I could not come out until I had finished it!!" Later on he married a charming woman with means who thought to reform the "fallen angel". Of course she failed. While still a young man he died in an asylum, and she was accidentally burnt to death through smoking in bed. As George Moore would say: "Why?"

Among the older members Buxton Knight was conspicuous. A fine painter in the English tradition, he did not owe anything to France, so though a little out of his element, he served to show the readiness of the Club to accept good work whatever its source. The extraordinary thing about him was that, after suffering a stroke, he seemed to paint better with his left hand than ever with his right.

Towards the end of the century Orpen, John and McEvoy, firstfruits of the Slade teaching, began to make their presence felt on the works of the Club. Each was remarkable from the first in his own way. Percy Young, chemist, colourman and general provider to the Slade School for many years, used to have a tale that John arrived there as quite an ordinary art student, but during his first summer holiday he went bathing, struck his head on the bottom, and returned a genius. Whether this is true or not, many have tried to follow him but none have caught up. His work at first was very uneven and I used to wonder whether he was quite sure of his reds and greens, but all that has passed. As time went on I was living more and more in the country so did not see much of the Club while Roger Fry and Sir Charles Holmes were working on the Committees. Then Fry went to America, and when he returned started his own club, with a following in the London Group.

Fry I never could follow in art though well aware of his ability, especially as exponent of a theory and as a writer. The truth is that for me Fry seemed to wish to turn art into a science, where everything can be docketed and explained exactly, and to which more and more can be added to clarify or refute as time goes on. This to me cannot be; the great rules of art may be as unalterable as those of nature, but the fact remains that the art in the drawing of a bull from the Altamira Caves or that in a Rembrandt cannot be repeated as an experiment no matter how well we understand the ingredients and the mixture. By this

"B.Sc. attitude" he transforms a perfectly understandable paper like Maurice Denis's "Cézanne" (in the book Denis calls *Théories*) and converts it into a treatise on geometry or higher mathematics where the poor artist may not follow. So that Cézanne's art, mainly a matter of beauty of colour and feeling, becomes lost in figures of speech. Worst of all, Fry started a school of critics who, however highly educated, know little about the craft of painting, and therefore try to discover in pictures what it is impossible to put in paint.

During most years of the nineties Sullivan and I endeavoured to keep in touch with what was going on in the art world in Paris by going over for an occasional week, usually when the Salons were open, and especially to keep our eyes open for what was being done then in black and white and in the graphic arts.

In the next chapter I propose to offer a few notes on what most impressed me at the time and since.

CHAPTER XIII

CHANGES AND CHANCES

The break-up of our careless Bohemian existence came suddenly, in a mixture of tragi-comedy, as it seemed at the time. Sullivan married. One morning, as we were getting up in Wentworth Studios, he asked me to put on my best clothes. This meant a "boiled" shirt, a frock-coat and striped trousers, etc., a most unusual, even formidable, proceeding. When in surprise I inquired what all this preparation was about, he told me that he wanted me to attend as best man at his wedding. Weddings of artists already in my experience were apt to be sudden and informal, but this was a bit of a "knock-out". Neither I nor any of his friends had a suspicion of what at the moment looked like a catastrophe. No females, except an occasional model, frequented the studio; and not one of these was suspect!

As a matter of fact, Sullivan, without consulting anyone, relation or friend, had decided to join up for life with a lady journalist whom he had met in connection with *The Pall Mall Budget*. Everything had been fixed up between them, so there was nothing more to be said or done, but to go to support a friend who asked for this kind of help. I don't deny that I was annoyed at being kept in the dark, but explanations had to wait; they would have been superfluous at the time. A very small party attended at a registry office; the knot was tied. Romance was sternly set aside; all were to go back to their jobs again as usual and at once. That night a small company of his friends, who had met in a "pub" for the occasion, sat round discussing life and its chances. The only way they could find to express their feelings was by singing a parody of a revivalist hymn of the period: "There ain't no flies on Jesus!"

I have no grievance; our paths had separated. Somehow, they

continued to diverge in the matter of making our livings. Though we continued to be the best of friends up to his death in 1934 the partnership of Hartrick and Sullivan was dissolved. I am not bandying compliments about a friend when I say that my considered opinion is that Sullivan was naturally the most gifted of the younger black-and-white artists of my time, not excepting Beardsley. Certainly, he could do anything with a pen. Old Godfroi Durand at *The Graphic* said he used the pen like a bayonet, for every stroke went home. There was no timidity about the handling of his instrument. A fully trained artist, he could draw anything that was set before him and do it with distinction. Why was it then that he was less successful financially than many who were not his equal in ability? There were two reasons, it seems to me, to account for the weakness. First, here was another illustration of Samuel Butler's theory that skill, getting in advance of judgment, even with artists of real talent, can kill art. In the second place, he was cursed with a sort of sardonic humour, or rather cynicism, that put the ordinary man off, even if it did not actually antagonize him.

The series of caricatures of the Kaiser, which he drew for *The Daily Chronicle* during the War, provides an instance of this. They were just a little too clever for ordinary consumption. Yet in his life Sullivan was as amiable and kindly as could be desired; moreover, he had a deeper note that he rarely got into his art. In volume two of the *Yellow Book* there is a drawing called the "Gardener" which brings out what I mean better than any writing. It was originally designed to illustrate the "Man with the Muck-rake" from *The Pilgrim's Progress*. Here is fantasy combined with depth of feeling, expressed with an originality of technique which is akin to genius. Unfortunately, it did not catch on as a money-making proposition. Probably it was too elaborately worked, not simplified in a way to display its intricacies, so as to be taken in at once and wondered at, in the way Beardsley wisely contrived. On the technical side the drawing is interesting. Made with a very flexible steel pen

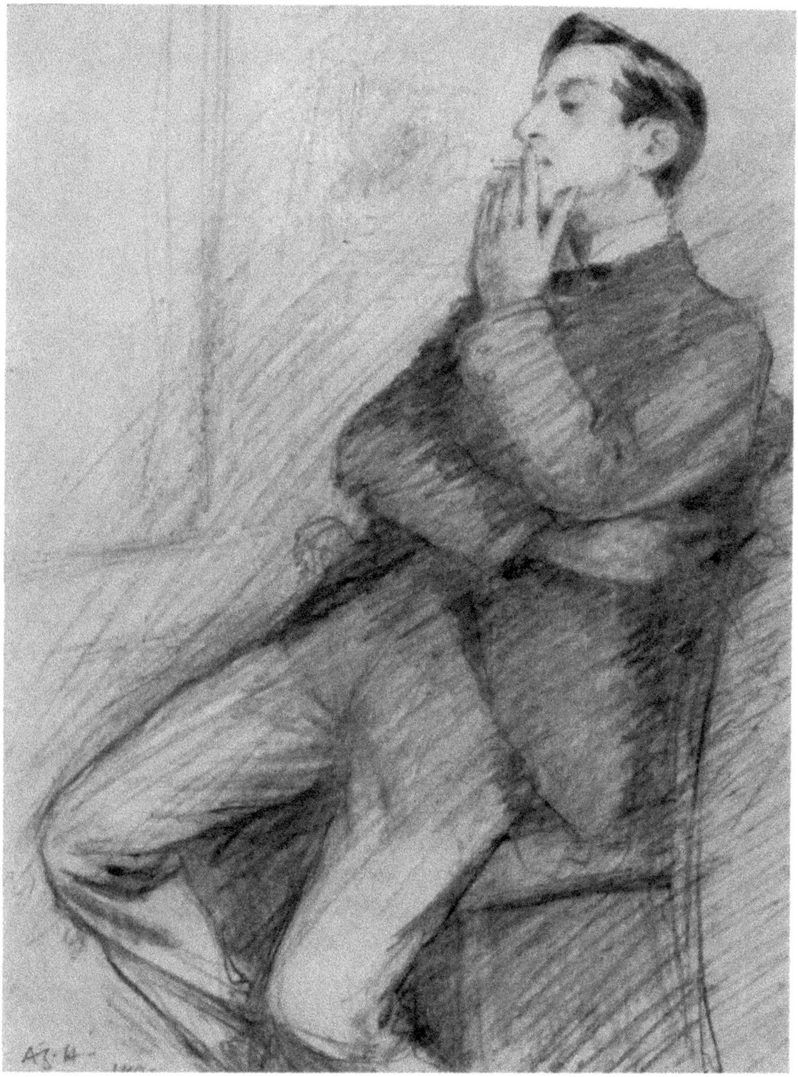

E. J. Sullivan

Pencil drawing of 1890

used by lithographers for their finest work, usually called a "bug" pen (because it was flat like its prototype), it could make a line fine as a hair or, with pressure, a quarter of an inch wide: and this combination made it a powerful tool in hands that could use it. Such drawings, however, did not stand much reduction, the varied thickness of the lines that gave the original quality being liable to be lost or thickened in reproduction by direct photography.

At that time the question of the reduction of the original by photography for reproduction was a matter of much debate among illustrators. The Americans in particular advocated an enormous reduction to give an effect of fineness, and this was all right in expensive magazines, like *Harper's* and *The Century*, which could print such illustrations.

Pennell did this for his Cathedral series of drawings, and I have seen Dana Gibson (the creator of the "Gibson Girl") drawing direct from the model, standing at an easel and slashing the lines in with a crow quill at arm's length. The original drawing was not pretty or really distinguished, but it was refined by reduction. Phil May did not care for much reduction. He often used pens of different thickness of point for coarse or fine work. In the end Sullivan worked for a comparatively small reduction. But it is probable that nothing but the most expensive photogravure would have done justice to drawings like the "Gardener" at that time. I myself always refused to draw for reproduction as if it were a virtue, holding that mechanical method must not be pandered to, but rather should follow what the artist gives it.

Soon after he was married Sullivan was commissioned by Macmillan's to illustrate *Lavengro*. Though it was unequal, I consider that he did some of his most strenuous and original work here. He had not yet formed a style of his own. Menzel, together with Vierge, to whose work I had introduced him at *The Graphic*, were his chief objects of study. In emulation of the practice of Menzel when illustrating his life of Frederick the

Great, he went down into the country near Hastings to make studies from nature of gipsies and their surroundings. As a result he brought back to town much material drawn from nature directly, which he translated into illustrations with his pen. I do not know of anyone before or since who has managed to convey the effect of gorse on an English common with a pen, and he made an almost impossible subject lend itself to that tool. The whole book is full of experiments; they vary in quality, but for that reason they are valuable as lessons for young illustrators as long as pen drawing remains in demand for the illustration of books. From this he passed to that technique with a German accent, which he invented out of a study of Durer's engravings, for his illustrations in *Sartor Resartus* by Thomas Carlyle. By these he became well known, and though he illustrated the same author's *French Revolution* and many other books afterwards, many people consider he never surpassed them, and the original drawings are now all housed in the Victoria and Albert Museum. He became a member of the jury of the International Society in its best days, and was elected an Associate of the Royal Society of Painters in Water-Colours several years before I was, though I attained full membership there many years before he did. During the nineties I made my only contacts with Germany and Austria. My elder sister did not care to live at home after my mother's second marriage, and as she was something of an invalid began to go to Schwalbach and Wiesbaden to take the waters, as was the custom of many in this country at that time. There she met a Russian girl, a Mlle de P—, who was in similar circumstances, and they began to live together and so remained for over forty years. The Russian died in Florence a year ago, but the association has continued with her sister. The Russians, of course, were ruined by the War. One summer I went to visit these two at Wiesbaden, and in this way made a tour of the Rhine, seeing Cologne, Schwalbach and Wiesbaden. This was my only sojourn in Germany, and I suppose I saw it at the height of its power and glory. About the same time my younger sister married a Freiherr von D—, who was an official in the Foreign Office at Vienna and the owner of vineyards in Hungary. To Vienna, therefore, I was also called for a visit. This time it was winter and I enjoyed everything about it, better than anything in Germany. There is no question, Vienna is a beautiful city, beautifully situated, and if you like baroque architecture you can enjoy it to the full. What attracted me most was the extraordinary number of picturesque types to be seen in the streets. Everybody seemed to have a uniform or a native costume, like a scene in an opera. Which reminds me that I saw a performance of "The Ring" by Wagner while there, at the Opera House, the finest entertainment of its kind I have seen or heard in all my life. The Imperial Gallery with its pictures is magnificent. The pictures themselves are on the whole the best preserved of any national collection I have seen; many pictures seemed as fresh as when painted, and they had not been cleaned in the way that is so common nowadays. I suppose the absence of coal fires in quantity has left the air pure and so preserved the paint. I am told that the Prado (which I have not seen) is the only gallery in Europe to compare in this respect. Rubens, Velasquez, Titian, Tintoretto and the elder Breugel there remain fresh in my memory to this day. All is now changed, the splendour is departed and Vienna desolate. My brother-in-law died of cancer in a bathroom, because all the spare rooms in the little house to which he had retired after the War had been "awarded" to the proletariat. His vineyards had been taken away and given to Roumania; my sister and her daughter make the best of things bravely enough; a proletariat family occupied half the house for years, and as she once informed me, paid a rent fixed by the state to justify their presence, which amounted to about the value of the stamp on her letter to me. I include these details to show why I have cause to know something of the state of Middle Europe after the War.

Dr Blatherwick had died in the summer of 1895, and the

home at Dunaivon, Rhu, was broken up, but my mother continued to live at Torwood Cottage on the Gareloch, which she had owned since early in the seventies. The following January saw me married to Lily Blatherwick, the eldest of the doctor's unmarried daughters. I had known her nearly all my life, for our homes had been side by side on the same hill at Rhu. She was already a painter of repute in Scotland and a member of the Royal Scottish Society of Painters in Water-Colours.

We started life together in lodgings at Chelsea, but retained 8 Wentworth Studios as our working centre. I had continued to live there after Sullivan's marriage, with R. M. Paxton, an old colleague from *The Daily Graphic* as my partner for the interval, but he also married and departed.

Besides working for any paper that would have my work I had a commission from Macmillan's to illustrate *Soldier Tales* by Rudyard Kipling, a selection of stories out of those little grey paper-covered books by which he first became known in England in the early nineties. I regret I never knew Kipling personally, as he went to live in America about the time I began these illustrations. Once I was introduced to him in the Queen's Club grounds at an Oxford and Cambridge athletic sports meeting. I cannot remember anything he said, since the occasion was not favourable for anything but looking on. Sullivan was a bit critical, but I was an admirer of Kipling from the first and once owned a set of first editions, including *Departmental Ditties*. Alas, they were borrowed from me and not returned.

I took a lot of trouble to get the local colour right for these illustrations, drawing on relatives who were still in India for the material. The book is now out of print, I believe, but years later a suggestion was made that I should colour the original drawings for a new edition. I even had the originals sent back to me to look at them, but I was not keen about it and the idea was dropped, I think wisely.

Again I was called back to *The Daily Graphic* as an outsider. My job was to tour through Ireland with a Railway Congress which had been assembled of representatives from railways all over the world, to write up and illustrate Balfour's light-railways, a new experiment to help the "distressful country". I had not been in Ireland since I was a small boy, but came back convinced that the Scotch had been maligned and that the Irish were keener after money than any other inhabitants of the British Isles.

The Irish journalists with the party were quite cynical about it, and the manager of the Cork and Bandon Railway, a brother of Boss Croker in New York, proved the keenest and most efficient advertisement agent I have ever struck. There were lighter incidents also that had nothing to do with railways, but politics had to come in. I saw Maud Gonne, at the zenith of her youth and beauty, escorted to the train by the Mayor and Corporation of Limerick in robes of state, after a luncheon in honour of one Daly, a Fenian who had just been released from penal servitude. I was shown a bog in Connemara into which several railway engines had disappeared before a line was laid across it. "And what do you call this?" asked an inquisitive member of the Congress. "Faith", said the foreman, "we call it the Radical Programme, because there's thorty-foive yards of Oirish rubbish shot there!"

Not long after my return I had the wire from *The Daily Graphic* asking me to go to meet Jameson at Las Palmas on his return to England after the Raid. As I have said, I did not go.

At last I was convinced that the only way I should find time to paint, as I was secretly determined to do, was to go to live in the country away from sudden calls by editors. My wife was only too willing, as London did not suit her and she wished to paint too. The way and the means opened clear; a sister of hers had married the Vicar of Acton Turville, a village near Badminton in Gloucestershire. They suggested that we should stay with them for a time; the vicarage was large and we could have rooms more or less for ourselves to paint in. I let my studio in London and off we went for an experiment which was to last ten years.

CHAPTER XIV

ACTON TURVILLE

This was my first real experience of English country life, though I knew something of that in Scotland. No introduction could have been better for my purpose than this through the parson and his family. The squire, the parson, and the farmer, in spite of the abuse showered on them, and even abuses for which they were responsible, formed a triumvirate control of life in the villages, with the parish church as a permanent centre, which, when each did his duty, made for a happy community in which all understood, and mostly helped, one another. It was not the first time I had been to Badminton, secluded and jealously guarded from the common herd as it still was. While I was on the staff of *The Daily Graphic*, some time about the end of the "silly" season and the reign of the giant gooseberry, in the early nineties, a correspondence had been started on the question "Should ladies ride astride?"—a knotty question at that period, but clearly settled to-day. To this correspondence the Duke of Beaufort, grandfather of the present one, a celebrity in London Society, as well as a great sportsman in the county, contributed. He wrote that he possessed a picture of some ladies of the Somerset family riding astride in Badminton Park during the seventeen hundreds. He suggested that the paper should send someone down to make a sketch of the picture. I was selected for the job. Accordingly to Paddington Station I made my way about 3 a.m. to catch a newspaper train to Bristol; it stopped at Chippenham, then the nearest point on the railway to Badminton, because at the time of its construction Badminton had been carefully isolated from the Great Western Railway, a condition which had to be expensively altered as time went on. Now, there is a station at Acton Turville called Badminton, and the distance by rail between Swindon and Bristol is shortened. Speed, of course, was winner in the end. At Chippenham, with difficulty I found a cab at the early hour to drive me the eight miles to Badminton Park: and there I arrived very early before breakfast. I was received by the house-steward, who presently informed me that I was to breakfast with the Duke and Duchess and that the former would be leaving early with the hounds for "cubbing" in the park.

It was interesting to observe the semi-regal splendour of a great ducal house of those days—a state of things passing rapidly now, or quite passed—the endless corridors, the snuff-colour and silver of the tall footmen's liveries—they had a most distinguished, rather Spanish effect—and amid it all the kindly and informal domesticity of the Duke and Duchess. An actor whom I did not know, but evidently an old friend of the Duke's, was staying at the house, and came in to breakfast with him. As it happened, the picture which was the subject of my visit hung rather high on the wall of the room in which we were breakfasting. It was a large landscape, with smallish figures of ladies in breeches and boots astride their horses. The Duke was full of interest and information about the picture, the names of the ladies and anecdotes of their lives. The serious business of the day—the "cubbing"—must not be delayed, so valuable explanation and breakfast went on together. In the midst of it the Duke's heir, the Marquis of Worcester, father of the present Duke, came in, a fine figure of a man of over six feet, dressed, like his father, in the blue and buff of the Beaufort Hunt. Though he was quiet enough at his breakfast, I learned that, with the reputation of the best M.F.H. in the country, he was anything but silent in the field; for his language was a terror to all delinquents, great or small.

His second horseman, later retired to the inn at Acton Turville, used to tell with respectful awe "that he had a *new book* for every day he went out". That he could unbend and be quite human is manifest by a story told of the present Duke as a little boy, apropros of a conspicuous feature of his father—the long nose which was an ancestral legacy from John of Gaunt. "You should see my daddy ring the bell with his nose", he is reported to have revealed. An electric bell had been fixed in the floor of the nursery to summon the kitchen, and the ancestral nose had been used to press the button by a happy father to please his infant heir. The old Duke was different, though his language could be lurid too; his popularity will be gauged by the fact that he could call every stone-breaker or road-mender in the Beaufort country by his Christian name as he passed on horseback.

Breakfast over, the huntsmen and whips, in their green coats so gay, rode up with the hounds on the drive before the house, the park with its oaks and elms making a vista behind. Everyone went to the windows to admire. The Duke and Lord Worcester immediately went out and, mounting their horses, rode off to the Verge to look for cubs. In those days the Duke owned the hounds, the hunt and everything, doing whatever he pleased with them. I was left with the Duchess and the actor. When breakfast had been cleared a ladder was brought in and I made my drawing from it. Afterwards the Duchess herself showed me the house and pictures. It was all interesting, of course, but the only special fact I remember was that the original drawings for the *Liber Veritatis* by Claude hung in a passage, apparently not much regarded. I remained for lunch, and, decorated with a bunch of violets given me by the Duchess, drove back to Chippenham to catch an afternoon train, after a strenuous day's work, the like of which neither I nor anyone will see again, for the conditions of that life have vanished.

To start work in new surroundings is always something of a stimulant for an artist, and Acton Turville up to that time had never seen an artist, certainly not one living there. Just outside the vicarage gate on the main road stood a milestone with "100 miles to Hyde Park Corner" inscribed on it. Badminton itself was only a mile away, and, even then, was a familiar name. The boundary line between Gloucestershire and Wiltshire was only a quarter of a mile back along the road to Chippenham. It did not take long to make up my mind that I had come to the right place to study English country life and character. Owing to the fact that I was living at the vicarage, I was soon on easy terms with all the village. The isolation from the railway, contrived for the amenities of the great house, resulted in the fact that most of the labourers were born and bred there or within a few miles. In these days of motor-buses it is surprising to remember how little people moved about in country places even thirty years ago—ten or twelve miles was the radius. It was like living with the characters in Thomas Hardy's novels, with most of which I was already familiar. I had even made a sketch of Hardy a year or so before at a matinee of a one-act play, the first of his efforts at playwriting. I used to go to London from time to time to collect work, and G. R. Halkett, who had become Editor of *The Pall Mall Magazine*, proved a good friend and helped me by sending me to illustrate most of the stories of country life which he was publishing in the magazine, and all the time I devoted to painting what hours I could spare from this pot-boiling. Thus I came on a place in a village not far off on the Wiltshire side, which both in itself and its inhabitants was a little backwater of the old life; this life was quickly passing, and must be seized on at once if any of it was to be recorded. Fry's Farm was its name, and for generations it had been known as the chief malt-house in the neighbourhood. In it lived four people, two brothers and two sisters, all over sixty. The house was large, fronting the main road like an inn, and, a thing unusual for the neighbourhood, was thatched, as were its barns and outhouses. Like its owners, who were of ancient yeoman stock, everything was in decay and business was declining; the land that had belonged to it also grew steadily less and less as field after field was parted with, till now but two or three remained. There was a tragedy about it, the facts of which were carefully concealed. The two brothers had quarrelled bitterly, and though living in the same house had not spoken to each other for thirty years. All communications were carried on through one or other of the sisters, yet both professed to conduct the business as maltsters. Through asking permission to paint on their ground—my wife and I did quite a lot of work there—we became well acquainted with all members of the family. The mother, we learnt later, had been the daughter of a clergyman, and so a strain of superior culture, as well as some fine old furniture, silver and jewellery, had been introduced; all of which had probably been useless, even fatal, to the qualities demanded for their business in life. I drew portraits of both the brothers, and they are included in a set of drawings of old English country types which, largely through the kind offices of Maurice Hewlett, were bought for the Print Room of the British Museum many years after, for Hewlett also was interested in the old English country life which was passing away. My wife painted one of the best oil pictures she ever did there too and called it "Fry's Farm". Of this John Sargent once said in a slow, surprised way: "Why, it's like a Cézanne!" At that time my wife had never heard of, certainly never seen, a Cézanne. That was in 1897 when Cézanne was unknown even to the art world in England.

I had great difficulty in persuading old Tom Fry to sit for his portrait, but he did so at last, with his whiskers cut in imitation of the old Duke of Beaufort's and in a brown hunting kit and boots of the early sixties. He had an ancient Welsh pony, thirty-five years old, he said, which was ending its years in one of the two last fields. If I would paint a portrait of this pet for him he would sit. So of course I did. The animal was prehistoric in appearance, blind, with a shaggy coat and hooves like slippers from not having been trimmed for years. Shortly after we left the neighbourhood, "Fry's Farm" was burnt to the ground; its

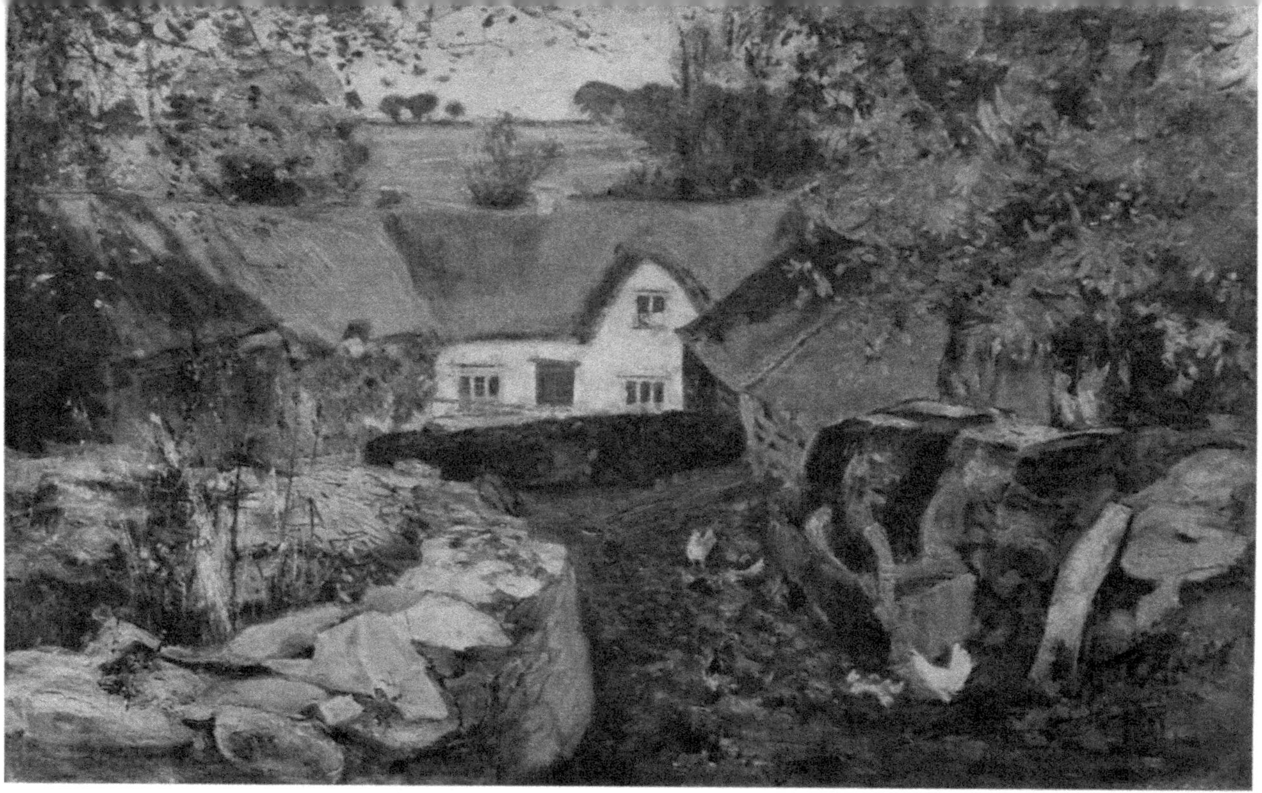

Fry's Farm

By Lily Blatherwick, R.S.W. (Mrs Hartrick), oil painting

owners scattered and died. Nothing remains to me but memories, and an old silver-mounted toasting-fork of eighteenth-century quality, that my wife bought from the sisters.

There can be no doubt, I think, that isolation in country places before the advent of good roads and cheap communications led to the making of people of extreme character, whether on the side of individual eccentricity in action or withdrawal from all contacts with their fellows to the extent of claustrophobia. The tales of Thomas Hardy are full of instances, and it was the case with the Frys. There is another incident of this period that comes back to my memory because of a portrait I was asked to make under very unusual circumstances. One summer afternoon I was seated in the garden of the Vicarage reading a London newspaper, which did not arrive till late in the day, when out of a shrubbery one of my wife's nephews, a boy of about fourteen, descended on me, out of breath and in a state of intense excitement. "Miss G. is dead", he panted. This I knew was the daughter of a neighbouring rector, of somewhat eccentric habits. The boy went on to tell me that the latter was away from home and the cook had sent him for his father, as being the nearest clergyman she knew of. My brother-in-law had gone out with the dog-cart to a place some distance away, so I prepared to go back with the boy to see if I could be of use. The shortest way was across the fields, but a mile or so in all, and as we went along my companion gave me some details of the tragedy. He had gone to the rectory about the arrangements for a cricket match. Miss G., a girl of about eighteen, was, it appears, mad about horses and riding. One of her amusements was to jump on to the backs of a couple of cart horses that were kept in a field that ran by the rectory grounds. The rector had gone away for a few days and, before leaving, had forbidden his daughter to do any more of her playing about with the horses—chiefly because he said it was undignified and he feared there would be chatter in the village. However that may be, the farmer still kept his horses in the field and the temptation, as usual, was too strong to be resisted. Miss G. caught a steed as she had often done before and riding about the rough ground was thrown violently, and broke her neck. As we drew near to the church and our destination, we entered a narrow path over a stile between banks of laurel that separated the graveyard from the rectory garden; then, passing through a little gate, we came out into the main drive. A strange noise drew me, so I went on down to the gate; there a still stranger sight was awaiting me. The rectory stood near the top of a steep hill, the road being flanked by trees that overarched above, making a tunnel. Up this hill came a weird-looking crowd; it seemed that the sick, the blind, the halt, and the lame of the neighbourhood, together with all the children, were advancing up the hill, waving their arms and making strange sounds of grief, for the girl had been much loved in the village: most of the able-bodied were at the harvest. We stood amazed; then, hearing a noise behind, I turned about and saw the curate. He was a tall, gaunt man of about forty-five, who somehow suggested a moulting jackdaw, with his black dundreary whiskers flapping like feathers about his neck. He had come from Nettleton, the village where he lodged, by the same route that we had followed. I just said: "Miss G. is dead." In a hollow voice he replied: "They tell me so, but I don't believe it." With that, looking apprehensively at the crowd advancing up the hill, he turned about, and with enormous strides hurried up the path again, to vanish into the shrubbery. He was not seen again in the village or at his lodgings for three days. I entered the house and interviewed the cook. She had kept her head, sent for a doctor and wired to the rector and relatives; some women from the farm were attending to the body, which had been brought home by labourers who had gone for the horses. There was nothing more I could do for the present, so with several others I went to inspect the place where the accident had occurred. In the middle of the field was a pond, like a hundred others in those parts. A high bank with bushes was opposite to the place where the cattle came in to drink. From marks left by hooves, we made out that she had ridden her horse up to the top of the bank; there we discovered, hidden by the long grass, a narrow gulley, made by a drain which ran down into the pond. Most probably she had tried to force the horse down the gully to the water, which was partly hidden by the bushes. The animal shied at the glitter or swerved back violently, throwing her off with her head against one side of the gully—this broke her neck. The marks bore witness to it clearly. When the rector returned and other relatives with him, among them a sister married to another parson, they all appeared to be as mad as hatters. To begin with they could not believe that the girl was dead.

A day or two after the accident I had a note from the sister begging me to go to make a drawing of the girl in her coffin. "She looks beautiful", she said. I went over at once and was shown into the drawing-room, where the coffin had been laid surrounded by flowers. There was a bad bruise on one side of the forehead and it was obvious that it was time the corpse was buried, so I did the best I could, using some water colour to make the drawing more attractive. Her people were pleased and grateful, but they still would not believe that she was dead. At length, they were compelled to close down the coffin, but still would not bury it for several days, and when they did, insisted that it should be bumped on the bottom of the grave in order "to waken her if possible" out of her last sleep. All was quite futile, of course, and only made for scandal; but at length the grave was filled in and the poor girl left to her rest.

Weeks passed into months, summer into winter: through all the pageant of the seasons we were growing into the life of the country just as should be done. In London friends and colleagues excited themselves about Kitchener's advance on Dongola, then on Khartoum, or perhaps about the Spanish-American War. The first Graeco-Turkish War brought up a more personal question, for to that I had been asked to go as a Special Correspondent; but in spite of all temptations I remained faithful to the job I had elected to learn—to depict the life of the English countryman. At Christmas time we found many of the old customs still in being. The "Mummers" with their morality play visited the house and gave the version that belonged to that neighbourhood. I could remember as a boy a play-acting by "Guisers", as they were called in Scotland, which in the main incidents was identical, though varied by local ideas and legend. The Wassailers, with their songs, were new to me. A Wassail bowl of wood, painted red, white and blue, was kept in Acton Turville, which was dressed anew with holly and a sort of Christmas tree each year, to be taken round the farms and houses by young farm hands to raise money for beer, and I made several studies of its keeper, a rather drunken old ruffian, appropriately named Woodman. One of these portraits is included in my set of Gloucestershire types at the British Museum.

Thus we remained at the vicarage, except for short visits to London, nearly up to the end of the eighteen hundreds. Then chance more or less led us still deeper into the country into a village on the edge of the Cotswolds. My brother-in-law had formerly been curate at Hawkesbury with Tresham, a parish on the Bath and Gloucester road, consisting of two villages, some five miles apart, just above Wotton-under-Edge. One of his friends, a farmer at Tresham, told him that there was a small unoccupied farmhouse belonging to a farm which he rented that he wanted to let. This was exactly what we had been looking for, so we went to see it and liked the place. The main objection was that the house was much out of repair, but we were told that we could have it for an almost nominal rent. We hesitated, because the place was so isolated. One night the farmer's son rode over to say that there was someone else looking at the house, and if we wished to have it we must decide at once. That little crisis made up our wavering minds: we took the house called Cherry Farm, and lived there for nearly ten of the happiest years of our lives.

The railway to Badminton, with the tunnel through by Chipping Sodbury to Bristol, had been begun just before our move. All the youthful labour of the countryside was absorbed as by a sponge, besides that of hundreds of navvies brought in from outside; progress had arrived at Acton Turville and the old life as surely departed.

CHAPTER XV

TRESHAM

When I discovered Tresham I believed that here at last was that *ultima thule* in England for which I had been seeking—a sure and lasting retreat from the fumes of industrialism. Built just under the edge, to escape the north and east winds that wither and destroy, though open to the strong but life-giving blasts that come from the west and the sea, the hamlet lies at the head of one of the many combes that run up into the Cotswold barrier from the Valley of the Severn, like the spaces between the fingers of an outspread hand. If you approach from the top, turn near to the twenty-third milestone on the Bath and Gloucester road, and you will come on it unexpectedly in the dip—after about a mile along a second-class road that leads through the village and to nowhere else, for the rest of the way to Wotton is blocked by gates which are usually closed.

Its inhabitants, too, we quickly discovered, conformed to the most conservative types. Several of its families had been there for many generations, and all were attached to the land in some way or other. Most of the property around belonged to General Robert Hale, who, lately retired, was now Colonel-in-Chief of the 7th Hussars, and formerly equerry to the old Duke of Cambridge when Commander-in-Chief of the Army. He was a bachelor and lived at Alderley House with two old sisters, who were rarely seen and never went anywhere. The family was descended from Sir Mathew Hale, the Lord Chief Justice to Oliver Cromwell.

Cherry Farm, the name of the house we had taken, stood in the centre of the village beside the little church; and 150 acres, the only free land in the place, went with it, but the garden of three-quarters of an acre was all we retained. The rest was owned by a family called Holborow, which had farmed in those parts for many generations, and whose members claimed that their name is

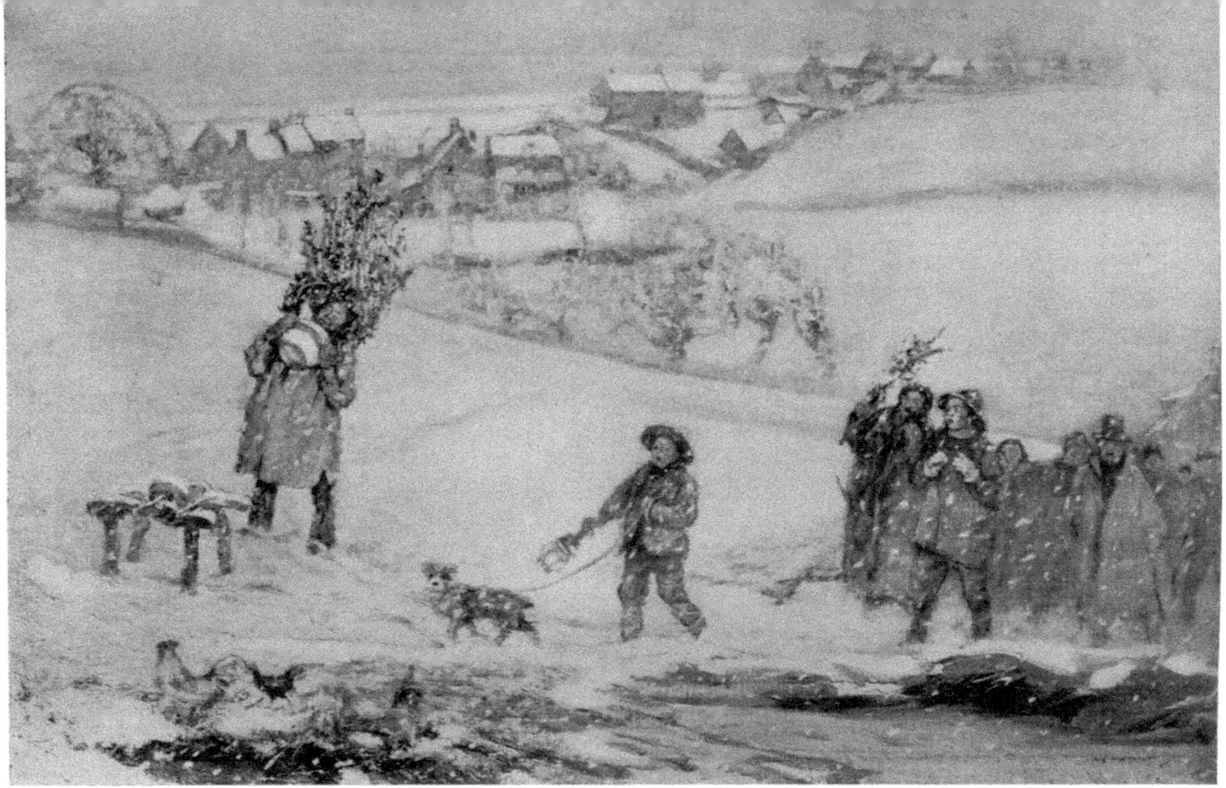

The Wassail Bowl at Tresham

Oil painting

registered in the Domesday Book. My landlord had been well off, but some time in the seventies progress tempted him, and he invested in a coalpit near Bristol. At first all was well, then water came into the pit, and fortune ran out. Another Holborow farmed at Burden Court, and the farmer next door to us, with a name equally distinctive, Robert Worlock, had married yet another Holborow.

In the village most names were of Saxon origin also, Stinchcombe, Hurcombe, Chappell, Shewell, etc. Several of their owners had never been in a train and one or two had never even seen one. It was one of these, who, at the death of Queen Victoria, being a contemporary of that sovereign, cried out in lamentation: "Ah! dear, dear! They do say our Quane be dead", but added quickly as true to type, "and who be goin' to get the job now, think ye?"

Worlock himself told me he was thirty-eight before he first set eyes on the sea. Tetbury, eight miles away, was the nearest station on the Great Western Railway. Most of the men had been there at some time, because there was a "Mop" or hiring fair there once a year, to which farm hands went who wished to change their masters. All this might have gone on just the same for another hundred years but for the internal-combustion engine. Alas! There was an aerodrome with hangars built at Leighterton, two miles away, during the War. This was dismantled later, but is being started to life again.

Twenty-five years after we left Tresham I revisited the hamlet. Not one farmer and only two old women remained of all we had known. I had hoped that no motor-bus would ever by vibration threaten the walls of these ancient cottages and farms; but now I learn that the Board of Education has undertaken to awaken the place with a bus. The school at Tresham has been closed, and all the children from Leighterton and Tresham, thirty-five in number, are to be sent daily back and forward to school in Wotton-under-Edge, 3½ miles away, by motor-bus. I am now waiting to be told what has happened after the next snow storm, for I have seen three or four feet of snow in drifts quite often on that road, and there is a hill up from Wotton steep enough to daunt the boldest driver in wintry weather.

But this is anticipating. After the house had been done up by local labour, we found it comfortable: the only water supply was a well which never did us any harm, though it gave trouble in times of drought. We got our furniture down from London and were soon quite at home and enjoying the life, especially in summer. Nor were we entirely without social amenities. The Squire, General Hale, called, and also his friend General Burn and his wife, both of whom lived at Alderley, about a mile away towards Wotton. After that a number of others came from places round about, though I fear we remained rather curiosities for those whose interests were mainly hunting (the countries of the Beaufort and Berkley Hunts both meet at Alderley); artists were an unknown species there.

The two generals we came to know quite intimately; their weekly walk together on Sunday often ended with tea at our house in Tresham, and for years, after the death of his wife, I dined with General Burn, a gunner and Indian Mutiny veteran, twice a week as a rule, thereby learning to know the country by night as well as by day in my walks there and back in all weathers.

By degrees I learnt to distinguish the bark of an amorous fox from the warning yelp of a vixen for her cubs to return to the safety of the earth; the snoring of the owls in the elms as well as their hoots on the wing; the agonized scream of a rabbit hunted by a stoat; all familiar sounds to the countryman. More unusually, I once on my lonely walks saw the shadow of a full moon reversed by the light of an extra brilliant meteor, to the dreadful alarm of an old cock pheasant as well as myself. On another occasion some sort of thunderbolt came down on the other side of the hedge from me. Its concussion nearly knocked me over. I did not investigate exactly what had happened as the rain in a deluge was running down my neck into my boots, and my one idea was to get back home and under cover. A smell of sulphur seemed to hang about the air afterwards.

Alderley House had a good library and I was given the run of it, so that during the winters I got through such unlikely books as *Wellington's Despatches*, Kinglake's *Crimea*, Mercer's *Journal of the Battle of Waterloo*, and from all of them I gathered information at first hand, which is what I prefer.

This, however, was but our recreation. All the time at Tresham we kept working: my wife painting, and I continuing with my real work of illustration, to keep the pot boiling, with painting during what intervals I could make. So I continued my series of country types, learning to know them personally and drawing them from life, before their kind became extinct with the mechanization of labour. Like the poor, the land is always with us, no matter how we try to wriggle away from its problems. One begins to suspect that the truth about it, as about other conditions of life in civilized countries, is, that there is still room and welcome for the thrifty and able man, starting even from the very bottom.

Unfortunately, the vast majority of mankind is neither the one nor the other, but prefers to wrap his talent in a napkin, to inveigh against the hardship of the system, and to excuse himself to the "Master" with the words of the parable: "Thou art an austere man, taking up that thou layest not down, and reaping that thou didst not sow."

But where are the men of the type of the former generation of tiers and pitchers, hedgers and ditchers, rick-makers, thatchers, and threshers? Skilled men all, with a personal pride in the doing of their work. The real sons of the soil, who lived and died content in one district, grew to know the fields in which they worked as their own gardens, and taught their sons and sons' sons the secrets to be won by patience and solid work, without which nothing can be done on the land. They were passing away, not to be recalled or recreated from any town-bred people by any number of lamentations or land bills: killed partly in the cause of progress by the introduction of labour-saving machinery, but also largely by a system of education which is of no use to them, however suitable for urban populations.

The genius of Thomas Hardy has rendered their characters immortal, but that, unfortunately, cannot preserve the men themselves to the country.

In many an old farmhouse you may still find hanging, in a corner, a framed card recording how some shepherd, cowman, or carter had served one family and one farm for fifty or sixty years: trusted and trustworthy was the rule more often then than now, I fear.

Some, no doubt, will hold these men to be dull fools, who allowed themselves to be robbed and exploited for their masters' gain. But judging by those of the old sort I have known, I fancy these could give this sort of critic points in shrewdness. Nor, while agreeing that the conditions of life for the agricultural labourer have vastly improved during the last thirty years, do I fancy that these old boys lost much in the way of enjoyment in their youth by comparison, and they were happier men at their end. They had been taught the work of their lives thoroughly, and found an interest in doing it well: a state that represents a higher degree of real education than is reached by four-fifths of those turned out of the schools to-day.

There is no need to pretend that these old ones had no faults. They were men first of all, with all the weaknesses of the flesh and their environment: secretive, suspicious, greedy and envious like most peasants.

I will try a sketch of two of the best known characters in my time. They were brothers and old inhabitants. The first, called Francis, was our gardener during most of our time at Tresham; his forbears were probably working on the land before the battle of Hastings. He was eighty-six years of age when we left and still good for a day's work at his own pace. Younger men laughed knowingly and hinted that he owed his present vitality

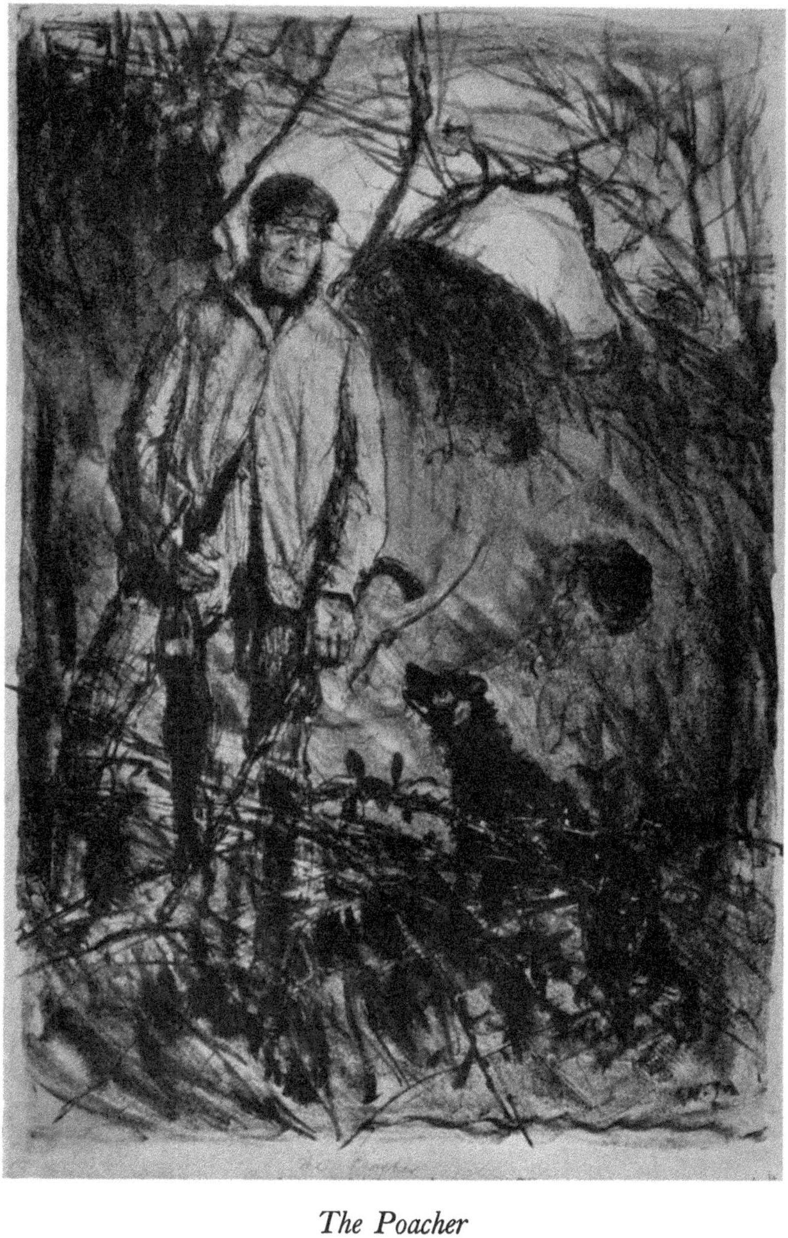

The Poacher

Lithograph

to the exceptional care he had always taken never to overwork himself. Not that he was lazy, for his toll for the day would still fall not far short of that of men thirty or more years younger; but long before the coming of trade unions he had decided exactly how much he need put in for a given wage, and nobody ever got more out of him. It cannot be said that he was beloved by anyone or was even popular with his neighbours. He had never been known to give anything away, and was believed to have quite a "tidy bit" of money hidden away in his cottage; not even his daughter who lived there knew where, or if she did, would not acknowledge it. To cut a cabbage from his garden was a trial to him, the smallest potatoes must be eaten first, and so on. Years before, it was reported that, as a man with a young family, he could rarely bring himself to cut a slice for Sunday dinner from the side of bacon in the rafters (he kept a pig always, of course) until the meat showed unmistakeable signs of being rotten. He had clothes that had served him for forty years, and the wrinkles in his corduroy breeches were as fixed, in spite of many washings, as those in his cunning old face. Deafness was his one infirmity, though his ears could always detect the magic word "beer", but his eyesight remained marvellous and nothing seemed to escape it near or afar.

He could read a little, he said, but his fingers were too stiff for writing. A radical in politics, he supported the chapel so far as he attended to his spiritual wants at all, but towards the end, for some reason never revealed to anyone, he attended the church as well.

His brother was nearly as ancient and quite as hale, but different altogether in character and temperament. Unsuspicious, he was hearty in every sense of the word. His job was that of woodman and carpenter to the Alderley estate, so he belonged to the aristocracy of the hamlet, and was generally given the title of the "Mayor of Tresham"—a real old-fashioned Englishman. He lived in a house of his own, that was held on one of those leases dependent on three lives, which used to be common and can only be excused on the grounds that they are English. A genial, careless fellow with a weakness for beer; truth to tell he was becoming a little senile at this time, and completely in the hands of his wife, a very respectable, practical woman with a strong sense of duty and appearances, but a bit too "managing" in her ways for the comfort of old Ted Evans. She kept him clean and would not permit him to enter the house in his muddy boots: they must be left in the scullery. Nor was he allowed to sleep on the sofa when in beer. Privately, we were told that she washed his great bald head every Saturday night, to be ready for church on Sunday. It cannot be said that he was grateful for these attentions, but he had reached that state of resignation or salvation that puts up with them. Having been sent to the vicarage with a parcel from his wife, who did dressmaking, one day of pouring rain, he was greeted by the parlour-maid with: "Well, well, it's a terrible wet day, Mr Evans." Turning up his eyes to the weeping skies, he answered humbly enough "We must take what the Lord does send us!"—"The Missus has naught to do with that", he added on a note of sly satisfaction that the weather at any rate was not under her control.

The son of this couple was a superior young man who had succeeded to his father's job on the estate and married the prettiest girl in the village. They had a little daughter and a baby son. All seemed well for another generation, and then the Fates, ravelling up the skein, cut it blindly, as is their wont. The girl wife had a brother, a soldier, who had been invalided out of the army in India with lung trouble; he came to live with this little family for the sake of the pure air. Within two years husband, wife, babe, as well as brother, were in their graves through tuberculosis, and only the little girl and the old people remained untouched. The irony of fate, it was called! But such close association with infection would not be permitted nowadays.

To turn aside to something pleasanter than the consideration of the inexplicable workings of fate, the Old Age Pension was first granted while we were living at Tresham. I am no economist, but am certain that this was the most beneficent piece of legislation of my time: the first real relief for millions from the haunting nightmare of old age. And especially for the old people in the country, most of whom, on 12*s*. a week or thereabouts, had brought up a family to be decent men and women like themselves. Man ought to end his days in thankfulness to God, for bitterness is a poison. So this was as a gift from Heaven, and I can bear witness that most of the recipients were thankful.

General Burn had a celebrated garden at the Mount House, which originally had been made by Miss Caroline North, whose paintings of flowers, done all over the world, are still preserved at Kew. Sir Joseph Hooker was a personal friend and used to send all sorts of rare plants from Kew to be tried out by her, as she was also a great gardener. When she died, the General took over the place as it stood, and it was his pleasure to send us both fruit and flowers from it every week. In this way my wife was supplied with flowers to paint of every kind, for every season. Thus it came about that she painted the series of twelve flower pictures, representing the months of the year, for Mrs E. J. Horniman, now in the drawing room of "Garden Corner" on Chelsea Embankment. This was one of the few chances that came her way to show the full range of her talent as a painter. In silver frames, they are let into a tall dado made of slate which Voysey, the architect, designed for the room, and they remain one of the most original and successful interior decorations that I know of.

She painted the feeling and spirit of flowers in a way that was unique, and a water-colour painting of an orchid, now in the Victoria and Albert Museum, will, I believe, uphold this statement for all who understand both painting and flowers. E. J. Horniman was at the Slade with me, and after my marriage, both he and his wife kept up the friendship, one of our most valued experiences. He came of Quaker stock and, though no longer conforming strictly to its rules, retained many of those qualities of the Society of Friends, which have gained for that body, that has always on principle refused to fight, the admiration of the world especially since the Great War. He was the best and most helpful friend I have ever had, and I owe much to him and his advice, which I can never repay. Although by a sort of mutual reserve we were never exactly intimate, we understood one another perfectly. I used to say that I was a radical by instinct but a conservative by conviction, while Horniman was a conservative by instinct and a radical by conviction—and I leave others to decide which had the better part.

The Boer War had begun when we went to Tresham and for a time Clement Shorter of *The Sphere* used to send me sketches from the front to work up into drawings for the paper. By an odd chance our postman came back to his duties after a wound from the battle of Pardeberg. As his round ended at Tresham about 10.30 a.m., and he started back again emptying letter-boxes on his return to Wotton at 4.30, he had a period of leisure during which he used to sit for me as a model.

Some time in the early nineteen hundreds I got a commission from Hallam Murray to illustrate Borrow's *Wild Wales*. To make the sketches for it I started out on a bicycle to follow his track through Wales early in October, that being the season at which he had made his walk. My impression was that Wales had not changed very materially in the fifty years since he had made his journey, and my opinion remains that Wales is by far the most foreign part of the British Isles. Welsh was universally spoken in the country places. I made a point of entering all the small inns which Borrow mentions, so far as they continued to exist, and it appeared that most of them did so. My entry into a bar was a sign for all to cease speaking, though they had been noisy enough before. I felt that I was a suspected character and obviously *de trop* for natives. True, I got on well with those who spoke English, after the first awkwardness had worn off.

The weather being changeable, as was to be expected at that season, the countryside looked interesting, though at times too stormy for pleasure riding on a bicycle. I had only one adventure:

that of being nearly lost on the road between Dolgelly and Dinas Mawddwy, which I believe can be one of the loneliest and most difficult in England. Bernard Shaw, I remember, was reported "lost" on it once also. I passed it in darkness, with a gale and pouring rain against me, and only reached my destination at Dinas Mawddwy by sheer luck, where I was taken in at a tiny inn—the Green Dragon I think was the name—and looked after with such kindness that I shall never forget it. Arriving at 10.30 p.m. (by a miracle they had not gone to bed) I was soaked to the skin, but they found me a change of clothing, then cooked me a supper of delicious little lamb cutlets, with tea, scones, butter and jam, all home made, dried all my clothes perfectly, and after a hearty breakfast of ham and eggs with scones, etc., sent me off at noon next day rejoicing, at a cost of *3s. 6d.* for everything. It sounds incredible, but later I met a Welshman going around buying pewter in Wales, who told me that this and another place near the Devil's Bridge, the address of which he gave me, were such that you could board there for 10*s*. a week all found, and be done well! Such places no longer exist.

I had continued to work for Halkett and *The Pall Mall Magazine*, and now I was called on to undertake most of the illustrations to *The Queen's Quair*, by Maurice Hewlett, which was being published as a serial in *The Pall Mall Magazine*. D. Y. Cameron drew most of the places mentioned in Scotland and Greiffenhagen also made a few drawings, but all the portraits and most of the subjects fell to my share.

I had already made Hewlett's acquaintance while he was still at the Record Office. He had not long been married, and was tossing his son, the future airman, high before the fireplace in a house in Notting Hill Gate. Now he had taken to literature for good and all, and I got to know him well. He was desperately interested in the life of Mary, Queen of Scots, and hoped to make from it his masterpiece. He told me he wrote and re-wrote the book six times. Although it never had a popular success, many good judges believe that he put his best work as a novelist into it. Thus it was I first became interested in the drawings of the French draughtsmen of the sixteenth century, especially those which are now at Chantilly, because they contain portraits of many of the men and women connected with the Court of France at that time. I have studied all the portraits of Mary, Queen of Scots, wherever available, and they vary exceedingly in fact as well as in artistic merit. The most convincing, for me, are the two drawings in red and black chalk now in the Bibliothèque Nationale in Paris; one of her as Queen-dauphiness, and the other in mourning, or *dule* as it was called in France. "La reine blanche" is the title given to the many paintings done from it, because white was mourning for the Queen. There is a good version in oil in the Wallace Collection, and a still better one at Windsor. At Windsor, also, is the miniature from the first drawing, which is a lovely work of art. Lastly, absolutely convincing is the death mask, now at Holyrood. The most interesting point about it is that it confirms the facts of the features in the two early drawings. The head of the effigy of Mary on her tomb in Westminster Abbey has a strong resemblance to that of Elizabeth in the same place, so that one can readily recognize that they were of the same blood and first cousins. The least attractive points seem heightened in that of Elizabeth, but softened in that of Mary.

Through the kind assistance of Lady Patricia Ramsay I had the opportunity to study the miniature at Windsor closely. This is square in shape, and exquisite in workmanship. Dimier, who is the authority on these portraits, recently took the drawing and this miniature away from the work of François Clouet and gave them to Jean De Court, chiefly because he is mentioned in accounts as painter to Marie Stuart. I cannot agree with this change, for the following reasons. The pedigree of the miniature is quite well documented. It is believed to be the one which Sir James Melville, the Scottish Ambassador to the English Court, brought to show Queen Elizabeth what her cousin the Queen of Scots looked like. Later it is mentioned as being in the possession of James I of England, her son, and is catalogued, among the works of art belonging to Charles I in the list which is still in the Records Office, as being by Janet. Now Janet is simply a diminutive of "Jean Clouet" (as we would say Johnny), an artist of Flemish descent who became Court painter to François I of France. On his death he was succeeded by his son François, and for long the works by both father and son were classed together and attributed to Janet, a sort of generic title, before experts began to distinguish between them. The miniature at Windsor is obviously done from the red and black chalk drawing of Mary as Queen-dauphiness now in the Bibliothèque Nationale, where it is still catalogued, and was shown at the French Exhibition at Burlington House, as by François Clouet. When examining the miniatures at Windsor I found that there are two others known to be by Jean Clouet. Now Jean Clouet, in these miniatures and also in his large portrait of François I in the Louvre, was fond of using a peculiar red (usually in backgrounds)—the tint is a sort of mixture of Indian red with crimson lake. All three miniatures at Windsor have this red in them, and it is used on the bodice of the dress in the Mary, Queen of Scots miniature. As artists at that time were accustomed to grind and mix their own pigments, I think this is enough to prove that it came from the Clouet Atelier, and as the age of the Queen makes it too late for Jean it must be by François Clouet.

Hewlett went to great trouble with the portraits of the characters in his novel, getting all he could that were authentic likenesses, and I used the photographs he had collected, only giving them new poses and new costumes of the period for their new setting. Some are certainly not authentic—that of Rizzio, I remember, was from an Italian painting that he thought gave the type he imagined Rizzio to be, but on the whole they are as accurate as any that are likely to be got together nowadays.

Hewlett was another good friend to us both, though he never came to see us at Tresham. I also made the illustrations in colour for the special edition of the *Forest Lovers*, his first real success. He was of the uncommon kind that fines down spiritually, as well as physically, with age. His aim was to be a poet and to capture beauty, and to this, the most difficult job of all, he at least came very near. Towards the end of his life, and as a result of the War, his interests turned to the common man and his problems, especially the English agricultural labourer, whom he admired above all. It was thus that my drawings of them made a common interest for us both. After the War I believe he crippled himself financially by assisting those about him to independence, with the result that he was suspected of Bolshevism by farmers and landowners, though his real opinions were far more tinged with the ideas of the Society of Friends, with whose labours for peace he had been closely in touch for some time. I have heard him hold forth on the theme that no man should have more than £150 a year, and though I am convinced that on that sum Hewlett would have died sooner than he did, there is no doubt he meant it in all sincerity. Though far from a rich man when he started out, for a time he made a very large income, especially in America, out of his romances, and he spent it royally. Then he struck, and refused to write any more of them; when he tried to put forward his new ideas in novel form, his public dwindled very quickly. There were those who found him too stand-offish, but he was simple enough when one knew him: his reserve was largely self-protection from the swarm of sycophants and idlers who pursue the fortunes of the successful. A master of many interests to which he could turn for change from writing, he was a first-class gardener both in the growing of plants and flowers, as well as in setting them out attractively. At the Old Rectory, Broadchalke, near Salisbury, he had the most beautiful garden I have seen anywhere. To begin with, the materials were ideal: an old-world rectory garden with lawns, a cedar and a tulip tree. Beyond this there was a river, large enough for canoes and bathing, not to mention many trout; this divided into several smaller streams, leaving islands between, and these he had joined by bridges. Near the house he added the more formal fantasies of a Dutch garden, and, leading to the walled kitchen garden, an apple pergola that was a dream of beauty in spring and autumn, in flower and fruit. As originally designed, all was set in a fold of the Downs, and seemed part of them. Unfortunately, in trying to prevent being overlooked by the curious, he lost this perfection. I have seen him, clad in a Moroccan *jelab*, walking in this garden early like a god, for in warm weather he slept beneath the cedar and worked before breakfast, so that he might play from noon on. If this sounds like posing, the fault is mine, for there was nothing of the kind about him. The iris was his favourite flower: he knew all about it, and at one time had seventy different varieties, for which he had contrived the right soil and conditions of living, for every month of the year save one.

Once I came on him in the rose garden, made on one of the islands, surrounded by a golden privet hedge, very private, with a lily pond in the centre. With him were the Laureate, Robert Bridges, and his wife. They were to write a new verse for the National Anthem, but it beat them!

When he lost the rectory and this garden, he moved into a smaller house still in Broadchalke, and I thought: "Now he is safe from trouble in his old age." He asked me to go to see it in the spring, but I could not get away. Then pneumonia got him in June, and he was dead in a week. He lies buried in a fold of the Downs he loved, a little further up the valley from Broadchalke.

Our parish doctor lived at Hawkesbury Upton, five miles away. He was over eighty years of age, so paid us only occasional visits in fine weather, when he made the journey in a farm cart in which an arm-chair had been placed for his greater comfort in travel. On his departure, the usual greeting between villagers was reduced to the question "Well? what did he gie ye, the pink or the blue?" He had two medicines for all emergencies, one coloured pink, the other blue.

Love tragedies or idylls there were none at Tresham, in our time at any rate. There were a few cases of births "without benefit of clergy", but such facts of nature were too much matters of common knowledge to become tragedies—comedies they might be perhaps. Several maidens, mostly those who had been in service, came back for the birth of an infant; but so far as I observed, there was usually a family of younger brothers and sisters into which the newcomer was simply absorbed, so that the affair was soon forgotten. Death, however, made an occasion that demanded serious attention of all, especially sudden death.

A man fell off a stack and broke his neck. It is surprising how easily the vital spark can be extinguished, though another time it is hard to kill, or may revive in a marvellous way. This accident, then, led to an inquest, and it was held in the public-house. I was elected foreman of the jury. We had to wait an hour or more for the Coroner, Dr E. M. Grace, the cricketer and brother of the great W. G. When at length he arrived he was full of apologies for being late, excusing himself with some remarks on a new midwifery bill of which he evidently did not approve. He went on to explain that he had been called out at 3 a.m. that morning on a false alarm to a farmer's wife some five or six miles away. "I would like to know what pleasure there is in that", he added, as a further reflection. "Ah!" piped the voice of a juryman with a big black beard, "It's in the makin' o' ee that the pleasure is, doctor", at which the Doctor roared. Then all adjourned to view the corpse, after which the verdict of "accidental death" was promptly returned. Some gave their shillings to the widow, but the rest was spent at the "pub" on beer.

To complete my cycle of experiences, we had a murder near at hand. Two men were in love with one woman; one, the husband, went out one summer evening on a bicycle ride from Stroud along the Bath and Gloucester Road. On the lonely stretch between the twenty-third milestone and Petty France (as it is called), the lover shot the husband from behind with a revolver, and throwing the body and the bicycle over the wall into a little copse by the roadside, rode back full speed to Stroud, and caught a train about midnight to London. Arrived there, he woke up his brother in his flat, telling him what he had just done on the road. The brother, after discussion, simply said: "There is a revolver in that drawer over there. You had better take it!" This he did and going out again, shot himself. There was trouble over this later. Early the same morning a shepherd crossing the Bath and Gloucester Road with his flock, when changing pasture, saw a spanner in the road. Picking it up he did not put it in his pocket, but laid it carefully in a crevice on the top of the wall, to pick up on his way back to dinner. On his return, seeking for the exact spot, he looked over the wall and saw the body hidden in some long grass close alongside the wall. So ended the chain of evidence and coincidence. But for this chance, the body would probably have remained concealed for months at least.

The murderer being already dead, there was an inquest at Hawkesbury Upton, in the same parish as Tresham. The jury had little to do but find a verdict of "Wilful Murder".

Towards the end of our ten years' sojourn at Tresham, it was borne in on me that there were only one or two tombstones in the churchyard there, for the rest were all green mounds that wiped one another out in time and came again, like waves of the sea. I suggested to the vicar that it would be a gracious thing to put a reredos in the church as a memorial to the unnamed dead buried in that churchyard. I offered to do a painting for it if the suggestion were approved. The idea was welcomed; it was decided to re-decorate the whole chancel as a memorial, and this called for some money to pay for alterations by a builder. A subscription was started to which everybody in the village, including the village idiot, subscribed according to his means. This, together with some larger sums given by kind friends from the large houses near who wished to help, produced enough money to do something more important. I designed it all: besides the painting for the reredos with an oak frame and the dedication, there was a new altar-table and altar-rails carved in oak and gilded by Mrs A. L. Bowley. My wife and I also painted a landscape of a stony desert with thorns—the outside world from which the little church was a refuge—in oil paint on the wall, as seen through four Norman arches, two on either side of the table. At last all was finished, and everyone was pleased when the then Bishop of Gloucester, Dr Gibson, one snowy day in March, before the whole village and many of the country round, dedicated the work "To the Glory of God and in Memory of the unnamed dead" buried in the churchyard.

CHAPTER XVI

THE INTERNATIONAL SOCIETY OF PAINTERS, SCULPTORS AND GRAVERS

Soon after the success of the Glasgow School at Munich in the early years of the nineties, the three leaders of that school, Guthrie, Lavery and Walton, moved to London, seeking as portrait painters a larger field for their work in the Metropolis. Of the three, only Lavery may be said to have taken root in the south; Guthrie became President of the Royal Scottish Academy and Walton returned north with him. All were admirers of Whistler, and their work had been influenced by his methods. About this time Francis Howard, a stepson of T. P. O'Connor, the Irish politician and journalist, founder of *The Star* newspaper and many other successful papers, came to London from America. He had been trained as a painter, but also showed talent for organization, which he wanted opportunity to develop. He saw that there was an opening for an International Society of Artists, with its headquarters in London, which might command the attention of the art world in both Europe and America. In touch with these Scotch painters and others who were already making reputations in European galleries as distinct from English, about 1897 he got together the nucleus of the kind of society all were aiming at, which should include the most important artists in every medium in both Europe and America. Whistler was approached and agreed to become President, and Lavery was made Vice-President.

It was the easier to persuade the elusive personality of Whistler to move in this direction, because the success of the exhibition of most of his most important pictures at the Goupil Gallery, New Bond Street, in 1892, had confirmed his reputation as a painter of genius, and the catalogue, with its amusing selection from the contradictory opinions of art critics on the different works when first shown, caused laughter amongst the general public and enhanced his reputation as a wit. The Luxembourg Gallery in Paris bought his portrait of his "Mother" for £160 (plus the honour!), while Glasgow Corporation had been screwed up to give 1000 guineas for his portrait of Carlyle. The Glasgow painters had been largely responsible for bringing off this latter sale successfully: Walton, especially, having worked valiantly on the Committee which brought forward the scheme.

I fancy it is the most successful purchase ever made for the Glasgow Gallery. I am told it draws many strangers to the city to this day. Nor was the portrait acquired without a final battle. When the Committee, consisting of Glasgow bailies (i.e. town councillors), arrived at the painter's studio to make their decision, one canny member, true to type and determined to bargain for a reduction of price, began: "But Mr Whistler, the picture is not very striking, nor is it highly coloured." In a second Whistler turned his eyeglass on him in a stare, to reply, "Are you striking-looking or am I highly-coloured?" No more was said, and the price demanded was paid.

This episode had rendered the Scotch painters *personae gratae* to Whistler, so his acceptance of the Presidency of the new society was effectively assured.

In the spring of 1898 Francis Howard, having consolidated his forces, financial and otherwise, obtained possession of the Princes' Skating Rink at Knightsbridge, and persuaded Admiral Maxse, the owner, to allow him to have it redecorated, to make a picture gallery during the summer months. Whistler, who had been living in Paris for some years with his wife enjoying the fruits of his success, had promised to interest the art world there in the success of the new society, but did not want to be bothered with too many of the details and actual work; thus it came about that he suggested that his friend Ludovici, a painter of Italian extraction, who had been born and brought up in England but spoke French perfectly and knew Paris intimately, should be sent over to make the contacts personally that Whistler suggested. This was agreed to, and after difficulties successfully overcome, Ludovici got promises of work from nearly everybody he saw except Degas who, as usual, was suspicious of all societies, native or foreign. At last the Galleries, decorated and hung more or less in the way that Whistler had invented when President of the Royal Society of British Artists, were opened with a flourish. This was the most important representative exhibition of modern Continental painting from the non-academic point of view that had been shown in London, and certainly proved to be an artistic success. Whistler had the place of honour of course: and all the paintings were carefully spaced and where possible hung in panels, as was the case with works at the New Salon in the Champs de Mars; but of course there was nothing like the amount of space that the hangers had there, and this led to trouble, because some did not get the places they expected.

The most interesting picture in that exhibition to me was Manet's "The Execution of the Emperor Maximilian". I am glad to have seen it; it was, in fact, the largest he ever painted, about 12 ft. × 8 ft., but afterwards it was cut up by the dealers and sold in fragments, two of which were bought twenty-five years later for our National Gallery. Although the picture was impressive, I suspect that the world no longer has room for works of this kind and size.

An exhibition of the same nature, with variations, in the same place was repeated for another year, but I believe the public support was not sufficient to make it pay.

The next home for the Society was made at the New Gallery, Regent Street, now a cinema. In my opinion, this was the best gallery for showing pictures there has ever been in London.

Although I exhibited in every show of the Society from first to last, I was not elected a member until after the first or second exhibition, so knew little personally about the early working of it. On my visits to town from Gloucestershire I used nevertheless to hear a good deal of what was going on from Joe Pennell, who of course was in the thick of it all. From him I gathered that the meetings of the Council were very lively and rows by disgruntled artists frequent. The methods of Mussolini and the Fascists in a small way appear to have been tried out here thoroughly, long before we heard of them politically. They made for excellence in the exhibits, I allow, so long as there was someone like Whistler, in whom the majority had confidence, to impose his will when necessary. After his death there certainly was a falling off in the standards as well as in the control by the Council. Even the jury grew slack in its attendances towards the end. I remember a Dutch member saying to me: "You English are an extraordinary people. Here is an important exhibition and only two, a Dutchman and a German, have turned up yet."

As one grows older nothing is more puzzling than to try to gauge the reasons for the way artistic reputations come and go. I suppose nearly everybody in the art world of Europe of that time, with any pretensions to talent, had some work shown by this International Society. Where are the laurels of most of them to-day? Even those of Whistler himself seem a bit faded. I am aware of course that there is nothing novel in this. We know that Raphael was ready to paint out the frescoes by Botticelli in the Vatican and replace them with his own, as did other masters on like occasions later. More amusing, as it seems to me, was the fact that El Greco had to leave Italy for good, having infuriated the Italians because he had the cheek to offer to repaint Michael Angelo's "Last Judgment" in the Sistine Chapel; and the irony of it was, no doubt, he would have done it well in quite another way.

Cézanne said of the painting of Van Gogh: "Assurément c'est la peinture d'un fou", and of that of Gauguin: "Il a chipé ma petite sensation." Yet Gauguin was the first painter of distinction who saw the qualities hidden in the apparently infantile clumsiness of Cézanne; in whom Whistler, alert though he usually was, could see nothing but "the work of a little girl who ought to be slapped by her Mamma!"

And so the wheel of fortune turns till the next name that is wanted becomes topmost. Van Gogh, I believe, was promptly turned down by those sent to Paris to select pictures for the International, and never had anything hung there; but Cézanne had some rather insignificant works shown once, I believe; a very dark picture by Gauguin was hung in the Gallery at Regent Street, when the obvious but uninspired painting of his brother-in-law, Fritz Thaulow (the Norwegian painter of snow), was on the line downstairs.

Yet these are the names that would be in the places of honour to-day. The vital spark must be in the work from the first, but awaits the time and conditions to fan it into life, when its brilliance becomes obvious and we wonder at our previous blindness. Nevertheless, it is impossible to make something out of nothing even by calling it an "ism".

Whistler died in the summer of 1903. He had been living in Chelsea since the death of his wife, and was ailing for quite a year before. He was buried beside his wife in Chiswick Churchyard, where Hogarth, his favourite among English painters, also lies. There was a commemoration service in Chelsea Old Church, which was crowded with a remarkably mixed company of artists and laymen, come to pay a last tribute of respect to the Master. In the pew with me, I remember, were Linley Sambourne of *Punch* and Alma Tadema, R.A. Afterwards, though not invited, with Sullivan and one or two others, I followed the coffin to its last resting place at Chiswick, looking on from afar. At the ceremony there was some disturbance because of the appearance of Maud F—, a former model and mistress, who before his marriage was known to his friends as "Madame". It was this lady who went with him to Venice when he was making his "Venice set" of etchings. Whistler was no saint, and he never pretended to be one. While there, another artist called Jobbins, or some such name, was much shocked at this departure from the proprieties, and proposed at the club there that Whistler should be "cut" to show its disapproval. Shortly after, Whistler was etching on the lagoon, just outside his lodgings, when Jobbins came along in a gondola. On seeing the Master, he could not resist the self-importance of greeting him with "Good morning, Mr Whistler", at which Whistler, looking up to a window above him, called out "Maud! Maud!" and Maud looked out. "It's all right," he said, "Jobbins isn't going to cut us after all!"

I dislike the attendance of any but relations at the grave; it leaves openings for these surprises, and in any case when weather is bad, many have taken their death warrants away with them, a strange way of benefiting the memory of the deceased. In Victorian times this sort of attendance was almost an obligation if one were invited. I can remember being astonished to see Mr Gladstone, then about eighty years of age, on a wintry day with sleet falling, at the funeral of the Lady Rosebery of that time. I had been sent to make some sketches of the celebrities present for my paper. Looking up from the lower level of a path I recognized with a start the familiar face and brilliant eye, round and set about with wrinkles like that of a parrot, of the Grand Old Man staring down at me. I had seen him previously in the House of Commons, but this was the closest I had been to him, and certainly he seemed to be taking undue risks.

Another funeral of that period also comes back to me, that of his contemporary, Tennyson; but here the settings and arrangements seemed all in tune. The coffin was being brought across a common to the station at Haslemere from the poet's Surrey home, where he died. It rested on a bed of autumn leaves and was carried in a pony cart followed by the mourners, all members of the family, on foot, not wearing mourning. There was "Sunset and evening star" also to complete the mood of the passing. I made a sketch of it, a feeble thing, for *The Graphic*, but I wish I had kept it, as the impression left remains powerful and clear to this day.

While writing on this subject of impressions at funerals, it may be of interest to recall that I saw the lying-in-state of King Edward VII in St Stephen's Hall, Westminster. I defy anyone with the feelings of an artist not to be profoundly impressed by the mystery and majesty of the ceremonial. The sense of awe, fear of the unknown if you like to call it, has nothing to do with politics, nor is it got rid of by verbosity, anarchist or communist. With their Lenin Tomb the Soviets endeavour to ape the mystery of a throne to impress their followers. In order to be allowed to draw, I had to attend very early in the morning before the passage of the queues began. It is difficult to decide which was the more impressive, the silence of the officers keeping watch alone, or the noises made by the multitude in a prolonged hoarse whisper as it shuffled by. I made two drawings in colour of the first effect, one of which was bought by the Countess Beauchamp and the other by Lady Crewe for her husband. I am told that the procedure followed for the passing of King George V was exactly the same.

To come back to the International, from which I have strayed. After Whistler, the question was to find the best man for his place as President; Rodin was invited to take it. It gave him a magnificent advertisement and he graciously accepted the honour. Certainly his name was the most prominent one at the time. But he was a poor speaker even in French, which was his only language, so as a figure-head he was ineffective. It was far more instructive to see him handle a bit of modelling. However, the Society became that of "Sculptors, Painters and Gravers" in honour of his presidency, and the Council did all the work, while Rodin remained at Meudon.

In the following year everything was centred on getting as complete a collection of Whistler's life-work as possible for the Memorial Exhibition at the New Gallery. The French Government lent the portrait of his mother, which they now valued at £5000 (for insurance); an almost perfect collection of his etchings and lithographs was got together, and a good collection of his later paintings; but some of the most charming of the early pictures like "The Music Room" and others of that period were absent, having been sold in America; but the "Little White Girl", one of his best, and the two "Nocturnes" now in the National Gallery, were then saved for this country by Arthur Studd, who had bought them after the Goupil exhibition. It was opened on February 22 with great éclat by the American Ambassador, Mr Choate. Rodin came over with several French officials, and they stayed for all the opening ceremonies, more to support Rodin and to glorify France rather than Whistler, I fancy. I doubt whether the general artistic opinion in France was ever so enthusiastic about Whistler and his work as he would have had us believe. There was a suspicion of the feeling that Degas formulated in his *boutade*: "You behave like a man who has no talent at all." Whistler could make mistakes, bad ones too; he once gave a small picture by himself to Ludovic Halévy, the French playwright and friend of Degas, and in reply to his effusive thanks, added, "You will never know how good it is!" Halévy said nothing, but was furious, and told the incident to a friend of mine as an instance of Whistler's outrageous egoism. Such details may appear trivial, but sometimes they can throw light in dark places. The French certainly did not put the portrait of his mother, a masterpiece, in the Louvre until much longer than ten years after his death.

This exhibition, in any case, was a great success and the peak point of the prestige of the International Society. King Edward VII and Queen Alexandra with all the court went to see it, and the attendance of the general public was such that there was a nice nest egg left for the funds of the Society of between two and three thousand pounds. I have no personal recollections about the exhibition, but I remember meeting John Swan there one day: he was dwelling on the valuation placed on the works there at that time, and comparing them with what Whistler had received, adding some reflections on his bankruptcy and struggle to live afterwards. He went on to tell me that he had just met in another gallery, off Bond Street, Durand-Ruel, the French dealer in impressionist paintings, and he (Swan) was looking at a pastel by Degas which belonged to Ruel. "How much do you want for that?" said Swan. "1200 guineas", was the reply. "Good gracious, Degas must be a rich man!" "Not at all", came the reply, "he owes us money!"

So much for the rewards of artists; and I remember that Swan went on to recall that Rembrandt was bankrupt when he died and Hobbema was buried from the workhouse.

The International Society did me some good turns after I was elected a member. Through the Society's exhibit, I got a silver medal at an International Exhibition in Milan for my set of English country types in 1906, and again two medals, one for oil, the other for water-colour painting, at the Chilean Centenary Exhibition, in the same way. My wife, too, who had also been made a member, had an oil painting of a snow landscape bought for the Gallery at Düsseldorf before the War. It was of this landscape that Thaulow, the Norwegian snow-painter, said to Pennell, "Mein Gott! I haf been trying to paint snow white for twenty years, but she has done it."

It was the War that finally killed the International Society, and in spite of valiant efforts since, it has not been possible to revive it in a stricken Europe, where art itself cannot decide whether it is worth living or not.

CHAPTER XVII

RETREAT FROM ARCADY

Now I come to the sad tale of our leaving Tresham and the countryside. All good things come to an end, and all bad things too, if given time. The immediate cause of our departure was the death of old Mr Holborow, the owner of Cherry Farm; the property had to be sold and divided up among his heirs, of whom there was none to take it on. We had not the money to buy a farm of 150 acres or the nerve to be tied to an encumbrance we could not manage. All the signs of the times were set for a change, though we hardly knew them, so I must try to recapture a few of the invisible forces at work against us.

The great victory of the Liberal party at the polls in 1906 and the first large influx of Labour into the House of Commons was the herald of a new movement all over the country. Queen Victoria was dead and privilege was threatened on all sides. I remember writing to Harold Cox, who had just been elected a Labour member, to ask what sort of a person Lloyd George was. His reply, I remember, was: "He complains that he is not loved" (i.e. as he thought he should be, I suppose). Cox himself soon left the Labour Party. He was the most destructive critic I ever met; very mild in manner, he would lead you to say something you flattered yourself was conclusive, and then he would destroy it root and branch with a few shrewd blows, while remaining as mild and inoffensive as before.

For a number of years now I had been dependent on illustration work sent me by publishers and editors in London, and on the whole had no cause to complain of neglect. George Halkett of *The Pall Mall Magazine* was a friend who did not forget. Leslie Wilson had started a series of illustrated books for Newnes, first of all small reprints of the classics with photogravure frontispiece and titles; these were a success; then he passed on to the illustrating of popular novels, each with eight illustrations, at sixpence. In this series I did the whole of Seton Merriman's novels, as well as some by Mrs Humphrey Ward and others. I remember in particular an edition of Rider Haggard's *She*. I rather fancied these illustrations, having laid myself out on them; but Haggard suddenly decided that he did not want another illustrated *She* to conflict with the original edition which was illustrated by Maurice Greiffenhagen, so the edition with my illustrations was withdrawn after about 3000 had been sold. I like to fancy it may become a rarity for the collector in time: for these sixpenny editions went all over the world and into unexpected places. An old schoolfellow of mine told me that he had bought one somewhere on the borders of Rhodesia when big game hunting. I had a number of strings of this kind to my bow and used to go to London pretty constantly, to try to renew them when they became worn: but slowly it was borne in on me that it was no longer so easy to do so.

The system of the art agent and the commercial studio was being introduced from America; these were soon ready to supply all kinds of work *en masse* and with less trouble for everybody, especially editors! On the face of it, this ought to have been to my advantage, and many illustrators employed an agent to get work for them as the authors already did with success. But drawing is not like writing. I hold, and always shall, that the personal contact between the editor and the artist is the vital point to ensure the best work; by this method the editor and the artist mutually educate each other. The agent does save the artist some trouble, and may raise his prices a little. But when his commission is paid there is not much difference in actual receipts.

Death, too, had been busy upsetting our social environments. Mrs Burn died at Alderley, a dreadful blow for her husband and General Hale and for all intimate friends of long standing. She was a charming woman and a perfect hostess, but more or less an invalid since we got to know her. A well-known woman once described her shortly and perfectly when she said, "She has the manners of a pretty woman", but there was much more to her than that. For my wife this was a serious loss, because Mrs Burn had taken a fancy to her and she was the nearest companion within easy reach of Tresham. Later on I designed a reredos in Alderley Church to her memory and it was carved in oak by Mrs A. L. Bowley. Not long after, General Hale, the squire, was struck down suddenly. He was a great gentleman, though he rarely asserted himself; he took the lead when a lead was required quite simply as the Squire of Alderley. He was succeeded by his brother, Col. Mathew Hale (Mathew with one "t" he always insisted, after his celebrated ancestor). A bachelor also, he lived mostly at the Army and Navy Club in Pall Mall, but came down for visits to Alderley. He was a great character in his way. He might have retired as a general like his brother, but carefully avoided doing so because he held there ought not to be two Generals Hale at the same time. General Burn, who was decidedly critical in such matters, used to say that his regiment, the Cameronians, was a model of efficiency when he had the command. In private life, ivy was his special enemy; he hated it, and at one time used to carry a little axe about with him in his walks on the estate with which he cut at the roots of any ivy he noticed embracing a tree. Shortly before he succeeded he also had a slight stroke. As he lay helpless in bed the first order, indeed almost the only one he gave, was that all the ivy on the "summer-house" was to be cut at the roots at once. Now this summer-house was one of those eighteenth-century imitation ruins set on the top of a knoll near the house. He was over seventy years of age and doubtless for long had desired to kill that ivy. Yet such was his punctilious humour that he never proposed to his brother, who would not have cared either way, to have it cut.

Art was one of the amenities he fancied and he had bought a few pictures, so he commissioned me to make drawings of himself and the general. They had to be full-length to show their figures, for they were both big men. His own round head, covered with white curls all over, was a feature of which he wanted point to be made. Though this was long before the days of plus-fours, he insisted that the knickerbockers he was wearing should be made to hang deep over the knees following some fashion he remembered in the sixties. General Burn and the rector, Mr Perkins, were the only two who continued on at Alderley. Of Perkins I am reminded whenever I visit the Victoria and Albert Museum; there is a room, in which I used to have tea, with a Chinese painted paper, taken bodily from a house that belonged to his brother in Wotton-under-Edge.

Bicycles were our chief means of getting about while we were at Tresham. When I went up to London, I rode my bicycle the eight miles to Tetbury and there got a train that took me to Kemble on the main line to London; and the bicycle I picked up again on my return. I was young, but I got to hate that bit of road, especially at night in rain and wind when returning from London. But this period was more distinguished in the country as the time of the coming of the motor-car. Of course, in a horse and hunting county, the car was at first both hated and despised. Farmers were always delighted to tell how one had broken down far from help, and then had to be towed back to some town by horse power.

The Duke of Beaufort was one of the first to own a car and he went to meets in it, rather to the disgust of the die-hards in the county. It was a French car with a French chauffeur, who drove at what was called a wicked speed, though I doubt if it exceeded thirty miles an hour or thereabouts. When his Grace was away he used to give joy rides to the girls round the park. The most remarkable specimen, however, belonged to a parson who lived a few miles away from us. He was one of the gaunt, red-bearded, eager-eyed, bespectacled kind. I doubt if he had any knowledge of mechanics at all, but he acquired a second-hand French car, something like a wagonette. Mounted on scarlet wheels it looked like a real devil-wagon coming along without visible means of propulsion. Horses shied at it wildly, but it usually had to be towed home by one. If they did not hunt, parsons in those parts seemed to develop eccentricities or hermitages. One, whose sale I attended after his death, had the stuffed head of an elephant in a sort of sentry box by his front door. It was almost impossible to get a strange horse up to it, for the day was fortunate if the horse did not run away in terror. I was told that this reverend gentleman had a lot of nephews in the army and in the Indies. I bought a fine set of Buddhist priest robes there for a few shillings; as for the elephant, no one would take it as a gift.

Shortly before we left I painted the portrait of another parson, a near neighbour and friend, Mr Huntley, the squire of Boxwell Court. This is one of the oldest and most interesting houses in the Cotswolds, going back in parts to the twelfth century. It is said to have been a Chapel-of-Ease of the Abbot of Gloucester, to which he might retire from the cares of the world or diocese. There was certainly a private chapel attached to the house; some of the original interior walls of the latter are wattled, though now covered by paper. The Huntley family has been there for many generations and I am thankful to say are still there. Boxwell is in the next valley to Tresham and takes its name from a large box wood, a sure find for foxes, where the box makes a gloomy covert of high trees all along the hill side, dark even in sunlight. An unusual and unexpected experience in painting Mr Huntley's portrait came about in this way: I had arranged a mirror behind me to reflect both the picture and the sitter as I wished. Mrs Huntley came in to inspect the portrait, which was nearly finished, and frankly mistook the reflection of the painting in the mirror for that of her husband until she saw my brush appear to touch it. This convinced her of the likeness of the portrait as nothing else could have done.

While we were living at Tresham my wife and I held an exhibition of work done there at the "Continental" Gallery in

Bond Street: it no longer exists, but was well known at the time. We called it "Flowers and fancies, facts and faces, round about Cherry Farm". My wife was responsible for the first and showed her set of flower panels illustrating the twelve months of the year, which was afterwards bought by Mrs Horniman for her house at "Garden Corner" in Chelsea. I showed most of my Gloucestershire types, besides landscapes in oil, pastel and water colour. Whistler honoured it with a visit; it was not long before his death and I think he was brought by Mrs Pennell; anyway, he was quite charming, and I venture to believe really interested in some of the things, from the way he spoke and looked into some of the work by both of us. He made no perfunctory tour; I have always held that, if Whistler believed a man serious, he would be quite serious too.

We had a good Press and the sales, though nothing to boast of, were satisfactory for our needs, and we were encouraged to go on.

A subject that excited some small interest at the time was my drawing showing a man working a breast-plough in the Cotswolds. Some people were sure that I had faked it, but this was not the case. I am not likely to forget how I looked over a stone wall one bleak March day and saw below me a man working with a breast-plough on the terrace of the hill-side beneath. It seemed like being put back into the Middle Ages. As a matter of fact, I found later that there were three breast-ploughs still in use in the village. They were brought out every year in the springtime to plant potatoes, a job for which they still proved to be useful. I afterwards bought the plough, together with the wooden "beaters" and "belt" that go with it. The man of eighty from whom I got it said he could remember twenty young men working abreast with these ploughs on the top of the Cotswolds, where the thin soil is suitable. It is the hardest work I ever saw and the man soon pours with sweat. I presented my plough to the Horniman Museum at Forest Hill, where they have made a collection of such relics.

Sometimes on my way back to Tresham from London I broke my journey at Reading to visit an old friend, Morley Fletcher, who had become head of the Art School there under a new scheme, by which it was made part of the new University College which was growing through the munificence of the Palmers, the family which had made a fortune in the town with their great biscuit factory. In this way I began to be interested in methods of teaching art. I had been intimate with Fletcher from his earliest steps towards art. He had begun life with a scientific training as an assistant to his father, who was Chief Inspector of Alkali Works, and was destined to follow in the parental footsteps. I fancy that, like Fry, he had his B.Sc. To the disgust of his parent he started off in this pursuit of art, a disreputable occupation and without prospects, but he would not be stopped. He had a first-rate brain for organization and all connected with it; but I fancy his scientific training always came in the way of his letting himself go freely, as must be the case for success in the emotional side of art. He made a name for himself with colour prints, however, done on wood in the Japanese manner; here his science became an advantage. He was moved from Reading to the Board of Education as an inspector of Art Schools, but did not like it, and moved from there to become the first Director of the new College of Art in Edinburgh. When within two years of a pension there, to the amazement of his friends, he resigned, to start a new kind of art scheme under the Carnegie Trust at Santa Barbara in California. As Pennell used to say, "When Fletcher puts his finger to his brow, we have the nonconformist conscience in being, and it becomes impossible to move him in committee or elsewhere." After a flourishing start in America he was let down badly when the slump came, but he is still there valiantly painting decorations and succeeding again.

His friendship was a valuable one to me and he persuaded me to write my book *Drawing*, published by Pitmans for a series he was editing. At least it helped me to formulate my ideas on the subject. It does not tell you how to do it because that, I am

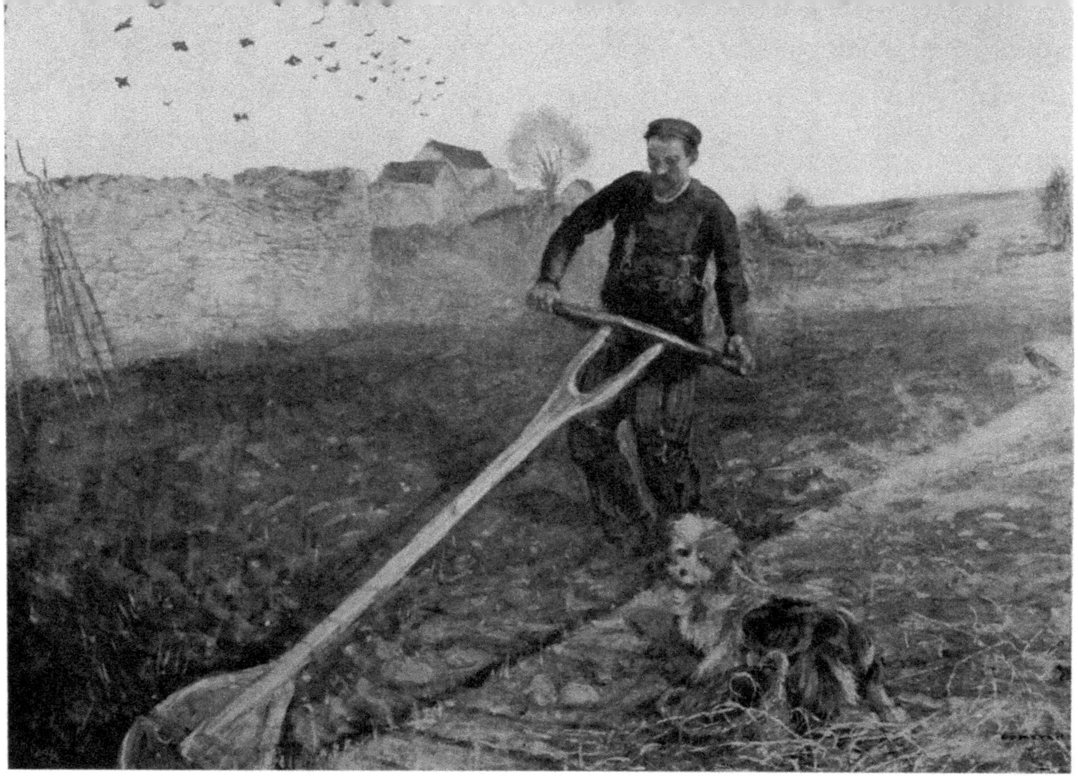

The breast plough

Water colour

convinced, is useless to attempt, but it does explain what drawing consists of, what to aim at and what are some of the pitfalls in its pursuit. It is now out of print.

My visits to Reading, moreover, had another result for me in after years, because I got to know Professor Alan Seaby, for many years head of the Art Classes of the University after Fletcher had left, and through him I used to pay an annual visit to Reading with W. R. Lethaby to examine students and grant diplomas. In this way my experience of the official management of art education as well as of the calibre of students themselves was much extended.

Finally, I was beginning to find out that the climate of Tresham in winter was too severe for my wife's health.

Such then were the facts, like straws blown by the wind, when some time in November 1907 I noticed an advertisement for a visiting teacher in head and costume painting at the L.C.C. School of Arts and Crafts, Camberwell. Unfortunately I possessed no diplomas or certificates of competence which are necessary on these occasions. I had never thought of teaching when a student and in Legros's time the Slade granted no diplomas. I had one experience of teaching when, at his request, I looked after a painting class in Glebe Place which Charles Furse used to visit, and carried it on for six months or so while he was away in South Africa for his health. In any case, I was forty-three years of age and thought I knew my business thoroughly, so was not specially nervous.

My next move was to get some testimonials of my capacity from artists of unchallenged position, and in this quest I was fortunate: Sir George Clausen, John Sargent, William Strang and Sir Charles Holroyd were all good enough to write testimonials and to promise their support.

Sir George Clausen has been one of my most valued friends from the first. No one has supported my efforts as an artist more generously and effectively.

Sargent I had known for a number of years through the New

English Art Club and at the Chelsea Arts Club. He was a very shy and reserved man considering his talents and his standing in the estimation of the world. Possibly this reserve was forced on him by his success as a portrait painter, though I can remember that he once said to me: "Every portrait is another enemy." This may have been in a heated moment, but it is true that towards the end he hated doing them or rather being forced to paint all and sundry. He took refuge with musicians, among whom were some of his most intimate friends, and he was a good musician himself. The efforts of those who to-day try to sneer away the position he won by his abilities will prove futile, though the reputation of one who has stood so high may fluctuate for a long time before it finds its precise level.

The end of it all was that I got the post at Camberwell, and as I had to take up my position early in January, we moved up to London at once, going into lodgings. But I still had a share in 8 Wentworth Studios as of old.

We had made our retreat from Arcady.

CHAPTER XVIII

LONDON AGAIN

It was now important to settle down in London with a permanent address. My tenure of 8 Wentworth Studios had for some time been insecure and I was liable to be turned out at three months' notice; because these sheds, for that is what they really were, together with the block of Trafalgar Studios, had been condemned and threatened with demolition for rebuilding at any moment.

To-day, thirty years after, they are still standing and going strong, while, by one of life's little ironies, Dorchester House, in Park Lane, to quote only one instance out of a multitude, which had been built at about the same time regardless of expense, to last at least 500 years, is demolished. In its place stands a huge hotel in modern taste, architecturally no more important than barracks. At the time, we certainly felt it was unsafe to depend any longer on this studio in Manresa Road; so my wife scoured Chelsea to discover a new home, but without success. After many disappointments she came upon 75 Clancarty Road, consisting of a comparatively new house and studio combined, beyond the "World's End" ("Where the angels are" as a facetious bus conductor used to announce it) and in the fastnesses of Fulham by Parson's Green. She feared I should find it too far from my new work at Camberwell, but as soon as I saw it no doubt remained to me that this was going to prove, in the Cockney tongue, a "bit of all right".

Parson's Green I already knew, because there, in a fine old house that formerly had belonged to William IV and Mrs Jordan, the actress, lived Theodore Roussel, a French painter and etcher of talent, with whom I had been acquainted for some years. This house must have been important in its day, with a large garden of which only a remnant remained; the interior decoration was admirable, with panelling, ceilings and brass work of first-rate quality, with the initials W. & J. worked in everywhere; in all of which Roussel took pride, though he lacked the money to restore them to their pristine splendour. The house has been sold, and, after being gutted of its fittings, has now become a girls' school under the Lady Margaret Beaufort Trust.

My new house and studio was not far from the Green, being built on the corner of the South Park, a recent gift to the Borough of Fulham by a Miss Sulivan, then living at Broom House; since her death this has been bought and incorporated with Hurlingham.

The last farm in Fulham stood, until after the War, at the end of Clancarty Road facing the park; and its last tenant, whose family had held it for two hundred years, died a fortnight after he left it! Its fields, with vegetables and fruit trees, stretched down to the river—indeed from my front door when the trees were in leaf you could see no more houses to the west, so that my friend Vereker Hamilton, the painter, named it "The last house in London"; to this day, in spite of new buildings all round, on account of the park alongside, it remains one of the most open spots left in town.

All this move, however, was not arranged in a day, and the house was not ready for us to enter until Easter 1908. Then I went down to Tresham alone for my Easter holiday to pack up everything there. Birchett, an old Chelsea character, who did most of the moving for artists—indeed he had moved my things to Tresham when I went there—came down with his vans and his sons, loaded up and took all my household belongings back to London, delivering them into the house in Fulham safely. Nothing could have been better managed. But my wife used often to say, with regret, that she had come up to London intending to stay there for a fortnight; she never saw Tresham again! She is now taking her last rest in the little God's acre about the church there, and it is my hope that my ashes will lie there too when my time comes.

To come now to Camberwell and my new work there. W. B. Dalton was my principal, a liberal-minded man, though trained on the old South Kensington system. I think I may claim that we got on well from the start, though some of the regulations in force seemed to me, as a newcomer, futile.

My engagement was for two days a week, two sessions a day; that is, from 10 to 1 and from 2 to 4.30, and I was engaged to give instruction in drawing and painting from the head, and drawing from the costume model for illustration or poster work, the latter being in connection with lithography and commercial art generally.

Although in the Paris of my time we were taught to draw altogether with charcoal, sometimes with a background as if we were painting, at Camberwell I returned to Legros's methods of teaching entirely with the point: and so pencils on white paper were the simple tools employed. By this time I was convinced that this is by far the best method of training pupils to draw. I also insisted on drawing by the character of the contour rather than the mass; it is the method of the old masters. The eye is very sensitive to convey and the hand to record the slightest variations in the outline, so the form, which is the object of all drawing, is more readily perceived, and so learnt. Again, this method does not favour mannerisms, which come from teaching methods of drawing in squares or by angles, phantoms that the incompetent and many amateurs love to pursue with fatal result to all real progress.

Although the basis of all good painting is drawing, the methods of thought which produce each work are different; in drawing you are working on a scale from black to white that has many more notes in it (so to speak) to arrive at complete modelling than in painting. In painting the gradation is from warm to cold colour or vice versa, the notes are fewer, and the effect of roundness will not be fully revealed until you stand well away from the painting, when the illusion becomes complete, though when close up you will perceive that the difference from light to dark pigment is very small.

There is a large nude back, part of a series of decorations by Paul Veronese, in the National Gallery, which illustrates these facts admirably. Cormon used to tell his pupils that Veronese is one of the old masters to choose for a teacher of the art of painting, and I should like to be told of a better example in the West. The most perfect examples I have seen of these facts in Eastern painting were exhibited in the Chinese Exhibition at Burlington House—four nearly life-sized heads depicting Genghis Khan and some of his relatives, painted on silk in the fourteenth century, apparently nothing but an outline with one tone, which varied slightly warm to cold: but the effect of roundness and solidity was amazing, and even the different quality of the skin of a young man compared with that of an old one was given. They were painted in a flat light without shadows. Such oppositions of warm and cold colour will be found controlling factors equally in chiaroscuro painting, whether by old masters like Rembrandt, Rubens and Velasquez or by the impressionists and post-impressionists of to-day, but it is a point which is seldom, in my experience, made plain to beginners, who flounder along in the dark asking "What colour shall I make this shadow?" or "How do I make that light?" If they once grasp the principles of warm and cold colours in opposition, most of this groping will be avoided.

Gauguin's advice to work with only three colours, a red, a yellow and a dark blue, on white paper, till the student gets the hang of these gradations, is a sound one.

The whole question of systems of teaching art in Government schools is again in the melting pot to-day. The man in the street, and many artists, are asking what is the use of them, when hardly anybody expects to make a living by painting pictures. Yet the longing for painting and sculpture lingers with a large proportion of men and women: there is no work in which man can lose himself with more perfect satisfaction, and many are willing to submit to incalculable hardships to be allowed to pursue it. Therefore, I believe, that no matter how mechanized the world becomes, art will never die out. At the same time there is much to be said for the view, to quote Gauguin again (an uncompromising but first-class brain), that there are only two kinds of artists, individualists and plagiarists, and the latter are there mainly for what they can get out of it commercially; so their work may be allowed to perish.

After twenty-five years of teaching and a working knowledge of the schools, I say frankly I believe that without the schools all knowledge of the handicrafts would be dead in a generation; and they are very difficult, if not impossible, to revive, as has been found even to-day when touch with the genuine old craftsmen has not been quite lost. Yet I am convinced that progress and invention are intimately connected with this training of the hand and eye; in the same way boat-sailing is now being revived for the training of officers in the navy and merchant service in the art of seamanship.

It is a parallel case with the so-called fine arts. All changes in painting that are permanent must arise out of the craft itself and not from theory, as is too often the case with those who seek short cuts to-day.

Not long after starting my teaching at Camberwell I had my experience of the educational field in art enlarged. Sir George Clausen, R.A., asked me to join the art advisory board of the Girls' Public Day School Trust, of which he was chairman. Professors Tonks and Selwyn Image were already on it, together with Vignoles Fisher. The idea was to draw up a syllabus which should be suitable for teaching art and aesthetics from a purely educational point of view in girls' schools. Clausen and Tonks designed a set of preliminary rules for the teaching of drawing in such schools, the aim of which, while including essentials, was to leave the mistresses a certain amount of freedom to exercise personal initiative in the direction wherein each felt she could get the best results. The object was to try to avoid that standardization which tends to become a slow death to all art. Some years later Thomas Derrick, who had experience in teaching at the Training College in Southampton Row, assisted us in a final amendment. This was accepted by the Education Committee of the Schools and sent to all the mistresses; with certain modifications it has remained in force to this day. Drawings by children make always a fascinating subject; the real difficulty is to teach them control without damaging the fresh interest and initiative which is always present in a healthy child. This can only be done by finding the right kind of mistress: that is, one who really can do what she teaches; indeed, the more accomplished she is herself as an artist the more valuable she will be, but she must also know how to teach. One of the best I have known said to me: "I am not afraid of the teaching. I can teach them anything: what I am afraid of is that I may teach them something wrong!" Such, I hold, is the creed of the born teacher, and she will take endless trouble to improve herself in the interests of her pupils, and they will respond marvellously. The other side must be stated also, that they will fall off equally rapidly in the hands of an indifferent or foolish one! I have come to see that the best results in such schools will be got by a mistress who combines sound drawing with a real flair for some craft that the children easily understand; and the best one for girls' schools, we have found, is embroidery. This must be taught thoroughly and progressively with no surrender to excuses for careless or slipshod work. To those who say there is no time for this, I reply that we have found that when properly taught the children do it as a pleasure in their own time. Where you have good embroidery a certain amount of taste will be found in the drawing also as time goes on, the fact being that in the craft the children have unconsciously learnt the necessity for selection and restraint in art.

This advisory board accomplished one thing at least, and I like to believe that it has been of permanent value to art education in this country: we persuaded the proper authorities to place all Secondary Schools on the roll of the Circulation Department of the Victoria and Albert Museum. This privilege had previously been reserved for the Art Schools proper.

This move put it into the power of all the art teachers in Secondary Schools throughout the country to borrow trustworthy models to set before their pupils. The suggestion originally came from Miss Beach, an excellent teacher of art in Putney High School, who complained to me of the lack of good models to set before her pupils and suggested that as the Art Schools had the right to borrow this sort of brain fodder the Secondary Schools might be permitted to gather up the crumbs that were left. I put her request into a report. Sir George Clausen at once saw the value of the idea and went to interview Sir Robert Morant, at that time head of the Museum and of the Board of Education. He was sympathetic, but, like most officials, feared it was impossible to do anything further because there was not enough material and no staff to handle such a scheme. Now Professor Image had recently been employed in sorting out thousands of excellent copies of objects and textiles in the Museum for which no use had been found. Here was the opportunity to use them. It took about two years for a scheme to mature, but one was finally evolved, and ever since it has proved, for those who know how to use it, most valuable for teachers in secondary schools.

In the spring of 1908 the stars must have been regarding me and my efforts with kindly eyes, though I cannot remember that my astrologer friend, H.M., advised me of it. Anyway, in March I was elected an Associate of the Royal Society of Painters in Water-Colours. I confess it has always been a matter of surprise to me how I managed to survive the searching tests, as I now see them, to which a candidate is called on to submit before election. All element of chance must be eliminated. Being frankly an individualist in art, painting just as I can and often not as I would, I must often, by my experiments, have shocked the eyes that guard the Society's portals. I fancy Clausen and Arthur Rackham, my proposer and backer, must have been bold to expect to persuade a majority to see that this work was certainly honest and that I did know my business. Once a member, you are free, the equal of any, having justified yourself as artist to the majority. A better set of friends and comrades I do not wish to meet, and now, as a veteran, I view the whole Society simply with affection, as a band of brothers working sincerely for the benefit of their art.

Water-colour is probably the oldest of all methods of mixing pigments, whether the binding elements be gum, egg, size or some oriental solvent; and it remains one of the most permanent, in that work done with it will be less changed by time from what the artist saw when he first laid his washes, than in any other medium of painting; always provided that the surface to which the pigments were applied was a sound one and has not been deteriorated by damp, or too long exposure to strong sunlight.

Water-colours are to be seen in our museums to-day, removed from temples or tombs in Egypt and China and especially from the lost cities of the Gobi Desert (which are reckoned to be anything up to 3000 years old), in which the colours have remained as bright and fresh as when first applied.

As for the ways in which water-colours can be used technically, they are almost as varied as the temperaments of the artists who use them. I see no sense in laying down rigid laws as to what is the right technique. What matters in the end is the result and that is decided by the artist. If he is competent, all will be well. The Chinese appear to have mastered the whole technique of water-colours from the earliest times, and their methods have been adopted and developed by the Japanese in particular with a skill that seems to leave nothing further to be discovered except that the perfection of the Chinese masters is inimitable. Indian and Persian painting also has been mainly in water-colours, so there remains no doubt that in water-colour artists of all nations of every degree of culture can find a perfect medium for all that they may wish to express.

In England until recently there was a curious popular superstition that water-colour painting was invented in this country; taking rise about 150 years ago, brought to its flower within two or three generations and since then fallen into a decline. I yield to nobody in my admiration of the work of Turner, Girtin, Cotman, and the founders of the old Water-Colour Society, but I would like to remind the forgetful that in Great Britain, at any rate, we had a school of illuminators from the eighth and ninth centuries A.D., beginning with the Book of Kells and the Lindisfarne Gospels, who understood the use of water-colour for their own purpose in a way that shows they were already supreme craftsmen in the medium. I myself would like to acknowledge that I have learnt much from a study of the Luttrell Psalter and other medieval manuscripts, such as "La Bible en images" belonging to the Earl of Leicester, with a picture of the Flood and the Raven returning to the ark, as original in design and as supernatural in colour as a Nativity by El Greco. These have mostly been worked without body-colour; but later, the use of body-colour became usual in nearly all Western illumination.

The question of the use of body-colour seems to me to have been settled by the medieval illuminators from the thirteenth century, I fancy because they found that it goes better with gold (which was not used in the earliest illuminations), and the colours in them could not have been more perfectly preserved. After these, we find development in the use of the medium in the surprisingly modern-looking landscapes by Albert Dürer, which are mostly dependent on transparent washes, as well as in gouache (miniature) portraits by Holbein, Hillard and the Clouets. And this brings me to a personal opinion in support of which I believe the above facts bear witness: that in figure painting in water-colour it is necessary to use gouache (i.e. body-colour) or else a pen line in order to keep the necessary control of form to suggest solidity.

The vagaries of fashion are inscrutable, but I should like to affirm my belief that, in spite of the present, or let us say recent, contempt for everything Victorian, nobody who has seen an English drawing-room in summer as I have, with chintz covers and water-colours by Walker, Pinwell and Birket Foster on the walls, or in winter, a room with a Morris paper and Pre-Raphaelite water-colours, will deny that such work in such settings was worth while. I am told by a friend that Mr Ruskin has said much the same thing; if so, *tant mieux*. I still believe that when he praised, as Sir Charles Holroyd taught me long ago, it is safe, nay wise to follow. This was an art of the home rather than of the gallery and we would be richer of the kind again to-day; but it is gone for ever, and no museums or stage plays can bring it back, though a breath of it remains in the pictures themselves, even when bereft of their proper setting..

My attention was first attracted to lithography as a medium to produce fine art by the appearance at irregular intervals of a little paper called *The Whirlwind*, which was sold for a penny in the streets, with pen drawings by Sickert and an occasional lithograph by Whistler. These latter had a novelty and charm which stood out at once in the rather drab surroundings of the period. The paper had been started by two young undergraduates, Erskine and Vivian by name, to air their youthful opinions, which were of a type more possible in Paris, where wit could be supported by the sword, than in this country, where it was more likely to be annihilated by the law of libel. The paper's efforts were certainly lively, but it perished soon after the institution of a ballot to discover and reward the ugliest man in London. George Moore's brother, Augustus, was in the lead for long, but was beaten on the post by an influx of supporters of the claims of Sir William Temple, an Anglo-Indian, prominent in the House of Commons of the time. After this the paper faded away from the streets, but the lithographs were not forgotten; they had been collected.

Then Macmillans, the publishers, experimented with *The Artist Engraver*, for which I did a lithograph, and at the same time Charles Shannon and Ricketts produced several lithographs in their occasional publication called *The Dial*, but the real effort to introduce lithography to artists did not come until F. E. Jackson returned from Paris and began to teach the whole craft of lithography in classes of the L.C.C. Art Schools. Before this, lithography was a commercial craft surrounded by secrets: its two sides, drawing and printing, being carefully separated in the lithographic trade shops. Now, as John Copley and his wife, Ethel Gabain, say, and have consistently and ably demonstrated in their practice, lithography is above all a printing medium; so the thrust towards perfection should be mainly from that centre. Jackson, with his classes, supplied the opportunity to learn all that was to be known about drawing on stone and about printing from it. In a few years there were a number of artists with their presses experimenting on their own behalf. In 1907 and 1908 Jackson, in partnership with Spencer Pryse, started *The Neolith*, a quarterly magazine in which both illustration and letterpress were lithographed. Nearly every artist in England who had done a lithograph contributed to it. I myself did two subjects for it before I left Gloucestershire, but probably the most attractive contribution from the collector's point of view (before it perished through having nobody to attend to its business side) was a short article in which Bernard Shaw describes football in Heaven. In spite of the decease of this magazine, it excited much interest among artists, especially those working in black and white.

Soon after I started work at Camberwell, where F. E. Jackson, among other schools, had a lithography class, we decided to call a meeting of all who were interested to form a society to advance the cause of lithography among artists. This was done at a fairly large gathering in Kerr Lawson's studio, Glebe Place, he being another of *The Neolith* artists who were enthusiastic. A nucleus in the form of a club was considered most suitable, and about a dozen artists, including several women, handed in their names on the spot. E. J. Sullivan named it after Senefelder, the founder and inventor of the craft, so once more the name of its originator was bound up in the fortunes of lithography. Inquirers often question the "why" of the name, so here is the history of its adoption.

Joseph Pennell was away from London at the time of this meeting, but he had begun writing a book on the history of lithography for the centenary of Senefelder's death and had made a lithograph for *The Neolith*, so his interest was engaged. On his return to London in 1909 he became one of the four founder members of the Club, namely, Jackson, Lawson, Pennell and Hartrick, and soon he began to make things move. First, the founder members bought a second-hand press and rented a studio in Chelsea, in which members were enabled to work for a small fee. Some experiments were made, enough to show that the scheme was feasible; but, like all artistic plans that need continued effort for a long period, it failed on the administrative side when enthusiasm had died down, and after a year was abandoned. An arrangement, however, was made with Vincent Brooks, Day and Son, an old firm of lithographers in Holborn, by which they became printers to the Club, and for a time space was set aside there for members to work and to keep stones on the premises. This worked better for a while.

Pennell now became President of the Club; and later, John Copley was elected the first honorary secretary: they both worked enthusiastically. A set of rules was drawn up and passed, and arrangements were made for the first exhibition at the Goupil Gallery, Regent Street, in January 1910. The standard to be aimed at was high, so from the first the Club's shows were international in character.

From now on Pennell used his marvellous powers of drive to enhance the prestige of the Club in Europe and America, with the result that this small club, in four years, became known through its exhibitions at home and abroad in a way that surprised everybody. Through his introduction of the "lay-member" print, by which subscribers of one guinea received a proof lithograph drawn by a member, which could not be obtained elsewhere, a body of collectors called "lay-members" were enlisted in support of the Club, and this method continues to this day. Thus all went forward swimmingly until the War came and for a time relegated the Club and all art to obscurity. But it is not my concern to give a history of the Club here.

A few episodes may be allowed to show how this connection with the Senefelder Club affected my life.

One of the first came about at the Coronation of King George V in June 1911. Pennell had interested Mr (afterwards Sir Robert) Donald, Editor of *The Daily Chronicle*, in a scheme to commemorate the Coronation festivities with a set of lithographs by members of the Club, to be published first in the daily paper as zinc blocks, and later in a portfolio as lithographs for a memorial of it all. MacLure Hamilton and Jackson were selected to do portraits of the King and Queen, while Brangwyn, Sullivan, Copley, Pryse, Pennell and myself were allotted various subjects. The one that fell to me was the last turn-out of the remnants of the Light Brigade (Balaclava Charge), saluting H.M. King George V in Fleet Street.

Some weeks beforehand, I was sent by car from the office of the paper to visit and draw portraits of such of the survivors as were living in or near London. Some were very feeble, and the trumpeter who sounded the charge indignantly refused "to be made an exhibition of", as he wrote. In this way I made drawings beforehand of six who were guaranteed to be equal to the occasion. On the actual day I was stationed in a ground-floor window of *The Daily Chronicle* office in Fleet Street and made sketches of the background in colour, and finally saw the veterans brought out from *The Daily Mail* office opposite, ten minutes before King George was to pass. The youngest was seventy-eight and the oldest eighty-seven, so it is not surprising that one or two turned faint and had to retire; but the majority were of tough material still. A ragged line they made in spite of a stiff effort at martial "attention". Many had the mutiny and other medals besides the Crimean, and their worn old faces were whiskered in the fashion of Commanding Officers of their time—Havelock, Outram, Lintorn Simmonds and such like—and some gave their salute in the old manner with the hand upright rather than horizontal. I am glad to say that a drawing which I made afterwards of the scene now hangs in the United Service Institution (presented by the purchaser), lit by the window through which King Charles I went to his death.

The Underground poster, as it was known for years, and its method of display in sets, belong to this period, being the result of a meeting between F. E. Jackson, with his technical knowledge, and Mr Frank Pick, at that time advertising manager of *The Underground*. No combination could have been happier, because Mr Pick had a more sympathetic intelligence in using art and artists effectively for his business than any other man I have known. A series of posters to advertise the railway was commissioned from members of the Senefelder Club. Brangwyn, Anthony Baker, Jackson, Pennell, Pryse and myself were each given a definite subject, and the set of six was designed to be set up together in all the stations at one date.

"Morris dancing" was the rage at that time, having just been revived in connection with Cecil Sharp's efforts to collect old folk music, so "Morris Dancers" was the subject that fell to my lot, and I designed a poster in colours with four printings.

This was really the first poster I ever executed as a commission, but twelve or fifteen years previously I had been responsible for the hanging of the first poster exhibition ever held in England, and moreover I wrote the preface for the catalogue. It was held in the old "Aquarium" at Westminster, where the Central Hall now stands, and was organized by a very enterprising agent of that time called Edward Bella, who had connections with "Lemercier", the chief lithographic printers in Paris. It was through Bella that, besides English posters, we had submitted to us a wonderful collection of the best French posters, including work from Cheret, Forain, Lautrec, and Steinlen.

The old "Aquarium" was an admirable setting and I doubt if there has ever been a better show of the kind in London. Raven Hill, Dudley Hardy and G. R. Halkett were on the Committee with me, if I remember rightly.

When this set of Senefelder posters appeared all together, they had an admirable effect and were noticed far and wide, both in the Press and by individual critics. The actual poster, however, that had most effect in giving a special *cachet* to *The Underground* poster was the large 60 in. × 40 in. poster by Spencer Pryse of workers going to their work, which he called "The Workers' Way": this, it has always seemed to me, is one of the best posters both as propaganda and as art that has been done anywhere.

My own lithograph of "Morris Dancers" also brought me a number of letters, among them one from Mr Percival Lucas, the Editor of *Folklore*, a delightful man who was full of information on matters in which I also delighted. One day, in the week before the War was declared, he came to see me and danced a whole morning for me as model for a drawing. Alas! I never saw him again, for he was killed at the battle of the Somme, but after the War his brother, E. V. Lucas, called to see me about that drawing. I made a replica for him, and the original drawing now hangs in the Folk Dance Society building, which they have put up to Cecil Sharp's memory, in Regent's Park.

CHAPTER XIX

THE WAR YEARS

There has been no more tumultuous upheaval in the art world of my time, at any rate in England, than that caused by the first Post-Impressionist Exhibition held at the Grafton Galleries from 8 November 1910 to 15 January 1911, and rumblings from it continue to this day. It will be well to note the title of it, "Manet and the Post-Impressionists", because Manet as the acknowledged leader of the successful revolt of the Impressionists from Academies was already a name to conjure with in the picture-dealing world; his works had a definite value in the market-place and money speaks a universal language; his name was there to justify this new revolt. A glance at the catalogue shows that the promoters of the exhibition were not sure of their ground. The names of the Hon. Committee have an asterisk referring to a footnote in italics below, which reads: *The ladies and gentlemen on the Hon. Committee, though they are not responsible for the pictures, by lending their names are good enough to give the project their general support.* Roger Fry, Professor (afterwards Sir Charles) Holmes and Sir Lionel Cust (Keeper of the King's pictures) are the chief names on the executive committee which brought the pictures from Paris, where they and their painters had been well known for years. Robert Dell of Paris had a preliminary show of some of them a year before at Brighton, where the Curator at the time, Mr Roberts, was much more enterprising than most officials.

As I have said, a few of the exhibitors had had work hung in exhibitions of the International Society, but most of the names and pictures were quite new to London.

At first they were all treated as a joke, but they soon began to create a stir. The Galleries were crowded every day with newcomers eager to see for themselves; sides for or against were taken up violently, and as little else was talked of in fashionable circles for weeks, the show was a success.

To mention a personal recollection, I met at the private view McLure Hamilton in correct morning dress, with two equally fashionable ladies, one of whom had her handkerchief stuffed in her mouth to try to restrain her mirth before Gauguin's painting of Adam and Eve (in the South Seas). His theme, "and they knew that they were naked", was presented with a frankness that in all probability would have produced a demand for the removal of the picture, but for a suspicion of the comic that might make objectors look foolish themselves. Anyway, in the rest of the Exhibition there were other canvases as disconcerting in other ways. Some good people were scared and thought the end of the world must be at hand. Opinions on the pictures varied fanatically, but the majority suspected a "plant". The introduction to the catalogue by Desmond MacCarthy explained this disconcerting effect by asserting that a good rocking horse has more of the true horse about it than a photograph of a Derby winner. I doubt if any horse-expert, stable-man or jockey would agree with that, and it is their job to know!

Painters of every school were equally divided. John Sargent, who by actual contact probably knew more about European art of all ages than anybody else in London, though his views on these moderns may have been coloured by what he heard from his friend Claude Monet, wrote that Gauguin was "a good decorator and his colour fine". Apparently he was not much impressed by any of the others, but ten years before this, I had heard him speak of Cézanne as "a strange and interesting painter".

I attended a crammed meeting of the Art Workers' Guild in their old hall, Clifford's Inn, where papers were read on these pictures and the usual violent discussions followed. W. R. Lethaby was Master and in the chair. Unfortunately I cannot remember his attitude at the time, but I knew him well in after years. He had one of the most acute brains, touching every side of art, that I have known, but from his affection for Gothic and medieval wall-paintings I believe he would understand what some of these men were after. His definition of art is the one I like best. "Art is doing the right thing in the right way, and beauty is the evidence of it." As one of the few present who had actually seen and spoken to the painters of these surprising pictures I was asked to say something, and I endeavoured to give an idea of what I thought they aimed at. Old J. W. North of the Royal Society of Painters in Water-Colours was also asked to speak; he would only say that he was very sorry for Van Gogh and thought they ought not to have let him out of the asylum!

One further personal reminiscence. I met Alan Seaby, who had become Professor of Art at Reading, in the Exhibition and at his request conducted him round it. He was so interested that he arranged for me to give a set of lectures to his pupils at Reading on the subject of Modern Painting, and the lectures some years later were published in *The Imprint*, after which J. H. Mason, the head of the printing department at the L.C.C. Central School, who was interested by them, set them up in a little book with the aid of his class, and a few copies were printed and bound at the School for private circulation.

It would be interesting to have a priced catalogue of that Exhibition to-day, to see how the values have moved. I only know the price set on one picture that I had been requested to inquire about. This was "The Rain" by Van Gogh, and the price then asked was £75. I saw it again last year in London, I am not sure whether "sold" or not, but the price was £5000, and there are pictures by him quoted higher than that.

A second Post-Impressionist Exhibition at the Grafton followed a year or thereabouts before the War. It was not so interesting as the first by a long way, being full of Cubism, Futurism and other "isms", most of them merely stunts, and dead or moribund to-day.

Among my best friends were Sir Dugald and Lady Clerk, now

alas both dead. Sir Dugald was the ablest man all round that I have ever been intimate with. Though his own subject was the internal combustion engine, there was little in life on which he could not speak with authority if he wished or could be persuaded to. Lady Clerk used to say that he liked talking to artists as it gave him a change of thought. Certainly, though he did not profess to know anything of the practice of painting, I have been surprised to note how readily he understood the intention and possibilities when I explained to him various theories and experiments which were present in modern movements. I made a drawing of him once, to commemorate for Lady Clerk a dinner which was given to him after the great case which gave victory to the Marconi patents in wireless over the American interests in the same. Clerk told me he had had a battle with the others engaged in the Marconi interests before the case came on, for he told them that if they followed a course suggested, they would lose the case. At last he had his way, with the satisfactory result of victory, after which Marconi said to him: "I believe, Clerk, you know more about wireless than I do." "Not at all," was his reply, "but I know more about the law."

In any case, Lady Clerk thought I had made him too fierce-looking. But I had been specially to see him speaking in action. Clerk was a Highlander. His people came from Loch Fyne side, he told me, and he was a "bonny fechter" as they say, when put to it. This drawing was done in coloured chalks and shows him making an important experiment in connection with his engine. I am glad to say that the drawing is now in the National Portrait Gallery of Scotland.

He was a good friend and patron to me in other directions also, buying several paintings, one of which, called "The Kirking of the Incorporated Trades of the Borough of Kirkcudbright", was bequeathed by him to the town of Kirkcudbright. It shows the procession of all the trades in the town to church on a certain day in autumn.

I can remember nothing of outstanding interest in art for the year before the War. True, Pennell believed the Golden Age for art was at hand again, and he was making things hum. He had made his Panama lithographs and had served on the San Francisco Exhibition jury as well as a hundred other bodies. In England we were under the shadow of the Home Rule Question —Ireland was in the foreground again. Ulster had refused to be coerced and everything seemed to be working up for civil war. There was the trouble at the Curragh when General Gough and others sent in their papers rather than fight against their fellow-countrymen. We were nearer then to what has since happened in Spain than we realized or can know even yet.

Spencer Pryse, ever since his "Workers' Way" poster, had been sought after by those who wanted a novel and striking method of propaganda. His secret was to use a little real art, but no one suspected it. I went to see him about this time: he was doing a series of posters for Ulster. One big upright one was called "The Widows of Ulster" and showed a dead man, with a gun, at the feet of an impassioned widow calling vengeance down from the skies; in addition there was a triptych with armed men on the march—the defenders of Ulster—with an ambulance in the centre panel. All very striking; indeed, I doubt if Pryse has ever done anything more dramatic. He had just been visited by a noble lord, a member of the Ulster Committee, who complained that the figure in the poster with the widow "had not the majesty of death". It was never actually displayed on the hoardings—one of life's little ironies again. We had escaped civil war by the skin of our teeth, only to plunge into a European War—but even that was the lesser of two evils.

By the end of September 1914 I was back in London and at work, teaching at the L.C.C. Central School of Arts and Crafts in Southampton Row. I had arranged to be transferred there in July, partly because it was the chief school under the Council, and partly because it was nearer to my home.

F. V. Burridge was the principal and I had several friends

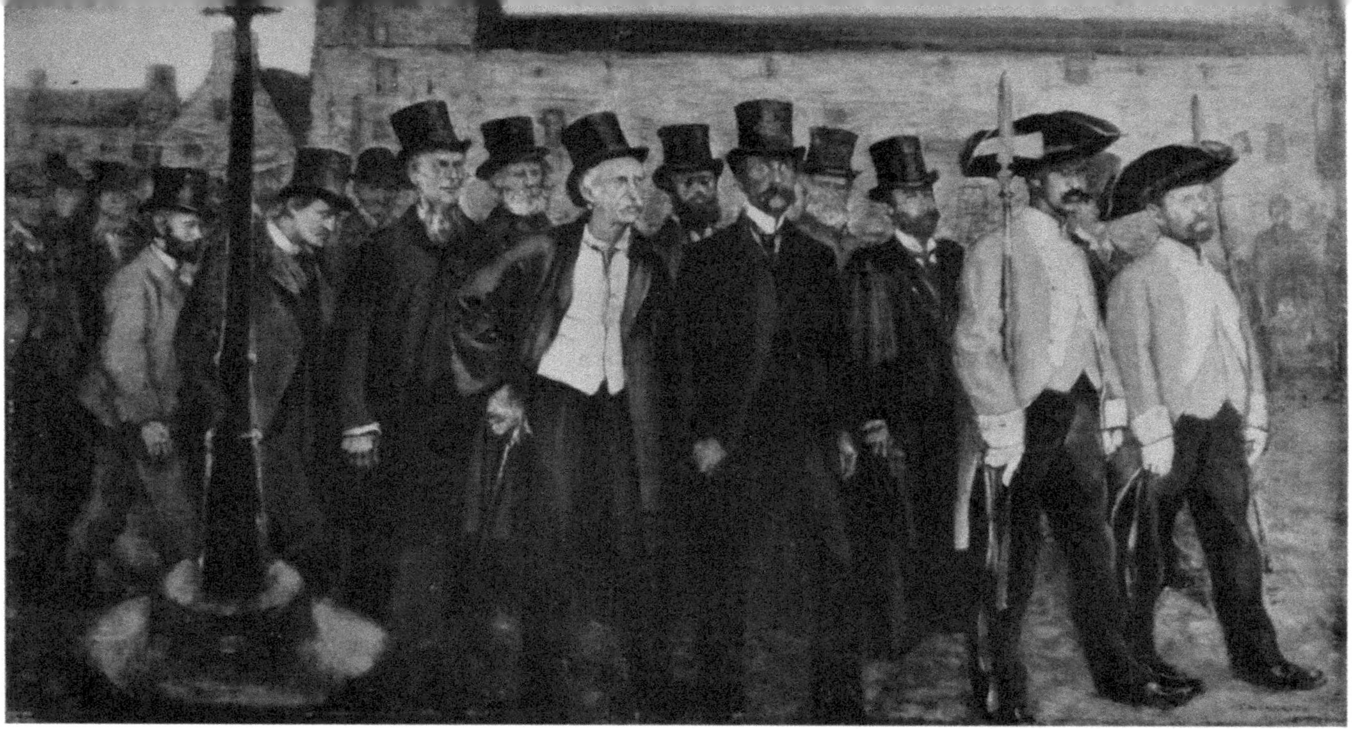

W. B. MacGeorge, R.S.A. ↑ E. A. Hornel ↑ James Aitken, nephew of Carlyle ↑ William Mouncey ↑ Provost ↑ Javelin men ↑

The Kirking of the Incorporated Trades of the Borough of Kirkcudbright

Oil painting

By permission of the Provost and Town Council of Kirkcudbright

on the staff, but I continued at Camberwell as well, until Christmas.

The enlistment for Kitchener's army, as it was called, was in full swing, so like the rest of those about me I tried to get something to do with the War, but I was far over age and had no special knowledge that could be used at such a time. I had two interviews with authorities, both of whom turned mé down while advising me to stick to my teaching, that being the most useful thing I could do. The School was still full of boys and girls, and their wants had, of course, to be served, war or no war.

My evening life class at the Central was always extraordinary, as much for the variety of trades represented as for the types of people to be found in it. The class-rooms were at the top of the building and one of my duties was to see that everybody was cleared out of them and conducted to certain passages in the lower levels as soon as warning of an air-raid had been given.

Nor was it very long before I had my first experience of this sort of excitement, although we had an idea of what to expect by what had happened at Antwerp.

The first air raid I remember as occurring on one of my evenings at the School was the coming of the Zeppelins in 1915, when bombs were dropped in a line from near the Lyceum, at the bottom of Kingsway, and across Lincoln's Inn Fields to Chancery Lane. Among those working in my evening class was a man called Bray, who painted miniatures for a hobby and in the day-time was a patent agent with a flat in Chancery Lane. He had drawn the specifications for Admiral Sir Percy Scott's "dotter" to control the shooting with big guns and now the Admiral was in charge of the defence of London.

Bray was absent from my class on the night of this raid but came along on the next, with plenty to say about it. His flat was high up in Chancery Lane, nearly opposite to the entrance to Lincoln's Inn. He was entertaining a few friends there when the alarm was given, and he heard the explosion of the bombs as they were dropped coming across from Kingsway. He even heard the whistle of a bomb falling as it came down into Chancery Lane beside him. All lights went out and some of his crockery was broken by the explosion.

Among his friends in the flat was one who had just been sworn in as a special constable. This man bolted off downstairs to see what he could do, and Bray followed him. When they got to the door all the lamps were out and water was rushing down the Lane with the wood paving, which was torn up, afloat in it—a bomb had just burst the main. A little farther down the road an incendiary bomb was blazing on the pavement. The special constable, seizing two blocks of wood from out the water, rushed up and with their aid pushed the bomb (which was enclosed in a sort of wire cage about four feet high) into the gutter, where the water put it out, or rather put out the flaming tow in which it was wrapped. Fortunately, the thermite was not yet ignited or it would not have been possible to extinguish it. When the flame was out the two men took the bomb out of the water, and though still warm, carried it up into the flat with a view to examining it fully. This action has always appeared to me astonishing, because Bray was to some degree expert and I suppose should have hesitated to bring a bomb into the building. However, that is what he did, the reason probably being that it was pitch dark in the street. They certainly did not see that the gate-keeper of Lincoln's Inn just opposite to them had been killed by the explosion.

Bray kept the bomb in his flat for two days, then wrote to Sir Percy Scott to tell him that he had got it. The next thing that happened was that an inspector of police came along in a hurry and removed the bomb in a taxi for examination.

One more incident remains to be reported. After a fortnight or so Bray wrote to Sir Percy asking if he might have his bomb back as a souvenir. I saw the reply to it. It ran: "The bomb is an exceedingly dangerous one: it has been sent to Shoeburyness for destruction."

The night of that raid had still other things in store for me. After it was over I had to take a number of girls to Holborn Tube Station, accompanied by several men students. When I got to the station they wished to go to the bottom of Kingsway to see what had happened there. Everything was still in darkness but just then an ambulance came along with lights full on, ringing its bell wildly. My friends followed it. One of them was an Australian, who had just returned for the War from Bolivia, where he had been working as an engineering chemist in the great silver mines of the Incas, which are still being worked. He was a dry, hard-bitten little man, with only one eye. When I inquired next evening what he had seen, he replied, "Not much—there were two great holes and in one of them a man striking matches, looking for a bit of bomb as a souvenir. I smelt gas so I came away!" Is not this a perfect picture of the unimaginative Briton?

As for the Underground, it was packed full, mostly with Italians from Saffron Hill, Clerkenwell—men, women and children lying in heaps, some of them hysterical. A few boy scouts were keeping order.

Besides this I saw several other raids, including the two daylight raids with aeroplanes. In the first of them I was taking "life" at the Central in the day-time. When the alarm went, my duty was to see all students off that top floor. I looked out of one of the windows towards Red Lion Square in which direction there was an explosion. I could not see any planes but there was plenty of noise. A bomb had come down on a school in a street quite near the Square.

On the other occasion I was in the New King's Road not far from Stamford Bridge when the second daylight raid by aeroplanes occurred. This time I saw the planes quite clearly. They were being attacked by some of our own planes, I believe, and looked just like swallows twisting about in the air, back and forward and up and down. I took refuge in a private garage that was open, but cleared out quickly as the gas-works as well as

Lots Road power station were not far off and I thought the enemy might make for them if they were returning.

The ammunition lorries were all parked in the South Park just beside my house in Fulham, so whenever there was a raid we knew of it at once, for all the lorries went out, and all through the raid a gun mounted on a lorry patrolled up and down at the end of the road by Hurlingham. We found some pieces of shell dropped near us, but fortunately no bomb. I suppose the parking place was never spotted by the enemy, and anyhow, all lorries were away from there during the raid. But the fact remains that it was too much for my wife, and she had a nervous breakdown after the War.

The worst explosion of the War, at any rate in this country, was that in Brunner Mond's Works at Silvertown. They were making high explosives, and the destruction from it extended across the river and for miles round. I heard the noise in the Central School, Southampton Row, about six miles away. By a curious chance I knew these works quite well, because from a lofty platform above them in July 1914 I had painted a picture of the lower Thames looking across to Woolwich and Shooters Hill—one of those pictures I painted for Sir Dugald Clerk's new house at Ewhurst in Surrey. I called it "Flood tide". Every portion of the works, I am told, was levelled to the ground, and for a radius of two or three miles an earthquake might have wrecked the neighbourhood, while windows were broken fifteen miles away, as far as Streatham.

Some time early in 1915 I answered a ring at the door to find Spencer Pryse on the doorstep in khaki: he told me he had just recovered from a shrapnel wound in the lung received before Christmas after an exciting time as a despatch carrier between the Belgian Government and our own, during which he had been present at the siege of Antwerp and the battle of the Marne; then back and forward until the line settled into stability in the Ypres sector. Now he had been invalided out and was being turned into a War artist, a change he did not much care for.

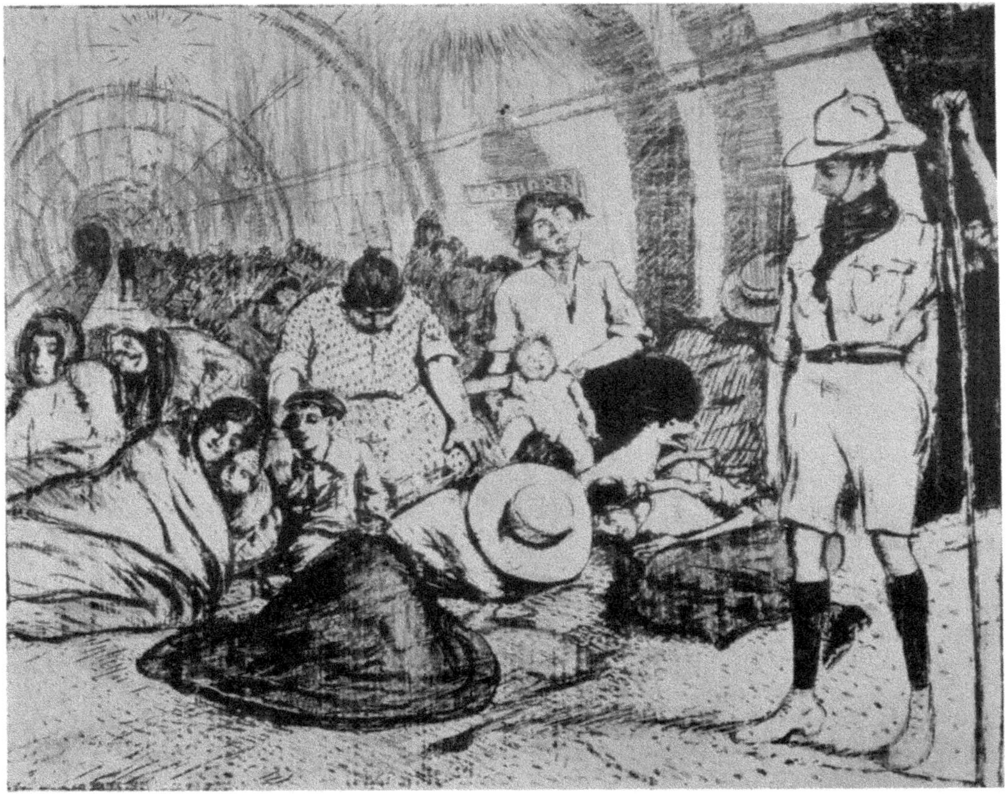

Underground in an air raid

Lithograph

Pryse is one of the few men I have known who enjoyed the War. He held that an artist should be able to fight as well as any other man and certainly bore it out. Within a few months he was back in the fighting line as an officer to undergo all sorts of trials in the trenches, through Paschendaele, from the mud of which he managed to emerge unscathed, in spite of the fact that his regiment, the "Post Office Rifles", was nearly wiped out there. He finished up with the retreat of the 5th Army, in which he got another wound, in the arm, that ended his fighting days. Only the good luck of being on the French side of the Ourc, he explained, had saved him from becoming a prisoner.

At the time of this visit to me he was hard at work finishing his first set of War lithographs. So far as I am competent to judge, these contain the most convincing records of the War in English art that I know. He actually drew the key-stones of some of them on the spot, from the back of a motor car. The "Railway Station at Ostend" is well known, but the "Northumberland Yeomanry in Ghent", with a crowd of refugees in the foreground, a stone on which he was drawing ten minutes before the German advance guards entered the city, is even more dramatic. My vote, as to which plate of the set is best, remains divided between this and that of a Senegalese private looking for wounded with a paper lantern on the battlefield of the Marne. A little later, with William Strang, I was hanging this set of lithographs in the Exhibition of the International Society. In the midst of our work Strang stopped and said: "But these are paintings on stone, not drawings", and it is true that they had a new note in them, which had not been seen in lithography before. He invented this technique. Their quality as art has not, I consider, been properly appreciated yet, though I can affirm that of all the works shown by the Senefelder Club in exhibitions on the Continent before the War, Pryse's lithographs excited most interest and were regularly bought for public galleries. So here I would like to salute his talent before I pass on.

As time went on, a number of artists were sent to the front to make records of the fighting or drawings to be used as propaganda by the Government. The results are to be seen in the War Museum to-day.

At length I was called on to do my bit in this direction. Thomas Derrick, who was editing the illustrations of a paper for the Ministry of Propaganda under Charles Masterman, drew up a scheme by which Britain's work and ideals in the War should be illustrated in a series of lithographs, to be called "British Work and Ideals", by a number of well-known British artists. Brangwyn, Bone, Clausen, Kenington, Nevinson, Pears, Rothenstein, Shepperson and Hartrick were selected to do "Work" and Brangwyn, Clausen, Dulac, Greiffenhagen, John, Moira, Nicolson, Rothenstein, Shannon and Sullivan to do the "Ideals" in a series of Posters. F. E. Jackson was in general charge of production.

"Women's Work", a series of six subjects to show what varied work women were doing in the War, was the portion that fell to me. A number of subjects was selected and I was sent to make the studies for the lithographs on the spot.

In most cases women were doing work which was usually done by men, and doing it well. What I remember as being characteristic of the point of view of nearly all the men in charge of machinery (and of course nearly all the work was done by machinery) was that they wondered what would happen when the men returned from the War to take up their work again. Most of the women did their work well and in some cases, it was said, stood the monotony of doing only one thing better than men. There would be trouble, these experts feared, except for the aristocrats of engineering, the gauge and tool-making men, without whom even the machine could not function at all.

Mrs Hewlett, who was one of the first women who learned to fly in England, was running an air-factory in collaboration with a Frenchman. She told me that the best all-round women workers in her experience were women who had been housemaids. Is this one reason why these latter are so scarce to-day?

One of the most interesting models I drew was brought to me from packing T.N.T. The work was so dangerous that I was not allowed to enter the hut itself, in case a nail in my boots or anything like that might cause a spark. She was a very pretty girl, though her hair and face were stained yellow with the chemicals, but she would not wear the sort of metal snout that had been supplied to workers. She preferred to tie a napkin over her mouth and nose; that was more comfortable, she said.

Another girl who attracted my attention was working at aeroplane engines. She was the daughter of a colonel and her mother was working beside her. Her devotion to work and her skill were remarkable, so that the chief engineer pointed her out as "one of the most faithful". When at the private view of all these lithographs at the Fine Art Society Galleries in Bond Street she, a fashionably dressed young lady, came up to speak to me, I did not know her without her overalls and hair tightly swathed in a silk handkerchief. Yet I fancied I had an eye that would not readily be betrayed.

These lithographs in sets of six were given to all the great museums of the Allied countries, and were also sold separately or in sets after exhibition in the same.

The spirit in which his pupils return to him in after years is often a source of joy to a teacher. Already several of those who had been with me at Camberwell called to see me on their return from the front, sometimes wounded or maimed.

One of the most interesting to me was young David Jones, who returned from the Somme, wounded at Mametz Wood. I had known him as a very small boy in knickerbockers, of Welsh nationality and a worshipper of Lloyd George, who was fished out from under a tram car one morning, fortunately uninjured. Now matters were more serious and he was still in hospital-blue, recovering from a wound in the leg. That wound was received under circumstances that almost developed into comedy, for he told me that Mametz Wood, which had been wired by the Germans, had then been shelled so that the tops of all the trees were cut off, and these, fallen, made an almost impenetrable thicket. In this Jones found himself lost, without knowledge of direction, hampered by his wounded leg and worried by terrifying noises. In the end he discovered that he and his colonel were stalking one another with rifles ready. He has gone far since then in art, and as a writer, chiefly in pursuit of the abstract, but as his first instructor I remain convinced that he is an incurable romantic.

In the summer of 1918 one of the inevitable catastrophes of life befel me—my mother died. She was seventy-five, full of years without being old. All her life she had enjoyed perfect health and did so up to a week before the end, which came in sleep. It could not have been more merciful.

"What I gave, I have", might have been her motto through life, for giving help, money, energy was her way, though I doubt if she ever thought about it. I am thankful to think that I never had a difference with her, though her temperament—half Highland, half Welsh—was wholly Celtic, enthusiastic with exaggerations, not cautious and reserved like my own. I suppose she would have been better pleased if I had gone into the Navy, for which I had a nomination, at the right time, and as originally planned; or if I had become a doctor later. But she eagerly supported my desire to be an artist, against the advice of the schoolmasters, who opposed it.

I think it was the milkman who brought us news that the War had ended. The maroons went off when it was officially announced, but there were no wild or noisy rejoicings as after Mafeking: like a nightmare, the War sat on the heads of everybody, and it seemed as if we would never be rid of it, but at last it had passed, and for long nobody appeared to care to recall any thoughts of it.

CHAPTER XX

THE PEACE AND AFTER

My first important work after the Armistice was to finish a portfolio of lithographs, a commission from the "Underground", to record the "War Work" of their people during the last four years. It was modelled somewhat on the lines of the one I had done on "Women's Work" for the Government. This time twelve types of workers had been chosen for illustration. Here again in the majority of cases women were doing work formerly reserved for men. Therefore I designed each print to show the work being done here, as superimposed on a scene at the War, in which the original workers were shown in their present environment engaged in military jobs. By the expedient of using two printings I could make the difference between the two places clearer.

For instance, I drew some women painting the station at Hammersmith, superimposing it on a subject with men camouflaging a tank at the front. When making studies for the former I was amused when one of the women in overalls went to a cupboard to fetch out several caps of differing shapes but matching the overalls, that I might decide which would be most becoming to her.

The quiet of Clancarty Road was interrupted and a small sensation created, when a motor-bus drew up at my front door to serve me for a model, together with its driver, one of the oldest in the company. Another important sitter was the Underground's V.C., for they had one at least. At ordinary times he was a platelayer.

After the war these portfolios, with a New Year Greeting, were sent to the managers and chief officers of railways all over the world. They seemed to be appreciated, to judge by the great sheaf of letters sent to me afterwards by the company.

But I must return to the Central School and my teaching: from this time on teaching was to be my chief activity in life. For a time a new type of student had appeared out of the tumult of the War; and I sometimes wondered if this was but another phase of what a Japanese friend had been seeking in his travels. He had been sent to Europe, officially, to report to his government the effects of the War on the art of each country he had visited. These students were older, and most of them had served through the War on various fronts: they came from various callings, and some from the Colonies, with scholarships to study art, in a three years' course. Some of these men were a study in themselves, and I took as much from them as I could give. I make no pretensions to any novelty in teaching, but I have done my best to teach my pupils their jobs thoroughly, so that they can make a living by it afterwards—not too much "high falutin'" talk about art and self-expression, as was threatening to be the rule. Recollections of many of these pupils remain with me; and though some, or even all, may not yet have made themselves notable in the public eye, some I am convinced will do so, and a few remarks about them may be worth while.

After many years of teaching art I am convinced there is no one way of reaching your goal. All men are different; what may open a road to one may close it to another. Some verses by Kipling in the old *National Observer* on the art of writing verse have the truth of it: I quote from memory:

> There are nine and sixty ways
> Of constructing tribal lays,
> And every single one of them is right,

that is, for the man who knows how to pull it off. At the same time I hold that it is best to teach one method of drawing thoroughly (it matters not which) in connection with some craft; this will ensure no nonsense about self-expression, because the craft will not permit it. When one method has been mastered, the pupil may experiment on his own in any direction he may wish, giving rein to self-expression, because the early training will have taught him to recognize bounds. My pupils, friends of my teaching I will call them, make up, after all, most of the pleasant memories of my life as an artist. From some of them, who are abroad, I hear at least once a year, often telling me in detail of their work, with its success or difficulties: that I count real pleasure, though the Benjamin Jowetts may still say that "artists are dull dogs". There was, for instance, Edmonde de Celle: his father is a French Canadian and his mother a Danish music-hall singer—himself a splendid looking man. Before the War he was helping his father on a melon farm in Alabama, but his goal was to be a painter and not a farmer. A sense of humour helped him on his way—soon after his arrival he wrote to a very serious little art student here "that he was crossing bees with fireflies in order to get them to work by night as well as day" and incidentally enrich his parent so that he would let him go back to painting! Not long after, having spent a night and a day hanging on to a corner of the house in a tornado which wrecked the melon farm, he was released by his father and went to Mobile, the nearest town. From there he wrote to me to advise him whether he should go to New York and start life in a studio there or remain where he was. Greatly daring, I advised him to stay in Mobile, for he was pretty well trained for making a living. Also, as he had initiative and originality, I thought he might do better in the south than as a member of a cosmopolitan crowd in New York, thinking only to copy the latest fashions in art for success. In a few years he wrote again that he was doing well. There is a chain of little islands in the Gulf of Mexico off Mobile, a veritable fairy land. The inhabitants, who are largely of French extraction, have a water pageant every year connected with the islands. De Celle organized the setting and decoration of this pageant with boats and cars. In six months' time, with the aid of half a dozen assistants, he painted and arranged all that was wanted, setting it afloat at the appointed hour. By these means he made enough money in the six months to allow him to paint landscapes, portraits, or whatever pleased him best during the remaining half-year, and so it continued for many years, until the slump in 1930. Another of his activities consisted in designing and painting scenery for an actor friend with a repertory company, which played in an immense tent. This actor was making about £20,000 a year by travelling round towns of 20,000 to 30,000 inhabitants with old-fashioned dramas like *East Lynne*, defeating the cinema apparently, and De Celle went round with him. That, however, has gone too in the slump. Recently he has been working under a Government-controlled scheme of art production, and has been painting murals in schools, using Mrs Traquair's method of oil paints with a wax medium which I taught him. He has been married for years, has a son and daughter, but they do not take to painting, he reports, which perhaps is just as well.

Only last summer I received visits from two of those soldier students of the years just after the War—both from Africa, but from places thousands of miles apart. One was Kenneth Robertson, who is attached to the Nigerian Educational Department and looks after a Craft School at Bida, in a climate that is not good for white men, but produces artists and craftsmen of uncommon skill in a race which is not Mohammedan. The other, the Rev. E. G. Paterson, is South African born but of Scotch extraction. He is an exceptionally interesting man. Before the War he was Town Clerk of Benoni, a small township near Johannesburg. Under General Smuts he fought through the East African campaign unscathed, but instead of returning to Benoni with the peace, and a salary of £700 a year, he decided to throw that up and to come to England to study art. Then he came to the Central School and worked under me for three years. As he clearly had both brains and initiative I thought he might make something out of art even in these days, but instead he returned to South Africa and wrote to me that he had decided to become a missionary among the natives out there, and that he had an idea to use his training as an artist in that sphere!

I was really astonished, because when I knew him he appeared to be uninterested in any religion whatever. I had given up all hope of hearing of him again, when he came to my studio to tell me that he was on leave with his wife, also a missionary. He had brought with him a very uncommon series of photographs of churches he had built and decorated with native labour in Bechuanaland. The Bechuanas, he explained to me, are Bantus, and belong to the most aristocratic blood in Africa; a pastoral people, more intelligent than the Zulus and other fighting races, though physically inferior. With their pastoral habits they take to Christianity naturally and the Old Testament especially appeals to them; indeed they consider themselves to be better Christians than the Whites, as they may well be! Artists by instinct, they take to a kind of low relief carving in wood; from this it is but a step to the problems of three-dimensional drawing. They make both the Christ and the Blessed Virgin black like themselves. They are the only body of natives in Africa who are not supported by a Mission Society in this country or in America, but support their own church out of their own efforts. They are gradually educating their own people properly to become priests, so there are few white missionaries among them now. Paterson, as one of these few, told me he had a flock of about 7000 souls to look after, and he helps with their schools, which are under church guidance. He also has been using his training at the Central School to help his congregations to build and decorate their own churches. The main part of each building is in concrete, but it is thatched in the traditional native fashion with excellent effect. From the photographs he showed me, all are interesting and some quite beautiful.

He has decorated the interiors by a method of wall-painting, direct on the concrete, using oil tempered with petroleum. There were also photographs of a kind of mosaic set in the concrete above the altars, which looked quite successful. I fancy Paterson is responsible for all the figure designs, but he tells me that the native takes to decoration with plant forms eagerly. Altogether the result is some of the most successful religious decoration that I have seen: the feeling of dignity and reverence is clearly present.

There were many others, of course; I cannot give all the names here, but Freddie Gray and John Goodchild of this period are in Australia teaching schools of their own as well as producing original works, of which they keep me posted from time to time. Francis Spear, Clarke Hutton, John Farleigh, James Fitton and R. Tanner are all with us still in London, teaching at the Central School themselves now.

Vincent Lines, who is of a younger generation, was awarded the travelling scholarship for painting at the Royal College and has kept me posted on his travels since then. He has a lively pen and opinions of his own which are well worth reading, as the following quotation from a letter on his seeing "The Funeral of Count Orgaz" by El Greco, in Toledo, will show. The visit was made a year before the present civil war in Spain.

The light is good, which is surprising because the rest of the Church is in that strange semi-darkness characteristic of Spanish buildings. Of course it is a very celebrated work and you will be familiar with the principal details of its composition. The dead Count supported by two very grand ecclesiastics, a priest robed in a white surplice, a monk, and a fine group of the noble's followers in the background. Heaven above, depicted in the Greek's own special manner—superb. I suppose all the portraits are of people who have paid for the decoration and so had to be well placed. They are, and they take their places easily; even the proximity of the Angels does not make them self-conscious! When I think of all the presentation pictures of groups I have seen—and this picture can, I think, be so described—only Rembrandt's "Night Watch" compares with this for imaginative treatment—Gainsborough, Goya, Frans Hals, all painted sets of *important* gentlemen but in every case they remained companies assembled hopefully for the delight of posterity. These three artists all did the thing superbly well....But Greco in this work transcends these limits and has made men and angels move together with ease and dignity.

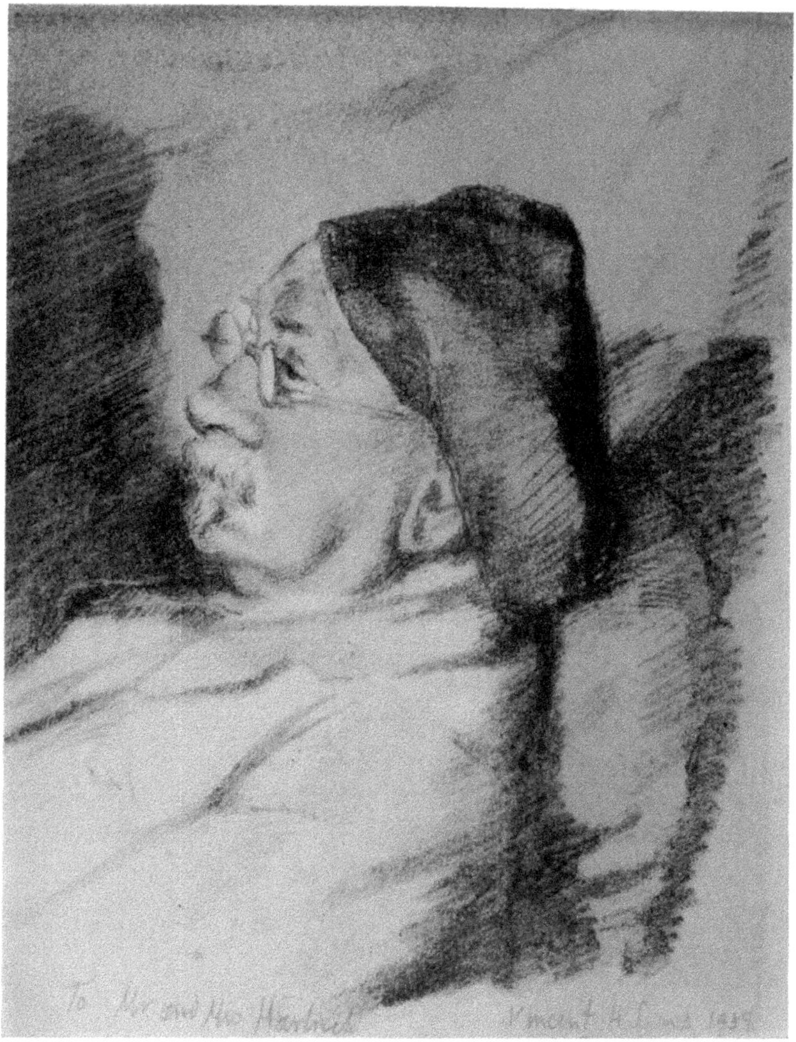

A. S. Hartrick by Vincent Lines

Lithograph

That, I think is well said. Lines now has a school of his own at Horsham. I do not wish to imply that I alone am responsible for the training of these men. They are products of the efforts of a number of experts teaching at the Central School; but as teacher of life drawing and lithography I had them all under my care at some time, and some of them have volunteered since that they have found my advice valuable, even that it grows on them with time.

Many of my pupils were women, and in my view women have a peculiar quality in their drawing and painting which has not been fully explored. It is a quality analogous to the literary power of Jane Austen or Dorothy Wordsworth—a kind of delicate strength which produces an effect of sharp surprise upon the observer. Lady Patricia Ramsay, who was my pupil, is an artist of this kind. With an eye highly sensitive to colour, and a quick reaction to any manifestation of beauty, it was a simple matter to teach her to paint.

Before I bring these memoirs to a close I should like to ask for attention to my latest love in art: the study of English medieval glass, especially of those remnants to be found in the windows of our parish churches. There is no glass in this country on the scale and of the importance of Chartres and that of other Continental cathedrals, though the glass in York Minster can challenge respect even in this direction. The truth is, display on a large scale is not a characteristic of the English genius; but on the intimate side of beauty and expression we have still a quantity of glass in our parish churches—more of it than might be expected, of high quality—which can often give the artist, and even the casual tourist, greater pleasure than the larger and more famous examples. The reason is that it can be taken in at once and appreciated without expert guidance.

For a number of years, especially since the War, I have made it my hobby to look for this glass in churches wherever I have heard of it, just as a labour of love. Though willing to get all the instruction I can in the craft, I have deliberately refrained from trying to work in it myself, because the consideration of difficulties with technical and financial questions might destroy or lessen my enjoyment of its beauty.

Some results of my researches may be found in the Print Room of the Victoria and Albert Museum, in a set of sketches which are only intended to try to give the effect of the glass in its present position, and to encourage those interested to go to see the originals themselves. In one short visit to the Museum, the character of a number of pieces, often widely separated in place, can thus be examined, and the curious can choose which he may prefer to visit. With a car much ground can be covered; but the ideal way, to get all the pleasure of an adventure out of this hobby, is to go on foot. The destination thus acquires romance and may become a haven of refuge, where one is glad of a rest—which will give time to attune oneself to the surroundings and to take in the beauty one has come often far to study. A pair of opera or field glasses is an important adjunct to such adventures: they help one to decipher the subjects in traceries high up. They also focus the object as in a looking-glass or picture and so enrich the impression received.

The late Professor W. R. Lethaby first set me on this track, and I was fortunate, because none knew the subject better. For a number of years I used to go with Lethaby once a year to examine and grant diplomas on work done in the art classes at Reading University. These visits I used to count among the red-letter days in my year.

The old garden of the Palmers' house, given by the family to the University, was an ideal setting. On the lawn before the Common-room, after lunch with Professor Seaby, we used to discuss questions of art, when we had finished with diplomas. Then Lethaby would give us of his best. His knowledge was of the kind that makes everything ancient live again—there was no dry dust about his teaching. His eager "Yes, yes, yes!!" when you found something that excited him, will remain with me always. I possess a copy of his paper on "Medieval Paintings at Westminster" which he sent me with a written inscription—"To A. S. Hartrick with great regard, W. R. Lethaby"—that I greatly prize. This brings me to one peculiarity: he was quite indifferent to what is known as "handling" in paint; I believe he actively disliked it. In looking at a candidate's work he frankly ignored it and left the appraisement to me alone. I can affirm that most of what I know of medieval art I learnt from him; and thereby came to understand that the English, far from being the inartistic muddlers we have been told they were by half-educated admirers of Continental methods, have from the earliest times produced work that is extremely personal, and need fear no detrimental comparison with contemporary culture in other European countries.

It is worth remembering that William Morris and Gimson, the architect and furniture designer, two of the most individual of English craftsmen in the later years, did not hunt round for aesthetes to carry out work for them, but took boys from the Cotswold villages near where they lived, or from the nearest board school in London, and they quickly discovered that many of these had the right instinct for craft in them, and were soon producing living work in the best spirit of the old, and not a mere re-hash of obsolete taste.

It seems likely that much of this natural hand-power has been made use of by the industrialists in the working of their machines to-day, but unfortunately this very facility in learning the machine also kills their former power of selection.

Now I believe I have said all I want to say. Of course there are many other friends and colleagues whom I have known, and by whom I have benefited, than those I have mentioned by name here. I can only ask them to forgive me for any seeming neglect: it is only that I try to follow a certain scheme in writing and must stick to it. As it is, I hear my critics saying: "The fellow likes too many things, he has no standards at all", or, "What are they?" By a surprising chance, considering how I fail to keep things except in my head, I recently came on that number of *Le Courier Français* in which Jules Roques, the editor in the early nineties, interviewed me. There, I find, I wrote out for him a sort of "Credo" which contains standards by which I have been guided all my life in art. Here they are, and I believe in them in exactly the same way to-day.

I am a modern and an impressionist in the sense that I wish to transmit and give to others the sensations I receive from what I see round about me. Personally I do not believe it possible for a man who buries himself in the past, be it only in the literature and art of times past, to be other than a mere reflection of those masters who drew their inspiration from the contemporary life about them. In saying this I do not wish to say that it would be impossible to produce to-day a work which is imaginative and mystical. Have we not material of this kind ready to hand in the strange forms of thought which have given us Theosophy as a religion, and Lourdes as a miracle? We await the man who by art can make clear the mystic elements—that is all. While waiting for him, truth lies open for us in the study of nature and modern life.

Nevertheless I do not think of lessening the debt we owe to the great masters of the past. In the faithful study of their methods we may hope to find the means to express the spirit of to-day.

As for my preferences as a draughtsman, I humbly adore a trinity: Holbein, Menzel and Degas.

The first, because he has said the last word in style on character in the silhouette.

The second, because he is able to realize the greatest number of facts in a drawing without weakening the dramatic interest of the whole.

The third, combining certain qualities of the two above mentioned, employs a method as convincing as that of Menzel while adding a sense of dignity and style to his line together with something quite new which is all his own.

I believe there are two distinct forms of artistic expression: one which charms, the other which convinces. This latter is only for people who are educated up to it; the pleasure which is derived from it is mainly intellectual.

For example, I would cite Watteau as a master who charms, Degas as a master who convinces. As a painter, I am perhaps most attracted by the form and colour of the primitives, though I cannot do other than render homage to such kings of painting as Rubens, Frans Hals and Velasquez.

All this, of course, was printed in French in the paper. In some ways I think Jules Roques's translation of my English is more pointed than the original. I have translated it back again here. He cut out something I said about Gainsborough and beauty being its own excuse—that artist is little known in France—also how no one can define the romance and the mystery of a painting by Rembrandt, who, a true Northerner, forbade his pupils to go to Rome.

As this is the sort of thing I have been saying to my own pupils for years, I restore them now. I like to believe that I understand the underlying motives in the art of all the great masters of all schools sufficiently to appreciate the greatness of their standards in each separate case. I hold that any thoroughly trained artist should by his understanding of the craft be able to do this. At the same time it may be of interest to name some picture by which I have been specially moved. The picture I should most like to have painted and to possess is that small blue "Madonna and Child" painted by Mantegna, belonging to Bergamo, which was exhibited in the Italian Exhibition in Burlington House in 1930. Sir Charles Holmes makes it the frontispiece to his work on Italian Art. Here is beauty in drawing and painting, with intellect and emotion, all at their highest. Comparisons are odious, indeed impossible in the case of great works of art, which represent the genius of a race as well as of an individual. Therefore I will not attempt to name another.

In 1936 Mr W. T. Creed, the Librarian, and the Committee of the Fulham Public Libraries offered me, as an old inhabitant of the Borough, a show of my work in the Lecture Hall of Fulham Central Library, from 14 May to 20 June. I gladly accepted the compliment and assembled as complete a collection of all my work in various media as I could under the title: FIFTY YEARS OF PAINTING: An Artist's Pilgrimage.

On 14 May, with the Mayor of Fulham in the chair, the Exhibition was opened by Lady Patricia Ramsay and her husband, Admiral the Hon. Sir Alexander Ramsay. I believe it did me real good. I think my friends were pleased with it, for which I thank them. The Press was kind. Speaking as an artist, I learnt something myself and was not ashamed. Beforehand I was afraid that being short-sighted my work might be short-focused, so would not "carry" well. To my surprise, most of it looked better than I had seen it before. Therefore all I would say is "Jubilate Deo". If there is really anything in it, it can now speak for itself.

Painters soon come to understand something, at least, of the significance of the parable of the labourers in the vineyard and to appreciate the force of the Master's decision: "The first shall be last and the last first, for many are called but few are chosen." Yet now, at the end of my labours, I prefer to dwell on that saying of the dying Gainsborough, who wrote to his rival, Reynolds, asking him to come to see him, adding: "We are all going to Heaven and Vandyke is of the company." And I believe Van Gogh will be there also.

INDEX

Lightning Source UK Ltd.
Milton Keynes UK
UKHW051309060519
341971UK00028B/105/P

9 781107 559783